THE MAKING
OF DOMESDAY
BOOK

Oxford University Press, Amen House, London E.C.4

GLASGOW   NEW YORK   TORONTO   MELBOURNE   WELLINGTON
BOMBAY   CALCUTTA   MADRAS   KARACHI   LAHORE   DACCA
CAPE TOWN   SALISBURY   NAIROBI   IBADAN   ACCRA
KUALA LUMPUR   HONG KONG

FIRST PUBLISHED 1961
REPRINTED 1963

BURGŪ HERTFORDE p̃ .x. hidis se defend̃ .T.R.E. 7 modo n̄ fac̃t.
Ibi erãt .c. xl. vi. burgenses. in soca regis Eduuardi.

De his ht in com̃ Alan̄ .iiii. domos. que t̃ 7 modo reddt cõsuetudin̄.

Eudo dapifer ht .ii. domos que fuer̃ Algari 7 t̃ 7 m̃ reddñ̃ cõsuetud. 7 tcia domũ ht ide Eudo que fuit Vlmar̃. non reddt cõsuetud.

Goisfrid̃ de bech .iii. domos. cõsuetud reddem̃.

Hunfrid̃ de Anneuille teñ sub Eudone .ii. domos cũ uno horto. harũ una decõmodata fuit cuidã pfecto regis. 7 altera cũ horto fuit cuidã burgensi. 7 in reclamatiõe ipsi burgenses sibi iuste ablatas.

Alii f. xviii. burgenses ht rex .W. qui fuer̃ hoes Heraldi 7 leuuini. omẽs cõsuetud reddt.

Petrus de ualonges ht .ii. ecclas cũ una domo. quas emit de Vluui de hatfelde. reddñ oms cõsuetudines. ipse Vluui 7 dare fuende potuit.

Goisfrid̃ de magneuile ht occupat̃ qdã. qui fuer Ilgari stalri. 7 vii. domos nullam cõsuetudine reddidt. nisi geldũ regis qdo colligebatur.

Radulf̃ bainiard ht .ii. domos. t̃ 7 modo ht arduin̄ de Scales ht .xiiii. domos. qs habuit Achi. T.R.E. nullã cõsuetud dabant nisi geldũ regis. de qbz aduocat harduin̄ regem ad protectorem. Adhuc unã domũ ht harduin̄ de dono regis. que fuit cuidã burgensi. reddens omnem cõsuetudinem.

Hoc suburbiū reddit .xx. lib arsas 7 pensatas. 7 iiii. molini reddt .x. lib ad numerū.

Ẽ do petrus uicecom̃ recep̃: .xv. lib ad numeru. reddebat T.R.E: vii. lib 7 x. sol ad numerū.

.i. Rex Willelmus.
.ii. Archiepc̃s cantuariensis. xiiii. Willelmus de Ow.
.iii. Epc̃s Wintoniensis. xvii. Willelm̃ de Odburgule.
.iiii. Epc̃s Londoniensis. xviii. Walterius flandrensis.
.v. Epc̃s Baiocensis. xxx. Eudo dapifer.
.vi. Epc̃s Lisiacensis. xxi. Eduuard Sarisberiensis.
.vii. Epc̃s Cestrensis. xxii. Goisfrid̃ de orarmeule.
.viii. Abbas de Ely. xxiii. Goisfrid̃ de Bech.
.x. Abb de Westmonast̃. xxiiii. Gosbertus de beluaco.
.x. Abb de S̃ Albano. xxv. Petrus de ualonges.
.xi. Abbatissa de Ceriz. xxviii. arduin̄ de Escalers.
.xii. Canonici de Lundonia. xxx. Edgar.
.xiii. Canonici de Waltham. xxv. Magno brito.
.xiii. Comes moritoniensis. xxx. Gislebrus filius Salomonis.
.xv. Comes Alanus. xl. Sigar de Crochet.
.xvi. Comes Eustachius. xli. Derman 7 alii Anglici regis.
.xvii. Comes Rogerius. xlii. Rohais uxor Ricardi.
.xviii. Robtus de Olgi. xliii. Seliz uxor hugonis.
.xix. Robtus gernon. xliiii. filia Radulfi taillgebosch.
.xx. Robtus de Todeni.
.xxi. Radulf̃ de Todeni.
.xxii. Radulf̃ de Limesi.
.xxiii. Radulf̃ bainiard.
.xiii. Radulf̃ annulfus fr̃ Ilgeri.
.xxv. Hugo de Grentemaisnil.
.xxvi. Hugo de belcamp.

TERRA REGIS. In BRAIDEWATRE hund.
WILLELM̃ REX ten̄ Wimundeslai. p̃ .viii. hidis se defd.
Tra ẽ .xviii. car̃. In dñio .ii. hide 7 dim̃
ibi sunt .iii. car̃. 7 xiiii. uilli 7 un̄
socs 7 vi. bord. 7 v. cot̃ hnt .xv. car̃. Ibi vi. serui.
7 ii. molin de xx. sol. p̃tũ .i. car̃. 7 ii. bob. pasta ad
pecun uille. Nem ad sepes. Hoc ẽ fuit in dñio eccle
S̃ WERBURGE de ceriz. sed Heralds comes abstulit inde
ut tota sira testat. 7 apposuit in hiz manerio suo
wyhe. annis ante morte regis Eduuardi.

Rex W. ten̄ Welleseie. p̃ .iiii. hidis se defd. Tra ẽ
viii. car̃. In dñio .i. hida 7 v. uirg̃ 7 dim̃ ibi sunt .iii. car̃
Pbr cũ ii. uillis 7 ii. cot̃ hnt .iii. car̃. 7 adhuc .ii. pot
fiert. Ibi .vi. serui. p̃tũ .i. car̃. pasta ad pecun uille
Silua .xxx. porc. Hoc ẽ iacuit 7 iacet in hiz hund
Higald tenuit.

Approximately half-size

THE MAKING OF DOMESDAY BOOK

BY

V. H. GALBRAITH

OXFORD
AT THE CLARENDON PRESS

© *Oxford University Press 1961*

PRINTED IN GREAT BRITAIN

TO G.R.G.

ACKNOWLEDGEMENTS

M Y interest in the administrative process which gave rise to Domesday Book was first kindled, more than half a century ago, by the late Professor James Tait of Manchester, whose review of *Domesday Book and Beyond* (*E.H.R.* 1897) remains today the most constructive criticism ever made of that great book. I am also indebted to a number of living writers, viz. Mr. R. Weldon Finn, Dr. R. S. Hoyt, Dr. R. Lennard, Professor Darlington, Mr. Peter Sawyer, and Professor H. C. Darby. Nor must I forget Mr. Mason, who read the whole book and made many valuable criticisms. To all these my gratitude goes far beyond their published works, a fact hardly apparent in the text, where they are normally cited only to record some difference of opinion! I also owe thanks for particular assistance to Mr. J. L. Kirby; to Professor Cronne and to Miss Clementi; to Professor Darby for the map on p. 216; to the Dean and Chapter of Exeter Cathedral for permission to reproduce Plate II; to Mr. Stanley Cohn; to the Editor of the *E.H.R.* for permission to reprint part of an article there published; to the long-suffering staff of the Clarendon Press; and, finally, to my wife, to whom the book—at long last—is inscribed.

V. H. G.

CONTENTS

LIST OF PLATES

NOTE

THE Frontispiece shows the opening leaf of Hertfordshire, with its numbered list of tenants-in-chief. Note the absence of the normal rubric 'Hic annotantur tenentes terras in . . .' the relevant county, which is lacking in all the counties of the third circuit except Middlesex (see p. 195). This rubric precedes the list of tenants-in-chief in all the other counties except Yorkshire, Lincolnshire, and, of course, Cheshire, which, apart from the Church lands, was held in chief by Earl Hugh. In Shropshire the rubric is more precise than elsewhere and reads 'Hic annotantur tenentes terram de rege in Sciropescire'.

There are various inconsistencies between the Hertfordshire list of tenants-in-chief and the text which follows. For example, the list omits the name of the Abbot of Ramsey, whose lands appear as no. xi in the text, and there are small differences in the names and spelling of the individual tenants-in-chief. The rubricator, however, made the numbers of both list and text add up to xliiii by marking two consecutive fees as no. xlii! See below, Chapter XIII.

The Plate opposite p. 32 shows only a selection of the scripts in Exon Domesday, and may be profitably compared with the photographs of Little Domesday in *Domesday Re-Bound* (H.M.S.O.), opposite p. 25.

ABBREVIATIONS

D.B.	Domesday Book
D.M.	Domesday Monachorum
E.H.R.	*English Historical Review*
Econ. Hist. Rev.	*Economic History Review*
I.C.C.	Inquisitio Comitatus Cantabrigiensis
J.R.L.	John Rylands Library
I.E.	Inquisitio Eliensis
Trans. R. Hist. Soc.	*Transactions of the Royal Historical Society*
V.C.H.	*Victoria County History*

NOTE

In the Record Edition of Domesday Book volumes I and II (1783) the original foliation of the manuscript has been scrupulously retained, and it was even attempted by a special record type to reproduce the original abbreviations of the manuscript. Both volumes are therefore, as it were, a facsimile in print of the original. Thus references to Volume I (which is in double column) are cited by the folio, the column, and the recto or verso of a leaf, e.g. a reference to f. 191 a 2 means that the entry will be found in the second column of the recto of the leaf so numbered in the printed edition, and a reference to f. 191 b 1 in the first column of the verso of that leaf as printed.

In the Record Edition of Exon Domesday the text is printed consecutively, though the folios are marked in the margin. References to Exon Domesday below, therefore, are to the page except in a few cases where, for special reasons, it has been necessary to quote the folio.

tells us that, '*had its returns survived in full*', it would have been 'a second and more detailed Domesday Book, giving an account of all England village by village and tenant by tenant'.[1] The words in italics explain, I think, why these later 'Domesday Inquests' proved abortive. Between the inquest of 1086 and all later inquiries of comparable magnitude there was a fundamental difference of treatment, the former condensing the returns to manageable proportions in an engrossed record, the latter conserving or attempting to conserve, the whole, overwhelming mass of 'original returns'. It is the unique distinction of the Domesday Inquest of 1086 that apparently no effort was made to preserve its 'original returns' in full. Instead, the practical genius of the Norman king preserved in a 'fair copy' what was little more than an abstract of the total returns, and by this wise compromise Domesday Book has outlived its later competitors.

Now this difference in treatment between Domesday and later inquests is a fact of cardinal importance, not only for the whole history of administration, but also for the proper understanding of the motives behind, and indeed the whole meaning of Domesday Book itself. The autocratic authority and the genius for government of William I pushed to completion a task that proved beyond the strength of later kings. Less than two years after the commencement of the Survey—in September 1087—the king died and historians have doubted, not unnaturally, whether so vast an undertaking was completed within a mere twenty-one months. But the alternative view, viz. that Domesday Book was completed by William II is, in the conditions which governed eleventh-century kingship, almost inconceivable and there are, as we shall see, strong, if not demonstrative, grounds for concluding that the whole enterprise was ruthlessly completed before the death of the Conqueror. Thus, in tackling the problem of

---

[1] *The Hundred and the Hundred Rolls*, p. 28.

I

THE EVIDENCE AND THE PROBLEM

IN the year 1085 William the Conqueror spent Christmas at Gloucester. There, according to a famous entry in the Anglo-Saxon Chronicle, he had 'very deep speech with his Witan about this land and how it was peopled and with what sort of men'. The result of these deliberations was the Domesday Survey, a minute and searching inquiry into the extent and value, both of the royal demesne, and of the lands held by the tenants-in-chief. For this purpose the king sent his men into every shire, and the information, extracted on oath from the inhabitants, was written down and returned to the royal Treasury at Winchester. The contemporary permanent record of this vast undertaking still survives in the two volumes of Domesday Book. For more than seven centuries they were preserved in the royal Treasury, from which they were transferred in the early nineteenth century to the Public Record Office in Chancery Lane. Domesday Book is thus our oldest 'public record' and the true starting-point of English administrative history.

The example set by the Conqueror was followed by his successors, and it is reasonable to suppose that the Domesday Inquest was the precedent and exemplar for those recurring special inquiries with which our history is punctuated to the close of the Middle Ages. Outstanding among these was the scheme for collecting a carucage in 1198, described by Stubbs as 'a new Domesday Inquest', and the repeated and detailed inquiries of Edward I, familiar to us as the *Quo Warranto* and the *Hundred Rolls*. Of the great inquiry of 1279, for example, Professor Cam

the making of Domesday Book we are attempting to explain a unique and, having regard to its early date, perhaps the greatest administrative achievement of medieval kingship.

Nor, oddly enough, is there a shortage of first-hand material for our inquiry. We start, of course, from the volumes of Domesday Book—for there are two—and the fact that these are not copies but the actual originals is all important. The two volumes, though accepted for 800 years as forming a single work, are utterly different from each other in shape, script, and scale, and seem to reflect successive stages in procedure. Read aright, much can be learned from these differences. We have, secondly and almost unbelievably, in the Exon Domesday for the south-western counties, a further original source, almost as big as Domesday Book itself, and actually anterior to it in date. This vital document, to which Domesday scholars have consistently turned a blind eye, bears a general resemblance to Vol. II of Domesday Book (Little Domesday), and though apparently it has always belonged to Exeter Cathedral is, like both volumes of Domesday Book, a 'public record' and an original of the Survey. Of rather later date and private provenance we have also two important documents from the church of Ely, viz. the Inquisitio Eliensis and the Inquisitio Comitatus Cantabrigiensis, while a certain amount of fresh knowledge has been gleaned from the examination of contemporary charters, especially royal. Finally, among the literary sources there has come to light (1907) an account of the Survey made by Bishop Robert of Hereford which illuminates and adds to the well-known contemporary notice in the Anglo-Saxon Chronicle. With these unexpectedly rich materials, then, we have to study the complicated process by which a vast mass of 'original returns' from what would later have been described as a 'general eyre' were epitomized and arranged as a permanent record in Domesday Book.

We may begin by looking a little more closely at them in order, and first at Domesday Book. Vol. I is a volume of nearly 400 folios (or 800 pages), written in double column on parchment measuring about 15 by 11 inches. It contains the record, county by county, of the whole of England,[1] apart from the three eastern counties of Essex, Suffolk, and Norfolk, which are dealt with in Vol. II. Normally each county begins with a description of the 'county borough', after which there is a numbered list of holders of land beginning with the king, followed by the names of archbishops, bishops, earls, barons, and so on down the scale to quite humble tenants-in-chief, who are grouped together as king's serjeants (*servientes*), thegns, &c. Each county record then proceeds to set out the manors held by the tenants, and marginal rubrics (often imperfect) indicate the hundreds to which they belong. Although there are a good many corrections and additions, by the same scribe, of manors originally omitted, this volume is written in a single distinctive set-hand (possibly even by a single scribe), which is not found elsewhere in our surviving materials. One is tempted to see in this script the copy-book hand taught to the scribes of the royal *curia*, but the hypothesis cannot be verified for lack of comparable evidence of so early a date. Altogether Vol. I is a handsome, well-executed book in spite of the fact that the writing is heavily abbreviated. The volume begins on folio I with the county of Kent and ends with the counties of Yorkshire and Lincolnshire.

Vol. II, the smaller volume, contains about 450 folios measuring 11 by 8 inches. Unlike Vol. I it is written in single column and in a number of greatly varying scripts, none of which is that of Vol. I. As an example of book

---

[1] The survey did not include the counties of Northumberland, Durham, Westmorland, and Cumberland, though portions of some of these are included in Yorkshire. The part of Lancashire between Ribble and Mersey is recorded at the end of Cheshire.

production it is in every way inferior to Vol. I, though no less accurately and carefully compiled. The possibility has recently been suggested

that we have in the smaller volume—in strong contrast to the larger —not a direct compilation from materials cast in a different form but an exact copy of a draft compilation of that nature previously made. That theory fits in with the comparative absence of Compressions, Corrections, Insertions and Interlineations . . . and it need hardly be pointed out that in the making of a straightforward copy of this kind one hand can cease and another take over at any point.[1]

Whatever one's conclusions about Vol. I, there is, as we shall see, good evidence in favour of the suggestion here made that Vol. II is essentially a fair copy of a largely similar original. Yet it lacks the style and finish of Vol. I, for while some of the scripts in it are fine examples of contemporary minuscule, others are extremely poor; and the difference between the two volumes is so striking as to render it highly improbable that they were products of the same office or administration. If Vol. I was produced by the royal *curia* at Winchester—and this is virtually certain—it is a reasonable inference that Vol. II was made somewhere else.

This conclusion, based on form and treatment, is confirmed by the contents of Vol. II. In place of the highly compressed summaries of Vol. I we have for these three counties the full, unabbreviated 'returns of the royal commissioners'. Comparison is difficult owing to the difference in size and shape between Vol. I and Vol. II, and a folio of the former is a good deal larger than a folio of Little Domesday. But each of the three East Anglian counties runs to over a hundred folios, while in Vol. I Kent fills only fourteen folios, and the great county of Wiltshire no more than twenty-one. It has been suggested that Vol. II

[1] *Domesday Re-Bound* (H.M.S.O., 1954), p. 45.

represents a first attempt to compress the huge bulk of the original returns, soon abandoned as being too elaborate. There are, however, no indications of any kind of abbreviation or compression in Vol. II, which has every appearance of being a straightforward and largely mechanical copy of the full returns. Thus the difference in scale between Vol. I and Vol. II, together with the difference in general treatment and in calligraphy, suggests rather that the two volumes are of wholly different provenance and, though so long associated, originally belonged to different stages of the inquest.

The Exon or Exeter Domesday, one of the treasures of Exeter cathedral, contains, though with many gaps, the full record of the Domesday Inquest for the five south-western counties, viz. Wiltshire, Somerset, Dorset, Devon, and Cornwall, arranged like both the Domesday volumes under the names of the king and the tenants-in-chief. It is still a very large volume of more than 500 folios and must originally have been larger still, for almost the whole county of Wiltshire has been lost, and much besides. Directly or indirectly it was the source of the epitomized surveys of the counties preserved in Domesday Book, Vol. I. It thus antedates Domesday Book itself and is the earliest surviving original document of the Domesday Survey. The outstanding characteristic of the Exon Domesday is its basic similarity to Little Domesday. In its arrangement of the material under tenants-in-chief, in the variety of the non-curial and non-calligraphic scripts in which it was written, in its very shape (for it was written in single column), it at once invites comparison with the East Anglian volume: and when we reflect that both contain the *full returns* of the Inquest these resemblances become very significant. Against these resemblances, however, there have to be set three important differences.

1. The manors whose particulars it lists in such detail are not assigned to any hundreds. With insignificant excep-

tions the hundreds are simply not mentioned in Exon Domesday; and this unique feature reappears in the shortened version of these five counties in Vol. I of Domesday Book.

2. The Exon Domesday, though something more than a first draft, is quite clearly not the finished return: the materials it contains have not yet been completely classified and are thus at an earlier stage than the final abstract in Domesday Book. From this it may be inferred that between Exon Domesday and Domesday Book there lay a fair copy of the same kind as Little Domesday.

3. The volume contains certain extraneous documents to which there is no parallel in Little Domesday. Of these the most important are the county summaries of the lands of Glastonbury Abbey and, for each county, the accounts of a geld collected in the same year as the Survey.[1]

Thus a cursory inspection of the surviving originals has revealed that the returns of the Domesday Inquest survive in part in two forms. First in epitome in Vol. I for all counties except Norfolk, Suffolk, and Essex; and secondly in full for the three counties in Little Domesday, and for five counties in the south-west in Exon Domesday. It has also shown a close general analogy in treatment and contents between Little Domesday and Exon Domesday, and a common contrast between these two and Vol. I of Domesday Book.

The significance of these facts becomes clear when we take into account the actual conduct of the Inquest. It has long been recognized that the royal commissioners or *legati* who made the Survey were in panels in much the same way as the later general eyres. Each panel dealt with a group of counties and so had its own circuit. Exactly how many such circuits were used in 1086 is still open to

---

[1] V. H. Galbraith, 'The Date of the Geld Rolls in Exon Domesday', in *E.H.R.* lxv (1950), pp. 1–17; J. F. A. Mason, 'The Date of the Geld Rolls', ibid. lxix (1954), p. 283.

question, but we shall not be far wrong in following the reconstruction suggested by the late Carl Stephenson.[1]

Group	Counties
I	Kent (1), Sussex (2), Surrey (3), Hampshire (4), Berkshire (5).
II	Wiltshire (6), Dorset (7), Somerset (8), Devonshire (9), Cornwall (10).
III	Middlesex (11), Hertford (12), Buckingham (13), Cambridge (18), Bedford (20).
IV	Oxford (14), Northampton (21), Leicester (22), Warwick (23).
V	Gloucester (15), Worcester (16), Hereford (17), Stafford (24), Shropshire (25), Cheshire (26).
VI	Huntingdon (19), Derby (27), Nottingham (28), Rutland (29), York (30), Lincoln (31).
VII	Essex (32), Norfolk (33), Suffolk (34).

The inference to be drawn from this table is not in doubt. There is at least a prima facie case for the view that both Exon Domesday and Little Domesday, which preserve the full returns, are the records of their circuits made locally and Domesday Book Vol. I, which preserves only abstracts, is the record made by the king's clerks at Winchester. If so, we can go a step farther and assert that Vol. I of Domesday Book *should* have contained an abstract of the returns for circuit VII of the same kind as that still found in Vol. I for circuit II. The most likely reason for the absence of Norfolk, Suffolk, and Essex from Vol. I is surely that the work was still unfinished at the death of William the Conqueror in September 1087.[2]

---

[1] *Mediaeval Institutions*, ed. Bryce D. Lyon (Cornell Univ. Press, 1954), p. 188. The numbers in brackets refer to the order of the counties in Domesday Book. Stephenson's list is taken from Ballard, *Domesday Inquest* (1906 ed.), pp. 12–13, who in turn had reduced the nine circuits proposed by R. W. Eyton to seven.

[2] That it was the latest circuit return to be received at Winchester is rendered likely by the extreme complexity of the free tenures in East Anglia. See below pp. 29, 71, 205.

The gap was filled by using the local return of this circuit, i.e. Little Domesday, which has thus been incongruously linked with the more calligraphic Vol. I ever since.

Such, in broad outline, is the explanation of the making of Domesday Book suggested by a study of the surviving 'originals', and it is safe to say that there is no other that will account for all the facts supplied by these three fundamental sources. It is more or less the view of Ellis, who edited the Exon Domesday, and it would never have been called in question but for the unfortunate omission from the record edition of Domesday Book of the famous document first printed by N. E. S. Hamilton in 1876— the Inquisitio Comitatus Cantabrigiensis. The I.C.C., like Little Domesday and Exon Domesday, is a more or less full record of the findings of the Inquest, but only for a single county, Cambridgeshire. Moreover, in the I.C.C. the information is set out in a unique way, for the separate manors, instead of being grouped under the names of the tenants-in-chief who owned them, are arranged geographically by hundreds and villages. It begins with a nominal roll of the eight jurors of Staploe hundred, and then sets out one by one the total numbers of hides in each village of the hundred, and a full description of each of them. It soon becomes evident that many, if not most, of the Cambridgeshire villages were broken up into a number of separate estates which divided between them the total obligation for the land tax or geld. Burwell,[1] for example, which answered for fifteen hides, was divided into five separate manors whose descriptions are succinctly grouped together in the I.C.C. The same facts, somewhat abbreviated, will be found on Vol. I of Domesday Book for Cambridgeshire, but only in widely dispersed entries.

[1] *I.C.C.*, p. 4. The five tenants are the abbot of Ramsey (10 hides 1 virgate); Alan (2½ hides); Geoffrey de Mandeville (1 hide 1 virgate); the nuns of Cietriz (½ hide); Hardwin de Scalers (½ hide); in all 15 hides.

The printing of this unique document in 1876 revolutionized Domesday studies, by diverting attention from the authentic, official survivals of the Inquest. The single manuscript of the I.C.C. was written in the twelfth century, and, though no doubt derived from the official proceedings of its circuit, is a document of private provenance from the archives of Ely Cathedral. The very fact that the information it contains appears in a form unknown to the engrossed originals of the Inquest implies that the original from which it descends belonged to some preliminary stage of the commissioners' activities. Such a document, when superseded by the final circuit return, might well fall into private hands, and thus survive as a solitary witness to the early procedure. A generation later scholars would have hesitated before building too much on a fragmentary survival unparalleled in the whole range of our private archives. These warnings, not unnaturally, perhaps, were disregarded in 1876, and, excited by the discovery that the I.C.C. was apparently derived from the full findings of the commissioners, J. H. Round was led to propound the view that the original returns sent to Winchester were not cast in the form of Exon or of Little Domesday, but rather as a great series of hundred rolls arranged geographically by hundreds and by villages. At Winchester, it was assumed, the information was regrouped, by an enormous labour, as we have it in Domesday Book, and then its bulk reduced by wholesale omission of unnecessary details. These hundred rolls, it seemed to follow, were thus the true return to the Domesday inquiry, whose fundamental object was thus shown to be a reassessment of the geld òr land tax. Domesday Book was in this way relegated to a secondary position, an afterthought made later on a different plan. 'The true key to the Domesday Survey and to the system of land assessment it records', Round wrote in 1895, 'is found in the *Inquisitio Comitatus Cantabrigiensis.*'

Round's view, quickly and universally accepted by Domesday scholars, became for half a century the classical exposition of the making of Domesday Book. There were, however, as we have seen, serious objections to it from the start,[1] and these have since grown greater with the more intensive study of the surviving originals of the Survey, and the new evidence of Robert of Hereford which only came to light in 1907. These, it seems to me, are insuperable and require a new hypothesis: but, before setting this out in some detail, we must examine more closely the older view.

[1] Not the least of these lay in reconciling the evidence of the I.C.C. with another private document from Ely, the Inquisitio Eliensis. This had been included in vol. IV of the Record edition of Domesday Book, but was reprinted by Hamilton along with the I.C.C. The titles of both documents are modern and have no contemporary warranty. The evidence of the I.E. is discussed below, pp. 136–42.

II

THE OLD HYPOTHESIS

WHOEVER writes about any aspect of Domesday Book treads in the footsteps of J. H. Round, whose *Feudal England*, published in 1895, is a landmark in Domesday studies. Few books have lasted better, and nearly everything written in later works about the purpose of the Survey and the process by which it was carried out repeats the arguments set out by Round. Until a few years ago his views were universally accepted, and they are the starting-point of all further inquiry.

Round's hypothesis, based fairly and squarely upon a single document, the Inquisitio Comitatus Cantabrigiensis, was worked out with remorseless logic in *Feudal England* in virtual detachment from the historical background and the other sources, in the manner of a mathematical problem. The effect of this essentially unhistorical approach was twofold. In the first place, his inquiries, pursued on such a narrow front, seemed to be conclusive and had all the force of scientific demonstration: and for the same reason they had, above all, the merit of simplicity. So long as the argument was restricted to the I.C.C. the logic appeared to be inexorable. And at first sight his theory had much to commend it, for it seemed to bear out the 'terms of reference' of the commissioners, who were instructed to inquire 'by oath of the sheriff of the Shire and of all the barons and their Frenchmen and of the whole hundred, the priest, the reeve, and six villagers of each village'. In the I.C.C. the account of each hundred, as we have seen, is prefaced by the names of a sworn jury of eight, followed by the clause 'and all the other Frenchmen and Englishmen swore'. What more then remained to be said? It is significant that Round saw no reason ever to develop or modify his original theory. Eleven years later in an Introduction to the Domesday text of Somersetshire —of all counties[1]—he contrived by a miracle of ingenuity to preserve it intact. In these considerations we have, I think, the explanation of its immediate and complete acceptance. It was simple, all embracing, and logical—and it took the learned world by storm.

A second effect of Round's peculiar approach to the problem was to give a new and decisive twist to Domesday studies. All eyes were henceforth focused on the study of the geld or Danegeld and its assessment. Round himself in *Feudal England* pursued the question through every county in England, elaborating the subtleties of the 'five-hide unit', the 'six-carucate unit', and the peculiarities of assessment in East Anglia. His views found favour with Vinogradoff;[2] but their influence was most decisive upon F. W. Maitland. In *Domesday and Beyond*, published only two years after *Feudal England*, the views of Round were accepted and developed in a book of far wider appeal than Round's. For Maitland the assessment of geld was not so much the chief as the only motive of the Domesday Survey.

All the lands [he wrote], all the land-holders of England may be brought before us, but we are told only of such facts, such rights,

[1] The folios in vol. I of Domesday Book devoted to Somerset, Devon, Dorset, Wilts., and Cornwall omit all reference to the hundreds in which the estates were situated.

[2] 'The Survey . . . is mainly directed towards ascertaining the data for the imposition and repartition of geld' (*English Society in the Eleventh Century*, 1908, p. 141). On p. 228 he states that 'the Exon copy of Domesday had been written for the use of the Abbey of Tavistock, or at any rate, by scribes prejudiced in its favour, and this at a time when all the operations connected with the Survey had come to a close'. Like many others he believed that Exon was a copy of Domesday, made much later than the Survey, but in fact its composition antedates that of vol. I, of which it is an indirect source. Three years later, in *The Growth of the Manor* (1911), p. 292, Vinogradoff repeated his statement about the repartition of the geld, but added that the Survey was 'something else besides'.

such legal relationships as bear on the actual or potential payment of geld. True, that some minor purposes may be achieved by the king's commissioners, though the quest for geld is their one main object. About the rents and renders due from his own demesne manors the king may thus obtain some valuable information. Also he may learn, as it were by the way, whether any of his barons or other men have presumed to occupy, to 'invade,' lands which he has reserved for himself. Again, if several persons are in dispute about a tract of ground, the contest may be appeased by the testimony of shire and hundred, or may be reserved for the king's audience; at any rate the existence of an outstanding claim may be recorded by the royal commissioners. Here and there the peculiar customs of a shire or a borough will be stated, and incidentally the services that certain tenants owe to their lords may be noticed. But all this is done sporadically and unsystematically. Our record is no register of title, it is no feodary, it is no custumal, it is no rent roll; it is a tax book, a geld book.

We say this, not by way of complaint against its meagreness, but because in our belief a care for geld and for all that concerns the assessment and payment of geld colours far more deeply than commentators have usually supposed the information that is given to us about other matters. . . . It seems then a fair supposition that any line that Domesday Book draws systematically and sharply, whether it be between various classes of men or between various classes of tenements, is somehow or another connected with the main theme of that book—geldability, actual or potential.[1]

In short, the purpose of the Survey was the collection of materials 'which would enable the royal officers to decide what changes were necessary in order that all England might be taxed in accordance with a just and uniform plan'.

Thus, under the influence of Round's dominating personality, Maitland reduced the motives for the all-embracing inquest of 1086 to the abstraction of Direct Taxation. The very brilliance of the writing, oddly enough, reveals Round's theory as just another Victorian

[1] p. 5.

anachronism, redeemed from absurdity only by the fact that whenever governments act on this scale it is—'your money they are after'. But in the eleventh century the geld was a far smaller fraction of 'taxable capacity' than in the age of Mr. Gladstone.

It may be surmised that even Round was rather embarrassed by the zeal of his distinguished disciple: for in carrying his views to such extreme lengths Maitland was, in fact, guilty of a *reductio ad absurdum*. It is quite unbelievable that the whole resources of an autocratic king should have been concentrated upon the details of an annual custom (*consuetudo*), paid largely by the lands of the unfree *villani*. The realities of royal finance in the late eleventh century were very different. They first come clearly before us in the Pipe Roll of 31 Henry I, but we shall not be far wrong if we carry back for half a century the system there set out.

The revenue of the Crown [writes Dr. Poole] was chiefly derived directly or indirectly from the king's position as supreme landlord. It included, first, the county farms, that is the composition of the rents and rights which the king anciently had in the Crown lands within each county; these brought in a total sum slightly less than £10,000 per annum. The lands held by the Crown were, however, constantly being augmented by estates which fell in by escheat; if a tenant died without heirs or was convicted of felony his land passed (escheated) to its lord. Though these escheated honours and manors were usually regranted to another tenant, they were kept in hand and farmed by the sheriff or by a specially appointed custodian for a time, often a long time, and the issues accrued to the exchequer. In the same category may be reckoned the revenue from vacant churches, from bishoprics and royal abbeys; and it became the practice of the Norman and early Angevin kings to keep them vacant frequently for long periods for the sake of the income. The king was also entitled to the feudal incidents—reliefs, the regular feudal aids, and wardships and marriages, which have already been discussed; to finance his wars he could take scutages or fines in lieu of military service. Danegeld, the earliest direct taxation, which had been called into existence to meet an emergency in the late Anglo-Saxon period, became under the Norman kings a very frequent, if not an annual, impost; it was normally assessed at 2*s.* on the hide, though occasionally it was as much as 4*s.* or even 6*s.* It was, however, subject to many exemptions: the demesne lands were exempted, so too were the lands of those responsible for its collection (the sheriffs) and its accounting (the barons of the exchequer); further, the tax was remitted by the king's writ in favour of certain individuals. Instead, therefore, of bringing perhaps nearly £5,000 into the exchequer, Danegeld was yielding little more than £3,000 in the early years of Henry II. It was fast becoming obsolete when it was taken for the last time in 1162. It was revived again as an emergency measure by Richard I in 1194 under the name carucage and still appears to have been levied on the Domesday assessment.[1]

The pattern of royal finance here traced from the Pipe Rolls is the true key to the Domesday Survey. The overwhelming financial concern of the king was with the manors of his own demesne, and the 'honours' of his great feudatories. Their 'honours' cut across the system of accounting at the Treasury by counties and sheriffs, and were therefore broken up according to the separate shires in which the lands were situated. Armed with facts recorded by counties in Domesday Book, both the Crown and the sheriffs were provided with the intricate details which fixed the annual value (*valet*) of each estate or manor, and so were able to cope adequately with the fixing of 'fines', wardships, and marriages from the tenants-in-chief, together with urban revenues, county farms, and the important revenue from the geld. It was the system of an aristocratic age in which the 'power and the glory' were concentrated in the hands of the few, under whose names the whole lands of each county were detailed, and with whom alone, generally speaking, the Crown directly dealt. The Domesday commissioners were

[1] A. L. Poole, *From Domesday Book to Magna Carta*, p. 417.

thus concerned (as indeed was every sheriff) with the
wealth of a small number of persons, whose names and
incomes, thanks to the Survey, are known to us. According to W. J. Corbett's[1] figures rather less than half the
total income from the land of England—£30,000 out of
£73,000—was devoted to the provision of 170 baronies,
'some great, some small', for William's feudal followers:
and rather less than £2,000 a year for the remuneration
of minor officials and personal servants later known as the
king's serjeants. Domesday Book is, in essence, the detailed record, first of the wealth of the Crown, and secondly
of these individuals.

The acceptance or non-acceptance of Round's view is
no small matter, if only because *Domesday Book and
Beyond* is still the most widely read book on its subject.
We can hardly doubt that it is worth while to consider
impartially and in a dry light the difficulties it presents.
But before listing our objections some things should be
made clear, and the first is this: that no one can doubt
that the procedure of the Domesday Inquest was based
on the immemorial local divisions of county, hundred, and
village. The commissioners, even if they did not tour the
hundreds, haled the hundredal juries before them and
extracted the information more or less in the form in
which it is presented in the I.C.C. They may even have
written it down in this form, in the Cambridgeshire circuit
for example, though not necessarily or even probably in
many other circuits; for it is both unlikely and unproved
that all circuits proceeded alike. It may help, then, if at
this point we define our terms. When Round wrote of
'the original returns' of the Inquest, he envisaged a single
and relatively simple operation: using a procedure based
on the hundreds, the commissioners (he believed) committed to writing their verdicts in the form of hundred
rolls: and the documents so compiled by each circuit,

[1] *Cambridge Mediaeval History*, vol. v. 508.

became, when forwarded to Winchester, 'the original returns' of the Inquest. Contrariwise, it is argued below that the administrative process was a more complex one, involving successive written drafts, the last of which alone, since it was sent to Winchester, became the 'original returns' of the Inquest. These are difficult matters on which there is, and is always likely to be, legitimate ground for argument. The sole point at issue is whether the returns made to Winchester were cast in the form of hundred rolls or arranged, as in the two volumes of Domesday Book and Exon Domesday, under the names of holders of land. Indeed, so great is our ignorance, that it is possible, if unlikely, that some circuits did the one and some the other. The inferences that Round and Maitland drew from the I.C.C. regarding the meaning and purpose of the Domesday Inquest would be invalidated by the discovery of a single exception to their rule.

There is one other preliminary point, perhaps, that should be made, though of academic interest only, as will appear, in this discussion. It is that even if it could be proved that the original returns *were* all cast in the form of hundred rolls, such a demonstration would only raise the view that the motive of the inquiry was a reassessment of geld to the level of a *possible* inference. It would not prove it. A possible theory was accepted, not illogically, as a necessary inference by the Victorians simply because, as we shall see below, it seemed to support a view they already held, if only as an unsupported assumption. This no doubt explains why Round, influenced by the climate of opinion around him, pushed the evidence of the I.C.C. to such extreme and dogmatic lengths. For no one knew better than he that no reassessment of geld could ever have been made from documents couched in the form of Domesday Book and the Exon Domesday.

What, then, are the objections to the theory that the original returns to the Domesday Inquest were a great collection of hundred rolls cast in the form of the Inquisitio Comitatus Cantabrigiensis?

I. It implies a complete change of plan between the making of the Survey in the counties and the compilation of Domesday Book at Winchester. For this there is no warrant in the literary authorities, and the huge task of converting these returns into the form in which we find them in Domesday Book could hardly have been completed before the king's death in 1087. The theory therefore requires the further assumption that Domesday Book was only a sort of afterthought compiled in the next reign, a contingency unlikely in itself, and one for which there is no earlier or later precedent. Failing demonstrative evidence.to the contrary, it is a reasonable assumption that William I's undertaking died with him.

II. It is no less difficult to explain the complete disappearance of these original returns. The I.C.C. apart, no remains have ever been found either in local or central archives of these hundred rolls, though very considerable portions of the full returns, in what may be called Domesday form, survive in the various Domesday 'satellites'.[1] Nor must we forget that the I.C.C. itself is a manuscript of only local (Ely) provenance, of later date (twelfth century), and that it is neither a complete nor accurate transcript of the full returns.

III. It is difficult also to explain the differences in form, script, and scale between Great Domesday (Vol. I) and Little Domesday (Vol. II). Taken together these suggest, as we have already seen, that Little Domesday is no more than the final return of the East Anglian circuit, and this view is supported by its colophon: 'In the year 1086 from the Incarnation, and the twentieth year of William, this survey (*descriptio*) was made not only through these three counties, but also through the others.'

---

[1] e.g. from the priory of Bath: see Reginald Lennard, 'A Neglected Domesday Satellite', *E.H.R.* lviii (1943), pp. 32–41.

It is sufficiently remarkable that so minute a record should have been made within the year: that it should have been recast at Winchester from a geographical to its present Domesday form is simply unthinkable. Round was well aware of this difficulty and evolved the ingenious quibble that the word *descriptio* had no reference to the book in which it occurs, but was a *post factum* record of the survey made in that year. Such an assumption was surely against the plain meaning of words, and the natural inference is that the survey of these three difficult counties arrived too late for inclusion in shortened form in Vol. I of Domesday Book along with the others. The only alternative to some such view as this is that the government, having already changed its mind by deciding to recast the geographical returns in Domesday form, made a false start, and having begun with these three counties decided on a radical condensation of the original returns for the remaining counties, using for the purpose other scribes and a different technique. So much change of plan and such hesitation puts too great a strain on our credulity and demands too much of the primitive 'civil service' of the age.

IV. The surviving traces in Vol. I of Domesday Book of several of the other circuits are equally irreconcilable with the theory of the original returns as a series of hundred rolls. There is, in fact, no evidence of any kind that the returns were made in rolls at all, which belong to a later age: but, contrariwise, every indication that they were made in books or sheets. Apart from circuit VII (Little Domesday) with which we have dealt, and circuit II to which we shall come, there are plain traces in the text of Great Domesday that the returns of circuits III and VI were made in book form.[1] All the counties of the third circuit, for example, are distinguished by the occurrence in the margin, from time to time, of a capital M. They have been added, it would appear, rather casually,

---

[1] Below, pp. 131–34, 175.

but they occur, however unsystematically, in every county in the circuit. Such marks are appropriate to an engrossed fair copy in book form where space is no object and it is reasonable to suppose that the abbreviators of Winchester took them over from just such a book as Little Domesday or Exon Domesday. In this connexion we may note that these marginalia are found neither in Exon Domesday nor in the abbreviated version of that circuit in Domesday Book. A more complicated and more systematic system of marginal capitals is also employed for the counties of the sixth circuit, which seems similarly to be derived from an engrossed record already in book form. The likelihood that the returns of circuits III and VI were broadly similar in form to Little Domesday and Exon Domesday is, moreover, raised to strong probability by what we may call the occasional appendixes which characterize the counties of East Anglia, Yorkshire,[1] Lincolnshire, and Huntingdonshire, as well as the five counties of the southwest in Exon Domesday. Norfolk, Suffolk, and Essex have each an appendix of *Invasiones super regem*; Yorkshire, Lincolnshire, and Huntingdonshire appendixes of *Clamores*, and in Exon Domesday Cornwall, Devon, and Somerset appendixes of *Terrae occupatae*. Why and whence these appendixes? If we suppose that the original returns were a series of hundred rolls, arranged by hundreds and villages, we are driven to the absurd conclusion that the Winchester clerks abstracted and arranged the facts in these appendixes from their uniform material on three cognate but varying principles, each with its separate terminology. Without assuming that all circuits proceeded alike it seems certain in these instances both that these appendixes were already completed and that the information was already arranged under the names of the holders of land before the original returns were sent to Winchester.

[1] See below, p. 177, for the Yorkshire *Index*.

V. The most serious, indeed the insuperable difficulty raised by Round's hypothesis, is the evidence of the Exeter or Exon Domesday. Here in an original and contemporary manuscript we have the complete findings of the south-western circuit already arranged, as in the abstract in Vol. I of Domesday Book, under the headings of royal demesne and the separate tenants-in-chief.[1] They have every appearance of being not the engrossed return of this circuit sent to Winchester, but an advanced draft, left behind when amended and recopied, at Exeter. That they are the source, directly or indirectly, of the shortened version in Great Domesday is beyond question. A collation with Domesday shows that, while the information has all been gathered and written down, the classification of the owners is still at an early stage, and Exon is thus the earliest surviving original fragment of the Domesday Survey. Exon Domesday, as we have seen, is closely analogous to Little Domesday, though at a less advanced stage. We know that behind Little Domesday lies an earlier compilation of the same kind,[2] of which it appears to be the fair copy actually returned to Winchester. We can infer from the frequent occurrence of the note *consummatum est* in Exon that it was itself the basis of a more finished volume.[3] The congruent testimony of these actual survivals of the Inquest compels us either to accept them as the original returns of their circuits, or to explain them in some other manner. We have already seen that Round's explanation of Little Domesday was far-fetched and unconvincing. How then did he reconcile the evidence of Exon Domesday with his theory of the original returns as a series of hundred rolls?

[1] The *Terra Regis* and the fiefs of the individual barons, however, though separately recorded for each county, are not yet arranged, as in Little Domesday, county by county, but grouped together. See below, p. 115.

[2] *V.C.H. Norfolk*, vol. ii, p. 4.

[3] *Palaeographical Society*, 2nd series, vol. i, pl. 70. The editors believed that the marginalia were probably the memoranda of those engaged upon a fair copy.

Exon Domesday, as an original fragment of the actual survey, could not be ignored: but neither, given his theory of the original returns, could it be explained. He accordingly ruled it out of the discussion as inexplicable, a compliment (I think) he paid to no other document of its time. It was, for example, omitted from the pedigree of Domesday manuscripts in *Feudal England*,[1] with the footnote: 'It will be observed that I do not touch the *Liber Exoniensis*.' To omit from the discussion about half the original evidence in the interests of a preconceived theory was plainly indefensible, and sixteen years later (1911) in his edition of Somerset Domesday he had the opportunity of reviewing his earlier conclusions. But his views remained unchanged and he concluded his preface with the words: 'It is greatly to be hoped that the Exon Book will some day receive at the hands of a trained scholar the full and critical treatment of which it stands in need and which may yet reveal its character, its origin, and its object.'[2] In this way Round in the interests of a theory made a mystery of Exon Domesday, and forty years later (1955) Professor Darlington, still championing Round's theory, in his edition of Wiltshire Domesday wrote: 'A more intensive study of the Exon Domesday than has been attempted as yet is needed before the relation of these two texts [i.e. Exchequer Domesday and Exon] can be determined.'[3] Exon Domesday in short is still to remain a mystery, since its prima facie character as a draft of the original returns of the south-western circuit is irreconcilable with Round's theory. We must, however, insist that no theory which fails to account for Exon Domesday is even worth consideration, and that Round's hypothesis must be judged to have failed until its adherents can show that Exon Domesday is something different from what it has every appearance of being.

[1] p. 146.   [2] *V.C.H. Somerset*, vol. i, p. 432.
[3] *V.C.H. Wiltshire*, vol. ii, p. 44. Cf. *E.H.R.* lxxii (1957), p. 94.

There are other objections to the view that the Domesday returns were a great series of hundred rolls: as, for
example, the date of the 'geld rolls' bound up with Exon
Domesday, the absence from the volume of hundred
rubrics, and the testimony of Robert of Hereford, which
was not even known when Round wrote. These are all
considered below. Here it is relevant to find just what
influenced Round to formulate and the learned world so
quickly to accept, his hypothesis. The explanation seems
to lie in the climate of learned opinion obtaining in the
Victorian England of his youth. The views of scholars
about the past were too deeply coloured by the world
around them, and they assumed an identity of purpose
between William's financial measures and the sustained
efforts of nineteenth-century liberal statesmen to purify
and rationalize the financial muddle which the new demo-
cracy had inherited from the past. Nowhere is this better
expressed than in Edward Augustus Freeman's *Norman
Conquest* (1876).

There is no need [he wrote] to depreciate the Survey and its
author by speaking of it as a mere vulgar instrument of extortion . . .
there is an evident connexion between the making of the Survey
and the great Danegeld which had been laid on two years before,
when Cnut of Denmark was threatening invasion. One great object
throughout the Survey clearly is to see that the tax was paid and
also that it was fairly paid. The reports which are made show at
once a wish to hinder the king from being defrauded of his right,
and a wish to hinder the subject from being made to pay more than
his fair proportion of the general tax. The payment or non-payment
of the *geld* is a matter which appears in every page of the Survey;
and it is perhaps not too much to say that the formal immediate
cause of taking the Survey was to secure its full and fair assessment.[1]

Ten years later there was a great 'Domesday Commemoration' whose proceedings were published (1888)
and dedicated (by permission) to Queen Victoria on the

[1] Vol. v, p. 4.

ground that Domesday Book was 'one of the greatest works of one of the greatest statesmen that ever ruled England, Her Majesty's illustrious ancestor and predecessor'. The first address was by Stuart Moore, who was concerned to explain away the awkward evidence of the only contemporary record then known, the Anglo-Saxon Chronicle.

This grumble of the Saxon monk, [he said] who like all his tribe resented all attempts to ascertain the wealth of the Church, must no longer be held up to the world as an instance of the rapacity and extortionate greed of the Conqueror. Thus all external evidence failing, we are driven back to the Record itself for evidence of the Conqueror's intention in framing it, and anyone who studies it will be driven to the inevitable conclusion that it was framed and designed in the spirit of perfect equity. . . .

In this situation his masterly and order-loving mind instituted this great inquiry, but ordered it to be taken (as I maintain the study of the Book will show) in the most public and open manner, and with the utmost impartiality, with the view of levying the taxes of the kingdom equally and fairly upon all. . . . He wished to ascertain in each case what was the old taxable assessment . . . but he directed his Commissioners to make a *new assessment*. . . . A more perfect method of assessment, a more just and reasonable basis of taxation can hardly be conceived, &c.[1]

The attitude revealed in these quotations was common to all students of the age. Everywhere there was talk of 'scientific' history and scholars were turning to the study of record sources, but without—as yet—any weakening of nationalist assumptions. History was still a pageant in which, though the costumes altered, the English 'nation' remained unchanged, and all 'good' kings (like William I) were 'patriot kings'. To historians in this frame of mind William I's avarice and oppression of the poor were offset, if not explained away, by his statesmanlike urge towards reform and the purification of the financial system. The idea that the deeper purpose of the Survey was to achieve

[1] *Domesday Studies*, vol. i (1888), p. 9.

a reassessment of the geld is far older than Freeman and long survived him. It was, of course, an anachronism foreign to the basic notions of the eleventh century and supported by no contemporary evidence. Geld was just one, though perhaps the most lucrative of a host of *customary* renders (*consuetudines*) of the most miscellaneous kind, and no consideration of equitable assessment arose. What was in question was the evasion of payment: the determination to record these obligations in writing and the pious hope—to quote the words of the commissioners' instructions—that more could be extracted than was being extracted at the moment ('et si potest plus haberi quam habeatur'). Nor, needless to say, was any reassessment of geld made. Nevertheless, Round learned from Freeman the current dogma of reassessment; Maitland in turn took it from Round; and even today it dies hard. To men in this frame of mind the (virtual) discovery and publication of the I.C.C. in 1876 was a godsend, for it seemed to bring much-needed proof to what they already believed. The geld was assessed and levied geographically from the top downwards: so much on the county; so much on the hundred and so much on the village; and so much on the manor where the village had been broken up. Supposing that 'scientific' reassessment had been the object of the commissioners, Round's hypothesis of the original returns was just what was needed. The assumption of an intended reassessment required geographic returns by hundreds. Domesday Book and Exon Domesday, which grouped estates in honours, were useless for such a purpose. No wonder, then, that Maitland complained of 'the curious compromising plan of Domesday Book', for he had completely misjudged its purpose.

The explanation of the making of Domesday Book suggested by Round is demonstrably inadequate; for it was based on a false assumption, and was irreconcilable with many, if not most, of the facts. The task now is to see Domesday Book in better perspective; and if so we must re-examine our basic sources. There are no short cuts to the truth in historical research, and the outlines of a new hypothesis set out in the following chapter were in fact the last part of the book to be written.

III

THE NEW HYPOTHESIS

THE objections to Round's explanation of the making of Domesday Book were not, and could not have been, apparent at the time when he wrote. Fundamentally they sprang from the over-simplification of a complicated administrative process, and this in turn was due to the Victorian preoccupation with purely constitutional history. In the last thirty years or more a new interest in administrative history and in original documents has gradually brought its shortcomings to light and corrected them.[1] Many problems capable of solution remain, but enough is now known to justify a more satisfactory explanation which at least covers all the facts. In the interest of clarity this new hypothesis is stated below, and demonstrated piecemeal in the chapters that follow. The evidence is technical and difficult; nor is it possible, as in Euclid, to proceed by deduction from a single premiss. Each inference in a matter of this kind depends upon a grasp of the evidence as a whole, and all lines of argument are interdependent. In the summary that follows, in order to help the reader, references are added to later pages where the more important arguments are discussed in detail.

The purpose of the survey

The new hypothesis is in essentials one of great simplicity. It asserts that Vol. I of Domesday Book—Great

[1] F. H. Baring, 'The Exeter Domesday', *E.H.R.* xxvii (1912), pp. 309–18; V. H. Galbraith, 'The Making of Domesday Book', ibid. lvii (1942), pp. 161–77, and 'The Date of the Geld Rolls', ibid. lxv (1950), pp. 1–17; Peter Sawyer, 'The "Original Returns" and Domesday Book', ibid. lxx (1955), pp. 177–97.

Domesday—preserves the official record of a royal inquiry made in 1086 into the lands and wealth of the royal demesne and of the king's tenants-in-chief: that this volume, written in a single, official script, and not improbably by a single scribe, was a direct abbreviation of seven (and perhaps more) very similar records, which differed from it only in containing a huge mass of detail, most of which was deliberately jettisoned in the final record. These seven (odd) 'circuit returns' were written on quires (or quaternions), as was Vol. I, in which each county was normally allowed one or more complete quires, according to size.[1] In the circuit return as in Great Domesday, each county began with a numbered list of 'holders of land', that is tenants-in-chief, starting with the king and then descending through archbishops, bishops, abbots, and other clerical holders, to earls, barons, and so on down the scale to the humblest tenant who held in chief. The smaller 'fees' were often grouped together under a single heading, e.g. 'king's thegns' or *ministri* or *servientes regis*. One of these huge circuit returns, that for the three eastern counties of Norfolk, Suffolk, and Essex, for some reason at which we can now only guess, was never added in epitome to Great Domesday. It may have been because the king's death in September 1087 abruptly brought the enterprise to a halt;[2] or it may be, as F. H. Baring thought, that the extraordinary complexity of socage tenure in East Anglia frightened the compiler from attempting to condense it. From the death of the Conqueror these two very different volumes have been unequally yoked together, and zealously preserved.

Such in a nutshell is the hypothesis the demonstration of which lies in the contemporary literature, the two precious originals of Domesday Book, the decisive but overlooked testimony of Exon Domesday, and lastly

---

[1] *Domesday Re-Bound* (H.M.S.O., 1954), Appendix 1.
[2] The evidence for the date of D.B. vol. I is summarized below, pp. 180–88.

but not least the climate of opinion obtaining in England immediately after the Norman Conquest. Before we attempt to summarize the evidence in detail, it is well to realize that the Normans were never so 'feudal' as when they arrived in England, and that they thought less of the ancient counties and hundreds than of honours or baronies or fiefs held directly of the Crown. Each of them was a single complex of separate estates or manors, wherever situated, and it was treated as a unit and normally had its *caput baroniae*. True, not all baronies were held of the Crown: there were mesne or honorial baronies, but these were in general the concern not of the king but of the great lord of whom they were held. There is scattered through Domesday Book a great deal about honorial barons, but it is there only to distinguish what was demesne from what was sub-infeudated in the larger baronies held in chief. And so a great revolution in the legal theory of landholding was put on record by Domesday Book, for when the royal demesne and the estates of the tenants-in-chief were listed, the whole of England was accounted for. After the Survey, in the Saxon chronicler's words, 'there was not a "hide" of land in England of which the king did not know who held it and how much it was worth'.[1] The presence of the king's chaplains, cooks, huntsmen, and other small holders at the end of each county must not obscure the plain fact that Domesday Book sets out the pattern of English society in the most aristocratic and autocratic period in its history.

We have already seen that the prima facie case for the new hypothesis depends upon the striking contrast which the one volume of Domesday presents to the other. Nineteenth-century scholars, working from the printed edition, gave little thought to the differences between the two volumes. Today we see them with other eyes; and their long association is manifestly fortuitous and accidental;

---

[1] *Anglo-Saxon Chronicle*, ed. Garmonsway, p. 220.

for both the script and the style establish their different provenance. The first volume is written in a single distinctive set hand; and, I think, a curial hand which has affinities however distant with the later official hands of the king's court. The second volume is the work of several different scribes, writing scripts of varying sizes and merit, with no common characteristics. There are in addition the widest differences in the style of the two volumes and in the rubrication. Finally it soon becomes clear that each is the product of a rather different operation: for while the scribe of Vol. I is proved to be directly compressing a larger original whose arrangement he alters from time to time, the scribes of Vol. II were doing little more than making a largely mechanical fair copy of a very similar exemplar. The *onus probandi* therefore lies upon those who would, against the evidence of their eyes, attribute both to the royal scriptorium.

The evidence of the original volumes is borne out by that of Exon Domesday, which was ignored by the Victorians, partly because it was irreconcilable with preconceived ideas, partly from a suspicion that it was not itself a surviving original of the Survey, but a later compilation.[1] This view, however, is disproved both by the palaeography and the internal evidence which provides ample proof that its compilers had not yet decided how to arrange the royal demesne or how to classify the smaller tenants-in-chief, and so had not arrived at the stage of compiling a numbered list of tenants-in-chief at the head of each county. The heading, *French Thegns*, for example, which we find in Somerset could not possibly have appeared after the Survey was completed. The only true thegns were English thegns, and the same people are thus classified in the abbreviation of these counties found in Vol. I of Domesday Book. Exon Domesday, therefore, was the penultimate version of the local circuit return

---

[1] e.g. Vinogradoff, *English Society in the Eleventh Century*, p. 228.

for the south-western circuit, and analogous to the compilation which we know to have preceded 'Little Domesday' in circuit VII. It antedates by a few months Vol. I of
Domesday Book, and it survives at Exeter because it was
superseded by a much revised version which became the
return of the circuit.[1]

On the evidence, then, of Little Domesday and Exon
Domesday, we may reasonably infer that the original
returns of the other circuits were arranged, as these
volumes are and as Vol. I is, by royal demesne and the
county fiefs of individual tenants-in-chief. That no two
of them were entirely alike is suggested by the existing
differences in the shortened text of Vol. I, which are the
only evidence of the number and grouping of the circuits.
But equally it is safe to assume that all were broadly similar to Little Domesday, in which each county begins with
a numbered list of the tenants-in-chief whose fees are successively set out in the text that follows. Thus as each
circuit return arrived at Winchester the abbreviator was
faced with the responsible, but not impossible, task of
compressing, by the omission of all but essential facts, a
text of 400 or more pages into something less than forty.
This he did directly from the larger text before him, which
it is vital to observe was already arranged exactly in the
form he required it. Turning to Vol. I, it is then possible
to see exactly how he went to work. On the first folio of
his county the abbreviator set out the particulars of the
chief town or towns, no matter where they were found in
the manuscript before him. The rest of the leaf was filled
by copying from the circuit return the numbered list of
holders of land, varying from little more than a dozen to
more than eighty according to the county. He then continued with his abbreviated text of successive fees. As
these entries were already marked and numbered in the

[1] All this below, Chapter VIII. Note too that the actual script of vol. I is
found on two normal leaves of Exon Domesday: below, p. 109.

animalia . & . lx . oues . & . xx . agros nemoris . & . C . agros p̄ti . .
& . C . agros pascue . hec manerio reddt . x . libras panni . & q̄rdo
.i. recepit eā . ualebat tantūdē .

& . ii . carr . Ibi hr . R . v . uitt . & . iii . bordar . & . ii . serui . & . vii . porc .
& . lxv . oues . & . iii . ag nemeti . & . xii . ag p̄ti . & . xii . ag pascue .
& uat panni . xx . sot & . qn . W . recep̄ . ualeb . xxx . sot .

p̄ . v . his . has posse arare . iiii . carr . de his hr . W . iii .
hidasi . & . i . uirgata . & . ii . carr . i d̄nio . & uillani . ii .

Abbas hr . i . mansionē q̄ uocat Talgar . q̄ tenuit Suuuin l̄atḃ ea dię q̄ rex ē f u.
+ . o . 7 reddebat Gildū p d̄m uirga hanc pot arare .i. carr . o̅ tenra ō ermenals se

11. Selected Scripts from Exon Domesday

margins of the text before him, the abbreviator did not in fact require to consult the preliminary list again. He simply followed the manuscript before him, leaving to the rubricator the final task of adding against each fee in red ink the name of the holder and the number of his fee from the preliminary list. Now it has often been noticed that the rubricator in Vol. I of Domesday Book has had repeatedly to 'fudge' his marginal numbers to make them agree with those in the list at the head of the county. This oddity suggested a careful comparison of the order and writing of the preliminary lists with the text that followed, and this disclosed the astonishing fact that the two very rarely if ever completely correspond. In some cases the list contains names absent from the text, in others names in the text are not found in the list. Sometimes the order of the names in the list differs from that in the text. Sometimes the same man is differently described in text and list, while in many counties the grouping of the smaller fees at the end of the list varies from that of text to which it should act as a guide. No one any longer believes that Domesday Book is free from errors, or expects that it should be; but those who have studied it most closely are best aware of the sustained effort made by its compilers to achieve accuracy. These persistent if slight discrepancies in virtually every county between what we should now call the Table of Contents and the text that follows therefore require explanation: and a close examination shows that the abbreviator also carried out a good many editorial changes, partly in the interests of uniformity, partly in the correction of local practice where that conflicted with the basic principle of the inquiry. Thus, when the name of a mesne tenant had crept into the circuit list, the abbreviator substituted for it the name of the tenant-in-chief; nor did he hesitate to alter the groupings of the smaller men at the end of the lists. With the full text before him, the abbreviator ignored the list he had copied from the circuit return, and the discrepancies were only discovered when the rubricator added in the text the numbers corresponding with those in the prefatory list. That this explanation is correct is finally proved by Little Domesday. There, by contrast, there is a perfect tally between lists and text for Essex, Norfolk, and Suffolk, since in the circuit return the preliminary list served as a guide to the copyist who, without it, would not have known in what order to arrange the fiefs.[1]

Thus in the prefatory county lists of Great Domesday we have our only surviving traces of the circuit returns before this material was epitomized: and a much closer scrutiny of them would yield valuable results. Meanwhile, they are of importance here as inescapable proof of the soundness of the new hypothesis.

So far we have established that in both the eastern counties and those of the south-west there were at least two successive versions of the circuit return, of which Little Domesday is the final copy of circuit VII and Exon the penultimate version of circuit II. But it is significant that both these volumes are engrossed records, written in the current minuscule of the monastic manuscripts of the time. They are then no mere first attempts or rough copies, and belong to the later stages of the Inquest. Behind them we can be sure must have lain earlier and partial drafts of which in fact some traces remain. From both Evesham[2] and Bath Abbey,[3] for example, we have rather baffling fragments, which are connected with the evolution of the circuit returns, though we cannot yet fully explain them. From Ely[4] and from Kent,[5] fortunately, more substantial fragments have survived, which throw a great deal of

[1] Below, pp. 192 sqq. It is worth noting that in Cambridgeshire the discrepancies between the prefatory list of tenants-in-chief and the text that follows are unusually marked.
[2] P. Sawyer, 'Evesham A, a Domesday Text' (*Worcester Hist. Soc.* 1960).
[3] R. Lennard, 'A Neglected Domesday Satellite', *E.H.R.* lviii (1943), pp. 32–41.   [4] Below, Chapter IX.   [5] Below, Chapter X.

light on the earlier, if not the first, steps taken by the commissioners. To understand their evidence we must attempt to reconstruct in some detail the actual procedure followed at the Inquest.

The procedure of the Inquest

We may begin with the Inquisitio Comitatus Cantabrigiensis which presents a striking contrast to our other sources of information. Instead of setting out the facts, as they do, under the headings of royal demesne and individual fiefs, it proceeds geographically by hundreds and by vills. The I.C.C. begins with a list of the jurors' names in the hundred of Staploe followed by the full manorial descriptions of the estates in each of its constituent villages. The other hundreds follow in order, each preceded by the names of its eight jurymen, four French and four English. A much shortened and reorganized version of the facts is found in Great Domesday, where each estate is found under the name of the appropriate tenant-in-chief. There are, however, clear traces in the Domesday text of the order of hundreds followed in the I.C.C., and also of a fixed order of villages within each hundred. Arduous research, too, has shown that this 'hundredal order' is characteristic of many other counties, and perhaps of all the counties surveyed.[1] Thus the supreme value of the I.C.C. lies in the unique proof it affords of the administrative procedure followed by the commissioners in every circuit. But we must not confuse the formal court procedure with the final record constructed from it, the circuit return. That was already arranged by fees, as we find them in our three basic and contemporary manuscripts. It is unlikely that any two circuits proceeded entirely alike, if we may judge from surviving fragments. The beginnings, however, are lost, and behind our basic

[1] P. Sawyer, 'The "Original Returns" and Domesday Book', *E.H.R.* lxx (1955), pp. 177–97.

documents in which the facts are set forth in a regular and almost unvarying form, there must have been earlier recensions. The I.C.C., although it has long been regarded as a partial copy of the circuit return to Winchester, is in fact a primitive fragment of one of these occasional survivals. To understand it aright involves a detailed examination of the Inquest procedure.

Soon after the Christmas debate at Gloucester in 1085, the king's commissioners (*legati, barones*) set out on their task in much the same manner as the general eyre of later days. Each of the seven (or more) circuits had its own panel of justices, though this term is never used by contemporaries. Everywhere, so far as we can judge, they dealt one by one with the group of counties assigned to them, sitting in the chief towns and holding special sessions of a reinforced county court. Of their numbers, and the personnel of each circuit very little is known. In the fifth circuit four considerable barons dealt with Worcestershire,[1] one of whom was a bishop; and another ecclesiastic, the bishop of Durham, was among the commissioners of the south-western circuit (no. II). But, apart from the fact that care was taken not to include the names of local magnates, we know nothing of the arrangements. In the terms of reference the operation is described as an 'inquest of lands by the king's barons', that is to say by the oath of the sheriff of the shire, and all the barons and their Frenchmen, and of the whole hundred, the priest, the reeve, and six *villani* of each village. The questions which the court had to answer are set out with precision:

1. What is the name of the mansion?
2. Who held it in the time of King Edward?
3. Who now holds it?

---

[1] Heming, *Chartularium*, ed. Hearne, vol. i, p. 288. Remigius, bishop of Lincoln, Walter Giffard, Henry de Ferrers, Adam brother of Eudo Dapifer, sent 'ad inquirendas et describendas possessiones et consuetudines tam regis quam principum suorum'.

4. How many hides are there?
5. How many teams—in demesne—of the tenants?
6. How many villans—cottars—slaves?
7. How many freemen—sokemen?
8. How much wood—meadow—pasture? How many mills? How many fisheries?
9. How much has been added or taken away?
10. How much was the whole worth? How much is it worth now?
11. How much had or has each freeman or sokeman there?
     All this is to be given in triplicate; that is, in the time of King Edward, when King William gave it, and at the present time.
12. And if more can be had than is had.

An inquest on this scale entailed the appearance of many hundreds of persons, who must have been summoned to attend on fixed dates according to a rigid time-table. The sessions of the court too must have been numerous and conducted with great formality, for the legal assumption behind them was that the whole county was bound by the sworn evidence tendered orally to the commissioners. Before we turn to the procedure of the Inquest, let us look at the questionnaire from which we can best gauge the intentions of the central government. First, we note that it is neither an inquiry into the geld, which is not even mentioned, nor into the village or the village community, on which the local assessment of geld depended. It is not in fact a geographical inquiry at all, but a personal inquiry requiring a cut-and-dried list of those who held land, by which was meant those who held in chief of the king, together with a full description (*descriptio*) of each *mansio*, manor, or estate held by them. The basic unit of the inquiry was in short the manor, of which there might be anything from one to half a dozen in a single village. Secondly, the questions asked fall into two distinct categories, viz. those to which a hundred jury of small landholders, half French and half English, can be reasonably supposed to have had the answers; and those which could only be answered by the sitting tenant of each manor. To the former of these belong the second and ninth questions, together with the final counsel of perfection—very imperfectly fulfilled—which required all the questions to be answered at three successive dates. These all relate to the past, and scores of entries in Vol. I of Domesday Book prove that the main function of the hundred jury was to testify to ownership, before the Conquest, and to subsequent disseisins, *invasiones*, and *terrae occupatae*. The interminable quarrels arising from questions 2 and 9, often involving a cloud of witnesses on either side, suggest that most of the formal sessions of the Inquest were occupied with their ventilation. They were a vital part of the information required, and the usual practice was to register with precision the conflicting claims, rather than to decide between them. The remaining questions were primarily the concern of the man who actually farmed the manor, though in several of them the jury also had an interest. But nos. 5, 6, 7, 8, together with the minute record of the animal stock upon the demesne, can only have been answered by the representative of each manor, whose presence at the Inquest we know to have been required by the commissioners. Nor is it realistic to suppose that many scores of illiterate bailiffs, or their masters (however intelligent), could have tendered these manorial statistics in open court within the time limits allowed to the Inquest. The more one thinks about it, the more difficult it is to avoid the conclusion that the bulk of the information was collected in advance of the actual Inquest. If so, much of the information, already arranged under the name of the owners, was already before the court in orderly form when the formal proceedings began;

and these were largely concerned with the heated quarrels of important persons so often recorded, amid the general waste of manorial particulars, in our texts.[1]

This sketch of the actual procedure is totally at variance with the views of Victorian scholars. Adolphus Ballard, for instance, from whose careful volume on the *Domesday Inquest* I have copied the list of questions, remarks:

> The jury for each hundred would answer these questions for each vill in that hundred, and their answers could be noted down in detail, as in the Cambridgeshire inquest. . . . The jurors would speak to all these details from personal knowledge. . . . When the returns had been thus compiled, hundred by hundred, and vill by vill, they were sent to the king's house at Winchester, and there rearranged.[2]

Since Ballard wrote in 1906 the criticism of records has made great strides, and it is now understood that records are normally complex compilations from earlier documents, however much they strive to hide the fact. Documents, too, involving the use of juries are particularly suspect, for the eleventh-century jury was not yet the sure shield of personal freedom which it later became. It was, contrariwise, a highly unpopular royal device to give legal justification to the despotic action of the Crown. No one today takes the medieval *proofs of age* at their face value: still less the *inquisitiones post mortem* in which the intricate details of real estate, known only to the dead man's steward and the escheator, are said to be declared in open court by a jury, whose names are solemnly set forth in the document.[3] If this is true of the thirteenth, fourteenth, and fifteenth centuries, it can only have been truer still of the eleventh, and there is therefore no reason to suppose that the I.C.C. bears any practical relationship to the actual processes by which the circuit returns were put

[1] Below, Chapter VI, p. 120, and Chapter X.   [2] *The Domesday Inquest*, p. 15.
[3] C. G. Crump, 'A Note on the Criticism of Records', *Bulletin of J.R.L.* viii (1924), pp. 140–9.

together. Like other documents which involve juries it is a purely formal record that sought to give a veneer of officialdom and legality to a mass of particulars compiled, more or less, in the manner suggested above. The court, perhaps, required a statement of its proceedings in legal form, stage by stage, as the interrogation of each hundred was completed; for there is evidence that each hundred was originally a separate document. However that may be, a close examination of the I.C.C. shows:[1]

(*a*) That it was never a complete record of the Domesday findings, nor was it copied from such a document. It systematically omits the royal manors of ancient demesne, and many other particulars which were added later.

(*b*) That the information it contains was already known to its compilers in what we may call Domesday form, for it mentions, more than once, the *breve regis* or schedule of the *Terra Regis*.

About this unique and late fragment we shall be wise not to dogmatize: but we can safely say that it is an early recension of most of the evidence, and that it formed the basis of the circuit return.[2] But that return, of which it formed the basis, was broadly analogous in its composition to Little Domesday, the local return of circuit VII.

The I.C.C., however, does not stand alone as a guide to the procedure followed by the commissioners. From Kent, and therefore from the first circuit, we have a sizeable fragment of what appears to be the earliest written record of the inquest proceedings. From this document we derive the constructive suggestion that the court proceedings

---

[1] Below, Chapter IX.

[2] The fact is finally proved by the shortened text in vol. I of Domesday Book, in which the discrepancies between the prefatory list of tenants-in-chief and the text that follows are above the normal. The fees of the forty-four tenants-in-chief in the list are all described in the text: but two of them (Peter of Valonges and Picot of Cambridge) are transposed: there are many differences of spelling, and some of title (e.g. Eudo fitz Hubert for Eudo Dapifer); and the marginal numbering of the fees is all at sea. Cf. above, p. 34.

in this circuit were concerned only to identify each estate, and to record the change of ownership since King Edward's day. Into this limited record were inserted the full manorial descriptions, which had been put together 'out of court' from the testimony of the local representatives attending the Inquest. The suggestion seems reasonable and practical; and it is strongly supported by evidence from Exon Domesday. In the absence of evidence from other circuits, we dare not generalize, but the Kentish document clearly lies nearer to what actually happened than the I.C.C. and it may well represent the practice of other circuits.

One last question, viz. How exactly was the information recorded in court? We have already ruled out the suggestion of the I.C.C. that the whole complicated mass of statistics was verbally declared to the commissioners, in favour of the limited geographical record made in Kent. This may well have been actually written out in court as the questions were answered. But evidence from Essex proves that there was another possibility.[1] In Little Domesday the twenty-one hundreds of Essex are recorded in each fief in an unvarying 'hundredal order'. Two of them, however, Dengie and Uttlesford, each occur twice, and at some distance apart, in the series. This can only mean that both juries were recalled to give further evidence, which, had the court record been made as in Kent, would have been added to the relevant roll of that hundred. We are thus forced to conclude that in the East Anglian circuit the particulars declared verbally in court were immediately recorded in court on separate sheets, one for each tenant-in-chief. The record for East Anglia was therefore arranged in its final Domesday form from the very outset. The same is almost certainly true of the south-western circuit, in which they did not even bother to record the names of the hundreds in which the manors were situated. It may

---

[1] Below, p. 158.

well be that this procedure was confined to these two circuits.

Amid many uncertainties one fact clearly emerges from the discussion of these preliminary documents, viz. that the final return for each circuit was only slowly evolved through several recensions. In some circuits, as in Kent, these began with a short geographical record which was turned by the circuit commissioners into a final return arranged by persons and fiefs: in others as in East Anglia and the south-west the facts were recorded right away in this final form. The earlier versions were of no further practical use to the commissioners when once this local return was completed, and some of them fell into private hands: the I.C.C. for Cambridge and Hertfordshire passed to Ely which also secured access to the parent volume of Little Domesday; the Kentish record to the three great churches of Christchurch, St. Augustine's, and Rochester; and Exon Domesday to the cathedral of Exeter.

Such then is our hypothesis of the making of Domesday Book. In the slow course of its elaboration over the years other important facts have come to light which are touched on in their place as they occur. In one important matter, however, viz. *the geld*, they all have a direct bearing on the main theme, and as such must be shortly summarized.

Firstly, the geld or Danegeld which was annual until the year 1051, and just as certainly collected annually in the twelfth century, was in the later years of William I once again an annual tax, or rather custom (*consuetudo*). The rate at which it was levied, that is to say the number of shillings charged on the hide, varied; but its levy which depended simply on the royal prerogative was annual and it is actually so described on the first folio of Staffordshire[1] Domesday, though the reference seems hitherto to have escaped notice.

[1] D.B., vol. I, f. 246 a 1.

Secondly, the geld accounts in Exon Domesday, which for a hundred years have been wrongly assigned to the levy in 1084, were unquestionably compiled in 1086,[1] from which it follows that the Domesday Inquest coincided with a geld levy. Indeed, the most contemporary of all literary references to the Domesday Inquest, that of Robert of Hereford, confuses or rather combines the two essentially separate but practically common activities: 'The whole land', he says, 'was vexed by calamities coming from the collection of the king's money.'[2]

This indeed is something new, the full implications of which must be left to the political historians of the reign. Here it is sufficient to point out that this discovery is still another corrective of the Victorian anachronisms regarding taxation which mar our textbooks. The geld was just one, and not necessarily the most profitable, of innumerable royal *consuetudines* or customs, automatically and annually exacted; and it would perhaps be more in keeping with the eleventh century to say not that it was actually levied in the year 1086, but that *of course* it was levied. Equally 'of course' it was essentially different from the Domesday Inquest with which it coincided, and whose purpose was to ascertain the wealth of the tenants-in-chief in lands and customs, with a view to their exploitation. In the avaricious mind of William I the information had, as we have seen, far wider possibilities than a reassessment of geld, but meanwhile, in the south-west at least, it served to tighten up the annual collection of geld that was taking place. Here, in fact, there was a special geld inquest, carried out apparently by the same or some of the same commissioners as were responsible for the Domesday Survey. How far this example was followed in other circuits we have, in the absence of other geld accounts, no means of judging; and it is significant that

---

[1] Below, Chapter VII.
[2] *Anglo-Saxon Chronicle*, ed. Garmonsway, p. 219.

the shortened text of Vol. I of Domesday Book for these counties would not by itself have led us to suspect that it had ever taken place. But we know more than enough to substitute for the pre-Gladstone reformer, the Saxon chronicler's stern picture of a king who, like his leading men, was 'fond, yea too fond of avarice' and would sell the same land three times over, as often in fact as he could find a higher bidder.[1] And he, like us, found these facts distressing to relate of a 'king of great wisdom and power who surpassed in honour and in strength those who had gone before him'.[1]

---

[1] *Anglo-Saxon Chronicle*, ed. Garmonsway, p. 219.

IV

THE FRAMEWORK OF THE SURVEY

AFTER twenty years of Norman rule it seems likely that the O.E. administration had been rapidly developed but not transformed. In England, as elsewhere, the Normans appear as an open-minded, highly adaptable people, ready, as we say, 'to try anything once' and to make it work. Coming from a small impoverished duchy, which had suffered as much as England from bad government and internal strife, they took over a more highly developed system of government than anything they had known at home. In Normandy before the Conquest there is no clear evidence of the keeping of any central written records, and the duke did not even possess a seal.[1] In England there had been some sort of Chancery department for nearly a century before the Conquest, which used sealed writs written in the vernacular to convey the king's orders to the shire courts. There was also a well-established financial organization permanently located at Winchester. This no doubt also used some sort of written records, though none has survived. The change of language (from English to Latin so far as records were concerned, and from English to French for social purposes) explains their disappearance, but the lone survival of a vernacular geld roll for Northamptonshire from the middle of the Conqueror's reign suggests that written tax records at least antedate the Conquest. The main task of the Winchester treasury was to collect the royal revenue: the profits of jurisdiction, the payments of boroughs, the render in

[1] There were, however, precedents in Sicily. See Miss Clementi's notes below, pp. 55-58.

money or in kind from the royal estates, and the geld when it happened. The later practice of the assay and of blanching the farm too were already known before the Norman Conquest, and all this may be presumed to have involved written records. It has been well said that the administrative machinery of the Anglo-Saxon kings is characterized by a 'rudimentary precocity'. But it remains true that we can easily exaggerate the degree of development reached by the central organs of government at this time. There were already written records in use, but the government was still predominantly customary and oral: and it is hardly before the thirteenth century that the government became bureaucratic in character. This is brought home to us by the fact that the great 'honours' or complexes of lands granted by William to his tenants-in-chief seem to have been made *sine carta*, that is orally and without written records. So too with justice; the transfer of more than half the land of England to a new nobility in this primitive fashion involved confusion, spoliation, and the seizing of land without title. From the great churches— Ely, Worcester, and Canterbury in particular—bitter complaints reached the king, and before 1086 there had grown up a well-developed habit of sending royal *legati* to investigate these matters in the shire courts. On these occasions a conjoined court of three or four counties would meet, and the sworn testimony of the English, who alone knew the facts, be taken as to the state of affairs 'on the day when King Edward was alive and dead'. Their findings, committed to writing, were returned to the king. In these primitive lawsuits oral evidence was the rule and written evidence exceptional and therefore especially valued. For this reason the side that could produce written evidence was likely to win, and the abbey of Bury attributed its success in its long struggle with the East Anglian bishops to the written evidence it was able to produce against the merely oral claims of the other side. We read too of Bishop Wulfstan of Worcester (1062–95) carefully repairing all the original deeds of his church, and having copies made for future use. Society was in fact at a 'betwixt and between' stage and a common formula of the Domesday jurors in disputed cases about land is that they have neither seen the king's seal (i.e. a royal writ) nor a royal agent to give livery of seisin. On all sides there was a growing awareness that it was a step forward merely 'to get the facts recorded in writing'.

In the localities each shire had its sheriff, who was essentially a royal agent. The shires in turn were divided into hundreds and/or wapentakes, each administered by its reeve or bailiff. But beneath this 'specious uniformity' both shires and hundreds were characterized by the greatest diversity in age, in customs, and in organization. By the time of the Conquest, says Professor Barlow, 'the whole organisation was riddled with immunities and complicated by anomalies and as a system existed no more'.[1] It may even be doubted whether the vanished 'system' to which historians look back had itself ever been more than an aspiration, for shire, hundred, and borough in Domesday Book are all marked by endless variety of ancient custom and practice vouched for only by the testimony of living men. Of nothing is this more true than the hide, the traditional 'land of one family', an immemorial unit of population, military organization, and taxation. There were large hides and small hides, though to the central government the hide seems to have meant a unit divisible into 120 acres. It was thus at once a measure of area and a unit of assessment, the fiscal hide. Every county had so many hides, and each hundred and village. In the whole system there was a marked tendency to round numbers, which tended to a village-valuation of ten or still more often five hides. These round numbers are hidden in Domesday Book by the fact that so many

[1] *The Feudal Kingdom of England*, p. 43.

villages were long since broken up into two or more separate estates, each with its separate lord answering for his own fraction of the total obligation. No doubt, then, that the Domesday hides are fiscal, for geld was paid at the rate of so many shillings on the hide: but a great many entries leave no doubt that this rating was assumed to bear a real and practical relationship to area, value, and the number of ploughs. Thus that the number of hides in each village was a matter of importance to its inhabitants as well as their rulers seems to follow from the fact that it was also the basis of fyrd service; and that it was a matter of common knowledge is suggested by the place-name Fyfield, which has evolved from the words *five hides*. Everything to do with hides was of high antiquity, and their use and meaning were by 1066 in confusion, deepened by the exemptions, or the practice of 'beneficial rating', to reduce an assessment by king and sheriff after the Conquest. For example, at Madingley in Cambridge-shire we read that it answered for 15 hides before the Conquest, though there were in fact no more than 10 hides, and that by 1086 this assessment had been reduced to 7½.[1] Add the fact that the village was further subdivided into a number of separate manors, each bearing its propor-tion of the unreal but reduced assessment, and the total picture is one of confusion thrice confounded. It was to deal with this jungle of custom that the Domesday Survey was undertaken and we can still dimly perceive the motives at work. The facts about each manor were de-manded at three separate dates: (*a*) at the moment of the Conquest, for no one dared look farther back, (*b*) when the present holder received the estate, and (*c*) in 1086. No doubt it was a council of perfection, very imperfectly achieved, but nothing less could hope to unearth the facts of the situation. We are apt to forget that the commis-sioners had not only to put on record the *status quo* at the

[1] I.C.C., p. 95.

time of the Conquest but to unravel so far as possible the anarchic changes of the twenty years that had since elapsed. The Survey was at one and the same time a fact-finding inquiry and a vast judicial eyre on the innumerable differences and disputes of the period 1066–86.

The extraordinary social muddle of 1066, illustrated above by the single factor of the hidage arrangements, could be equally well pursued into the still darker questions of hundredal organization (*manerium cum hundredo*), of social status (*socmen*), of jurisdiction (sac and suit), of *feorms*, and so on. All further inquiry carries a warning not to read back into a remote past a conception of state action, which was at the time impossible. The very notion of reform was still unthought of, and all obligations were either religious, or found their sanction in custom and the past. The practical Norman genius by its Domesday inquiry sought simply to enforce that sanction by putting the facts beyond dispute, and putting them down in black and white.

In striking contrast with the variety of local custom, and the attendant confusion from the slow accretion over centuries of independent states into a single body politic, was the relative simplicity and efficiency of the administrative machinery superimposed upon it in the course of the tenth century. Considered in relation to their age, the shire, the hundred, and the manor, each with its court, formed a system for enforcing the king's will, doing justice, and collecting taxes which was probably without parallel at the time. It was the Norman inheritance from the past; and the most impressive, though not the earliest, evidence of the energy with which they developed and exploited the machinery is found in the Domesday Survey. The result was an admirable and exhaustive record of the royal demesne in each county, and comparable, if rather less satisfactory, summaries of the land and revenues of his tenants-in-chief. This difference sprang from the fact that the honours and baronies created after 1066 followed the 'feudal' principles of the Continent, whose introduction constituted a social, if silent, revolution. The king became the supreme landlord and the scattered lands of each tenant-in-chief a single fief, held by homage and fealty in return for a *servitium debitum* of knights, and subject to a variety of other feudal customs and services, yet with a wide sphere of internal autonomy, including important rights of jurisdiction and service from those honorial barons whom great magnates in turn enfeoffed. All this is very imperfectly reflected in Domesday Book, which merely lists and describes the lands of the tenants-in-chief, great and small, county by county, and the chief sub-tenancies. With fiefs as such (the *caput baronie*, the *servitium debitum*, and tenancies at more than one remove) it is not concerned,[1] with the result that only in living memory have scholars painfully pieced together the main lines of the feudal system of the age.

The story of Domesday Book begins with a famous entry in the Anglo-Saxon Chronicle,[2] written by an English monk, who for a time had 'dwelt in King William's court and looked on his face'.

The King spent Christmas (1085) with his councillors at Gloucester, and held his court there for five days, which was followed by a three-day synod held by the archbishop and the clergy. At this synod Maurice was elected bishop of London and William bishop of Norfolk and Robert bishop of Cheshire: they were all chaplains of the King.

After this the King had a great council and very deep speech with his witan about this land and how it was peopled, and with what sort of men. Then he sent his men all over England into every shire to ascertain how many hundreds of 'hides' of land there were

[1] Domesday does sometimes tell of sub-sub-tenants and at Lubbenham in Leicestershire of a sub-sub-sub-tenant (Vol. I, f. 230 b. 2, cited Stenton, *William the Conqueror*, p. 447).

[2] *The Anglo-Saxon Chronicle*, ed. B. Thorpe (R.S. 1861); and, in translation, G. N. Garmonsway (1953).

in each shire, and how much land and live-stock the king himself owned in each county, and what annual dues were lawfully his from each shire. He also had it recorded how much land his archbishops had, and his diocesan bishops, his abbots and his earls, and—though I may be going into too great detail—what or how much each man who was a landholder here in England had in land or in live-stock, and how much money it was worth. So very thoroughly did he have the inquiry carried out that there was not a single 'hide', not one virgate of land, not even—it is shameful to record but it did not seem shameful for him to do—not even one ox, nor one cow, nor one pig which escaped notice in his survey. And all the surveys [gewrita] were subsequently brought to him.

The author of the Chronicle rarely wastes words, and the mere space he gives to the Survey is significant. It was clearly without precedent: and, reading between the lines, we gather that our author was both resentful of the inquiry and suspicious of the king's intentions. Did he suspect the levying of further taxes? He almost seems to have taken it for granted, for in the entry of the next year (1086) he tells us that before the king crossed over to Normandy, he 'levied very heavy taxes on his subjects upon any pretext, whether justly or unjustly'. A year later when the king was dead, he again refers—in a long obituary—to Domesday Book as one of his greatest achievements, comparable with the subjection of Scotland and Wales. And once again he stresses his financial extortions.

> A hard man was the king
> And took from his subjects many marks
> In gold and many more hundreds of pounds in silver
> These sums he took by weight from his people
> Mostly unjustly and for little need
> He was sunk in greed
> And utterly given up to avarice.[1]

[1] *The Anglo-Saxon Chronicle*, ed. Garmonsway, p. 220. William II, immediately after his coronation, visited the Treasury at Winchester in order to inspect 'the untold wealth there gathered in gold, in silver, in vessels, in costly

Until fifty years ago the account of the English chronicler was our only reliable literary evidence on the Domesday Survey. Then, in 1907, W. H. Stevenson[1] discovered in a Bodleian manuscript a new Latin account which had eluded all previous inquirers. It occurs in a technical treatise on chronology written in the very year of the Survey: and its author was Robert, bishop of Hereford, who, as Sir Frank Stenton remarks, must have been present at that 'deep speech' in Gloucester after Christmas 1085.

In this, the twentieth year of his reign, by order of William, king of the English, there was made a survey (*descriptio*) of the whole of England, that is to say, of the lands of the several provinces of England, and of the possessions of each and of all the magnates. This was done in respect of plough land and habitations, and of men both bond and free, both those who dwelt in cottages and those who had houses and some arable land and in respect of ploughs and horses and other animals; and in respect of the services and payments due from all men in the whole land. Other investigators (*inquisitores*) followed the first; and men were sent into provinces which they did not know, and where they were themselves unknown, in order that they might be given the opportunity of checking the first survey, and, if necessary, of denouncing its authors as guilty to the king. And the land was vexed with many calamities arising from the collection of the royal money.[2]

This notice, though more precise, is in close general agreement with the Chronicle to which, however, it adds two striking pieces of new information. First, that there were two successive eyres of the royal commissioners to prevent or minimize collusion and fraud; second, and even more startling, that the Survey coincided with a tax levy, since 'many calamities arose from the collection of the royal money', *ex congregatione regalis pecunie.*

robes and in jewels, and in many other precious things which are difficult to enumerate' (ibid., p. 222).

[1] *E.H.R.* xxii (1907), p. 74.

[2] Stubbs, *Select Charters*, p. 95, for the Latin text. There is an echo of this account in *Florence of Worcester* (ed. B. Thorpe), vol. ii, p. 19.

The importance of Stevenson's new text for Domesday studies is not easily exaggerated. Round's *Feudal England* had appeared in 1895 and Maitland's *Domesday and Beyond* in 1897—both too early to make use of the evidence of Robert of Hereford, which is even more authoritative than that of the Chronicle. Both writers are describing the actual Survey, and both insist that the last year and a half of William's reign was marked by extortionate taxation. From their combined testimony we may infer that the actual conduct of the Survey coincided with the levy of the geld; and this inference is at least partly substantiated by the discovery that the geld rolls, bound up with Exon Domesday, belong, not as was long believed to 1084, but to the very year of the Survey (1086).[1] Thus, the Survey appears as an extraordinary measure, independent of the apparently ceaseless process of financial extortion which marked William's later years. And this, if we read carefully, is precisely the tenor of the Anglo-Saxon chronicler's description, which records his suspicions of still heavier exactions as likely to result from the inquiry.[2] Finally, it is worth noting that neither writer even mentions the word geld, and that both conceived of the Inquest as a writing down [*descriptio*] of the lands of the king and his magnates, so comprehensive and minute that every acre, nay every cow, ox, or sheep had to be recorded. The text of the Survey more than bears them out, for it contains a mass of detailed information about most of the towns and cities, though not of London or Winchester.

Domesday Book, then, records the results of an inquiry

[1] Below, p. 91.
[2] The verdict of contemporaries on William I's avarice is fully endorsed by the writers of the early twelfth century—Florence of Worcester, William of Malmesbury, Henry of Huntingdon, and Orderic. On the other hand, the absence of any outcry against the use of the sworn Inquest as such is a warning not to accept too lightly the common assumption that the use of a jury of men who knew the facts was first introduced into England by William I. Cf. Pollock and Maitland, *History of English Law*, vol. i, p. 143.

into the whole wealth of England, actual and potential. The administrative framework, and more especially the pre-Conquest financial system, determined the way in which the Inquest was carried out, and to some extent the form in which it was recorded. The unit of record was inevitably the county, and the procedure was by hundreds and by villages. But the actual returns to Winchester were arranged according to the 'fundamental dogma'[1] of feudal tenure, viz. that every acre of land was held mediately or immediately of the king. Thanks to the Norman lawyers Domesday Book is formally not a record of the king and his magnates but of the king and his tenants-in-chief.[2] Mesne tenants and mesne tenures are systematically listed under the names of the relevant tenants-in-chief of the Crown, while the tiniest holding of the humblest of the king's tenants-in-chief was separately recorded. A direct, intimate relation existed between the king and his tenants *in capite*, both great and small, and they thereby possessed a special status. Domesday Book thus set forth for the first time the legal theory of the new feudalism, which was followed in public documents for more than a century. Henry I's charter of 1100, for example, is substantially a grant of privileges to his 'earls, barons or other men who hold of me', while the famous fourteenth clause of Magna Carta (1215) undertakes to summon 'archbishops, bishops, earls, and greater barons singly, and generally by the sheriffs', not as is often said the lesser barons but '*all those who hold of us in chief*'.

[1] *History of English Law*, vol. i, p. 232.
[2] In some counties the circuit returns to Winchester included in their prefatory list 'great men' (e.g. the abbot of St. Mary's, York) who held no land in chief of the king, but this was invariably deleted in the final abstract in Vol. I of Domesday Book. See below, p. 198.

Notes on Norman Sicilian surveys

by D. CLEMENTI

For the twelfth century the question whether there was in existence a survey for the island of Sicily presents no difficulty, because it is a well-established fact that records of this type were kept by the royal financial department known as the *dîwân at-tahqîq al ma'mûr*, μέγα σέκρετον, or *duana de secretis* (nearest English equivalent exchequer). These survey records contained the boundaries (in Latin *divise* or *divisiones*) of places; the names of the serfs who went with the land, in lists known as *garâ' id*, πλατεῖαι, or *platee*, and details concerning the extent and value of estates with their description as cultivated or uncultivated, pasture, or woodland.[1] A number of twelfth-century references to them show that they were used by royal officials for settling disputes concerning the ownership of land and by the purchasers of real estate to register a sale.[2] In addition it is extremely interesting to find that these survey records were kept in Arabic, witness in particular William II's privilege of May 1182 to Monreale: 'has autem predictas divisas' (set out in the privilege in very great detail) 'a deptariis nostris de saracenico in latinum transferri, ipsumque saracenicum, secundum quod in eisdem deptariis continetur, sub latino scribi precepimus.'[3] Amari[4] when he studied the Arabic version of the privilege, which duly followed its Latin text, pointed out that, on reaching the sentence quoted above, the Arabic rendered it with a clear statement, that the boundaries were copied from the *dafâtir*, i.e. the survey records, kept by the *dîwân 'at tahqîq*. Moreover, during Roger II's reign, 1105 to 1154, when this department issued a document in favour of a private individual, it was frequently written in Arabic, irrespective of the

---

[1] M. Amari, 'Su la data degli sponsali di Arrigo con la Costanza . . . e su i divani dell' azienda normanna in Palermo', in *Atti della R. Accademia dei Lincei, Memorie della classe di scienze morali, storiche e filologiche* (Rome 1878), vol. ii,. pp. 430 ff., and *Storia dei Musulmani di Sicilia*, ed. C. A. Nallino (Catania 1937), vol. iii, pp. 326 ff. L. Genuardi, 'I defetari normanni', in *Centenario dalla nascità di Michele Amari* (Palermo, 1910), pp. 159 ff.

[2] *Le pergamene greche esistenti nel Grande Archivio di Palermo*, ed. and trs. G. Spata (Palermo 1862), Chiesa e vescovado di Cefalù, nos. IX, XI.

[3] *I diplomi greci e arabi di Sicilia*, ed. S. Cusa (Palermo 1868), p. 202.

[4] *Atti*, p. 431, and *Storia*, vol. iii, p. 329, 3.

language normally used by the recipient[1] and until 1149 its leading officials were known by the Arabic title ṣāḥib, since their Greek and Latin styles of σεκρετικοί and magistri duane de secretis were subsequent.[2] Further confirmation of the initial strength of Arabic influence can be found in the fact that the section of the dîwân unquestionably established by the Normans, namely the duana baronum or σέκρετον τῶν ἀποκοπῶν, had apparently no arabic form for its name, whereas for the dîwân at-taḥqîq al ma'mûr only the Arabic name is found in the earlier references.[3]

The conclusion, very reasonably drawn from the fact that the bulk of the survey was recorded in Arabic, has been that it must have existed before the arrival of the Normans, who therefore merely adapted it. The surviving evidence for its existence in the eleventh century is, however, as is usual for these years, slight. But Amari[4] accepted as conclusive a phrase in a privilege of Roger I, 1087, July, indiction 10, which granted the casale of Regalbuto[5] to the episcopal church of Messina as: 'casale sarracenorum, quod dicitur Butah cum omni tenimento suo et pertinentiis suis secundum antiquas divisiones sarracenorum'.[6] Chalandon,[7] however, after accepting Amari's conclusion that Count Roger's document provided adequate proof of survey records (referred to at various times as διφθέραι, dafâtir, deptarii, or quaterniones) in existence for Sicily before the Normans arrived in the island, went on to question whether they had originated with the Arab occupation, as Amari[8] inclined to think, or were derived from the preceding period of Greek rule. He based his suggestion on the fact that it was customary for a Byzantine administration to keep a 'cadastre complet',

---

[1] Cf. Cusa, op. cit., passim.

[2] E. Jamison, Admiral Eugenius of Sicily, 1957, p. 40.

[3] Ibid., pp. 51, 39.

[4] Atti, p. 430, and Storia, vol. iii, p. 326.

[5] Province of Enna.

[6] I diplomi della cattedrale di Messina, ed. R. Starrabba (Documenti per servire alla storia di Sicilia, 1a serie, diplomatica, Palermo, 1890), p. 2, from a presumed original. Amari, followed by Chalandon, quotes the document as printed by Pirro in Sicilia Sacra, ed. A. Mongitore (Palermo, 1733), p. 384, from Fazello's copy, and so they both date it by attribution to 1090; the Sicilian law courts have twice condemned this version as a forgery, see G. Salvioli, Le decime di Sicilia (Palermo 1901), p. 40.

[7] La domination normande en Italie et en Sicile, vol. ii, p. 531.

[8] Storia, vol. iii, pp. 329, 331.

compiled at the end of each indictional period, containing 'la délimitation des terres et la liste des πάροικοι qui les habitaient'. As this practice was still in force in the reign of the emperor Alexius I (1081 to 1118) he presumed that surveys of this type must have existed for the south of Italy, at least until the 1060's, when the Greeks were driven out by the Normans. He therefore shifted the search for evidence to the mainland, where at Cava he found a document,[1] which appeared to meet all his requirements by referring to *quaterniones fiscales*. But in fact his case remained unproved, because the manuscript is clearly a forgery, probably of the Swabian period. Monsieur Ménager, however, who has conclusively established this fact,[2] has knowledge of Greek and Arabic documents, which prove the existence, at the very beginning of the twelfth century, of surveys for Calabria and in his opinion they derive from Byzantine precedent. Further support comes from work done by A. Lizier[3] on the history of south Italy during the last centuries of the Byzantine occupation, for in his opinion the Greek government levied a land tax in the areas it occupied with any continuity, and he argues that this could not have been done if the administration had no survey to work from.[4] The assumption, that the survey of Sicily was not merely pre-Norman but also pre-Mussulman, can again be strengthened to a certain extent by Amari's[5] identification of the Arabic word for the survey records, namely *daftar*, or *diftar*, pl. *dafâtir*, as derived from a corrupt transcription of the Greek word for a pell, διφθέρα.

As to the procedure employed in making such a survey, for the south of Italy and Sicily the methods used initially are, of course, lost in the mists of time, but when later on it was thought necessary to check such records an inquest was used. A particularly detailed example of the process survives for the year 1176, when *Eugenius*

[1] Archive of Cava, C. 12.

[2] L. R. Ménager, *Diplomatique et catalogue des actes des ducs normands d'Italie, 1059–1127, no. LI*, a forthcoming publication. I am much indebted to Monsieur Ménager for this reference and for the information concerning the Calabrian survey.

[3] *L'Economia rurale dell' età prenormanna nell' Italia meridionale (Studi su documenti editi dei secoli IX–XI)* (Palermo, 1907), pp. 142, 143.

[4] Arguing on the same lines, Genuardi, op. cit., p. 159, quotes Salvioli, *Le decime di Sicilia e specialmente quelle di Girgenti* (Palermo 1901), pp. 45 ff., for the existence of a land tax in Byzantine Sicily.

[5] *Storia*, vol. iii, p. 329.

magister duane de secretis settled a boundary dispute by summoning the elders from the neighbouring villages and sending for *scriptum dohane mamur id est doane secretis*. After which he read out the *scriptum*, while they all tramped the boundary, so that the elders might identify on oath the place-names it contained.[1]

There is, therefore, a very strong presumption, that the Normans found detailed administrative surveys in existence, when they made their first settlements in the Greek territories of Apulia, *c.* 1042, and Calabria, *c.* 1048. Experiencing the advantages of the use of such records, they could have passed on this knowledge to their compatriots in Normandy, even before the conquest of England took place. But the analysis of the evidence from Sicily and the south of Italy produces in addition two main themes inimical to the theory that the Domesday Survey and the procedure for making it were innovations in eleventh-century England, since the Sicilian experience shows that a conqueror tends in matters of administration to follow the line of least resistance, by adopting and adapting the system he finds already in force. This first fact therefore strengthens the probability, which arises from the speed and general efficiency of the Domesday inquests, that the process of making a survey was not entirely new and strange to the Anglo-Saxon population. Secondly, there is the widespread opinion among historians of the Norman Sicilian kingdom that the existence of a survey kept for general purposes can be inferred, when an administration is found to be levying a land tax, and since the government in England before the Conquest is known to have raised such a tax there is a strong possibility that at least an elementary survey was in existence. Consequently, seen from the perspective of the wealth of detail necessary for Norman Sicilian administrative purposes the Domesday Survey presents itself as a measure intended to improve, by revision or replacement, routine administrative records damaged or destroyed during the Norman Conquest, or become obsolete through the passage of time or through the drastic changes in the ownership of land which had followed on the invasion.

[1] Spata, op. cit., Chiesa e vescovado di Cefalù no. XI = a Latin translation made in 1286, from the original Greek and Arabic charters in which the happenings of 1176 had been recorded. It is interesting to find that the Arabic version was fuller than the Greek. For *Eugenius de Calo* or *toû kaloû* see Jamison, op. cit., pp. 56 f.

V

THE CIRCUITS AND THE
TERMS OF REFERENCE

W E have already seen that for the purpose of
making the Survey the counties were combined
into a number of circuits, each with its separate
panel of commissioners (*legati*). The analogy of the
'general eyres' of later times, the text of Domesday Book
itself, and the time factor, as well as a few scattered names
of individuals employed, put the matter beyond dispute.
It is, however, a most difficult problem to determine the
number and composition of these circuits. Stephenson's
reconstruction, printed above,[1] has much to commend it,
but is not necessarily definitive. We have to bear in mind
that no number of common characteristics proves that all
the counties sharing them formed a single circuit. Stephenson's total of seven circuits is thus a minimum: and of
these, while numbers I, III, and VII are hardly in doubt,
there is less certainty about numbers IV, V, and VI.
Number VI in particular seems a heavy assignment for
a single body of commissioners, and it is possible that
Yorkshire and Lincolnshire formed a circuit of their own.
Historians have paid too little attention to these circuits,
which are of great administrative importance and a constant warning against easy generalization. It is unscholarly
to assume that all proceeded exactly alike, and unlikely
that all seven returns (if that is the correct number) were
identical in form. On the other hand, it is a reasonable
assumption that the king's clerks at Winchester abstracted

[1] P. 8.

and epitomized the original returns in Vol. I of Domesday Book so far as possible in a uniform manner. Thus the differences between the county summaries, especially, as we have already seen, in regard to the appendixes of *clamores* and *invasiones*, are due to differences in the original returns. There are indications that the abbreviators tended, so far as possible, to iron out the variations in the form and nomenclature of their material, but great complexities—it is obvious—underlie the superficial uniformity of Vol. I of Domesday Book.

However great the differences in procedure between circuit and circuit, they were limited in the last resort by the commissioners' terms of reference, a copy of which, by incredible good fortune, is preserved in the Inquisitio Eliensis, and, in translation, runs as follows:

Here follows the inquisition of the lands made by the king's barons viz. by the oath of the sheriff of the shire and of all the barons and their Frenchmen and of the whole hundred, the priest, the reeve, six men (*villani*) of each village: in order, the name of the estate (*mansio*): who held it in the time of King Edward: who holds it now: how many hides: how many ploughs on the demesne: how many among the men (*hominum*): how many *villani*: how many *cotarii*: how many slaves (*servi*): how many free men: how many sokemen: how much wood: how much meadow: how much pasture: how many mills: how many fishponds: how much has been added or taken away: how much, taken altogether, it used to be worth and how much now: how much each freeman or sokeman had or has. All this three times, to wit, in the time of King Edward, and when King William gave it, and how much now: and whether it is possible that more be had from it than is being had.[1]

Inasmuch as the I.E. contains the findings of the Inquest for the six counties in which the church of Ely held lands and these counties fell within three different circuits, there can be no reasonable doubt that we have here the official instructions, both for the scope of the Inquest, and

---

[1] Stubbs, *Select Charters*, p. 101; *I.C.C.*, p. 97.

the method of its procedure. The text of Domesday Book bears out this inference, although it is noteworthy that nothing is laid down about recording the livestock on the demesne—the pigs, sheep, oxen, &c.—which so annoyed the Anglo-Saxon chronicler. Yet there is ample proof that the stock was generally recorded: it was perhaps found necessary in order to arrive at the annual value (*valet*) of each manor. But it is no less significant that these particulars were omitted from Vol. I of Domesday Book, the permanent record of the inquiry which preserved no more than was asked for in the terms of reference.

The instructions are, as we might have expected, precise and explicit, and reveal the inquiry as a record of estates or manors. More than twenty questions are asked about each estate, and as the answers are required at three different points of time, it follows that a perfect return for a particular estate might, in fact, require more than sixty answers. The first five questions in order are the name of the estate (*mansio*), the name of the holder T.R.E., who holds now (1086), how many hides and how many ploughs on demesne, and these, it is interesting to note, are the very questions and in the same order to which the answers are given in Exon Domesday. Moreover, the word translated as 'estate' is *mansio*, which is that uniformly used in Exon, though Domesday Book, Vol. I, according to its usual practice, preferred to use the word *manerium* or manor. From this we may infer that the instructions issued to the south-western circuit were identical with those for eastern England. The perfect correspondence between the contents of Exon and the instructions could be similarly demonstrated in respect of the remaining questions, but the first five are enough for our purpose. Next, it is noteworthy that nothing is said in the instructions to justify the emphasis laid by recent historians on *hides* and *geld*. The word *geld* is not even mentioned, and the assessment of hides in each estate, which was asked for, is just one more particular in the long *questionnaire*. Nor is the assessment of the whole village demanded; still less a return of the number of hides in the hundred or county. The fact is that these particulars were already well known to the authorities from the geld accounts which marked each levy of that tax. The inquiry is simply of estates or manors under the names of their holders, exactly as we get the information in Exon Domesday. Nor, for that matter, are the instructions concerned with the collection of any particular geld, from which we may infer that the collection of the tax for the south-west, recorded in the Exon volume, apparently coincided with the Domesday Survey, but that the two are essentially unconnected.

The procedure used to elicit this information is less exactly defined. All evidence was apparently given under oath, though it is possible that the evidence of the priest, reeve, and six men was not so given: and, ignoring the new feudal grouping of the 'honour', the commissioners proceeded according to the old, pre-Conquest administrative organization of the village, hundred, and county. The text of Domesday Book yields much valuable information on procedure, which is examined in detail below. Here it is sufficient to note that this procedure by sworn inquisition (*inquisitio*) can be traced back to the early years of the Conqueror's reign, but no farther; and is therefore supposed to be a Norman innovation, derived ultimately from the prerogative procedure of the Carolingian kings. In theory, at any rate, the Domesday inquisition was a description (*descriptio*), or writing down, of a vast collection of facts gathered orally in the public sessions of the royal commissioners (*legati*). No convincing proof has yet been produced for the widely held view that written returns were also made by the king's tenants-in-chief, though some of our evidence—examined below[1]—points in this

---

[1] Pp. 82–85.

direction. Indeed, it is difficult to imagine how such a vast body of minute particulars about many thousands of estates could have been collected orally and systematically digested on parchment in the time allowed. A great deal of time was spent in deciding conflicting claims and still more in the search for convincing evidence for claims, which, while not in dispute between parties, lacked the support of clear oral testimony or of writs and charters. Yet the almost invariable formula used is that X or Y says (*dicit*), or that the county says this or that, or—and in some counties invariably—that the hundred says this or that. Moreover, as we know from the I.C.C., this oft-recurring evidence of the whole hundred was given by a sworn jury, which in Cambridgeshire and Hertfordshire consisted of eight landowners, four English and four French, whose names it is careful to record. The time spent in the process of fact-finding, as well as in the settlement of conflicting claims by rival landowners, must have been enormous, and it is scarcely conceivable that the minute particulars of innumerable manors were committed to writing from verbal testimony in open court. The commissioners, we are almost driven to think, must have held their session with some sort of draft return already before them. But here we enter the field of conjecture, and the single conclusion on which all scholars are agreed is that everywhere the actual procedure followed by the commissioners was governed by the hundredal divisions of the shire. In Cambridgeshire, for example, the abbreviated text follows much the same order of hundreds as the fuller version, arranged hundred by hundred in the I.C.C., and does so both for the royal demesne and for the baronial fiefs. In Buckinghamshire, too, royal demesne and baronial manors are set out in the same consistent order of hundreds, and Mr. Sawyer[1] has lately demonstrated the same

---

[1] 'The "Original Returns" and Domesday Book', *E.H.R.* lxx (1955), cf. below, p. 160.

procedure in nearly twenty other counties. These facts scarcely support the common and reasonable assumption that the landowners made separate preliminary returns of their fees to the commissioners. In most cases these would be unlikely to follow a constant order of hundreds. The consistent hundredal order of the baronial fiefs is thus rather an argument against the likelihood of baronial returns to the commissioners. But, if they *were* made, it is obvious that they must have been recast in advance by the commissioners in the hundredal order in which they carried out the inquisition.

All this suggests that the taking of the Survey was a more complicated and perhaps varying process than has been imagined: and even though the oral procedure was everywhere carried out hundred by hundred, we must recognize the possibility that the written record was either simultaneously converted into lists of manors under the names of their holders, or, in some cases, that the information was immediately committed to writing in that form. The second possibility is clearly suggested by Exon Domesday, which omits all reference to the hundred, and has no hundred rubrics, a unique feature which reappears in the shortened text of Great Domesday for these five counties. There are other circuits,[1] as we shall see later, in which the first written record may well have been under the names of tenants as in Domesday Book, and it is even likely that the geographical record of the third circuit, the Cambridge part of which survives in the I.C.C., was a solitary exception to the general rule.

Thus an examination of the various factors treated above gives no ground for doubting the broad inference suggested by the surviving original documents of the Inquest. Contrariwise, every angle of approach has suggested that the original return required from the circuits was a list of manors, county by county, arranged under

[1] e.g. the East Anglian (No. VII). See below, p. 178.

the heads of royal demesne and the names of tenants-in-chief. A return of this kind was in conformity with the administrative framework, first fully laid before us in the Pipe Rolls, but already in the Conqueror's reign sufficiently well known from the geld accounts, where the money is charged against persons and collected by counties. That the commissioners based the procedure of their inquiry upon hundreds and villages has never been questioned, but in that feudal world, then in its hey-day, a return of 'hundred rolls' would have been an anachronism. Society was dominated by the fief or honour, which was a complex of manors. In this connexion the evidence of the satellite surveys from the abbeys of Bury, St. Augustine's and Christ Church, Canterbury, Evesham, and the cathedral of Worcester, which everywhere record the results of the Survey in feudal and personal form, is decisive.

So far we may now feel that we are on hard ground. But this examination has brought to light the extraordinary complexity of the process by which the information was brought together. The ruling class was no more than a few score of great men, each of whom was vitally interested in the results of the Survey. One of these, Robert Malet,[1] in East Anglia actually mentions the day on which he was enrolled (*inbreviatus*) and there is no doubt that we can easily exaggerate the importance of the role played by the middle landholders, who formed the hundredal juries, while overlooking the testimony and influence of the only men who really mattered. The conviction of almost all scholars that some sort of written returns were made by these great men is a reasonable one, though, as we have seen, not easily reconciled with what we know of the procedure adopted; and, if and when made, the barons concerned must have answered at a single county court session for the whole of their fiefs. We can hardly doubt that a vast deal of preliminary lists, copies, and valuations,

---

[1] D.B., vol. ii, f. 276 b.

long since perished, lie behind the more or less engrossed
originals of the Survey which still survive: and that these
varied with the special circumstances obtaining in each
separate circuit. To this early stage of the Inquest is to be
ascribed the original from which the I.C.C. is derived and
which, in the general consensus of all the other evidence,
begins to assume the character of a 'sport' or at best an
early expedient adopted in circuit III or part of it.[1] It
is significant that the Inquisitio Eliensis, whose compiler
was able to draw upon the full returns for the three
separate circuits in which the Ely lands lay, and to whom
we owe the 'terms of reference' quoted above, was only
able to quote the names of the hundredal jurors for
Cambridgeshire and Hertfordshire. No jurors' names are
given for East Anglia or for the circuit in which the county
of Huntingdon lay, and the natural explanation of his
silence is that only one of these three circuits recorded the
full findings of the Survey in I.C.C. form. The I.C.C. is
examined more fully below, but we have next to consider
in some detail the evidence of the Domesday text regarding the written and oral testimony offered or extracted in
accordance with the commissioners' terms of reference.

[1] Below, p. 161, n. 1.

VI

ORAL TESTIMONY: THE EVIDENCE
OF THE DOMESDAY TEXT

THE clearest proof that the 'terms of reference'[1] are preserved for us by the Ely inquisition lies in their exact correspondence with the final text of Domesday Book. The statistics there preserved are in fact the answers to exactly the questions set out in this document, and to no other. Two centuries later, in the time of Edward I, a copy of them would probably have appeared on f. 1 of both Great and Little Domesday, but in the eleventh century the king's servants saw no need to justify or explain their actions. That this was so is evident from the text of the Survey which, broadly speaking, is no more than a vast storehouse of bare statistics, summarily epitomized in highly contracted writing. There is no title or heading. Folio 1 plunges straight into the description of Kent; f. 382, the last, completes the description of Yorkshire. From the form of the record one would never guess that each fact recorded—and they must run to millions—was the sworn answer to a separate question. By far the greater part of the information is set down dogmatically as a matter of fact: but here and there we find interspersed among the bare facts explanatory passages in which the commissioners were moved to cite evidence for their conclusions. Most of these, though by no means all, are due to a conflict of evidence. Thus, for example, in Hampshire (f. 44 b 2):

William de Chernet claims this land saying (*dicens*) that it belongs

[1] Above, p. 60.

to the manor of Cerdeford . . . and on this matter he brought forward the evidence of the best people (*melioribus*) and the old men
of the whole county and hundred; and Picot opposed him by the
testimony of villagers and rustics (*villanis et vili plebe*) and reeves
(*prepositis*).

These passages are of great interest, for by their careful
wording, they often skilfully suggest without actually deciding which party had the greater right. But not infrequently, a simple claim (*calumpnia*) or a statement of fact
is qualified by the words 'as he himself says' (*ut ipse dicit*)
and we are left to guess whether this implies some doubt
on the matter in the minds of the commissioners.

Entries of this kind occur in practically every shire and
are the only proof in the text of the Survey that the information was derived from oral statements made in court
under oath. Nineteenth-century historians, romantically
attached to a simpler age when the 'unfogged memory' of
rustics made 'paper work' unnecessary, accepted this formal notion of the Domesday Survey at its face value. But
there are few historians today prepared to believe that this
waste of statistics in Domesday was achieved without some
preliminary written information. All other considerations
apart, the time factor compels us to postulate some
preparation in writing of the evidence before verbal evidence was given in court: and when to this we add the
exact and logical arrangement of the material in both
Little Domesday and Exon Domesday, the argument for
some system of preliminary records is very strong. The
evidence, such as it is, invariably states or implies that the
information tendered to the commissioners was given
verbally, apparently in open court. The decisions, too, of
the commissioners are verbal. Thus, in Herefordshire
(f. 181a2): 'This land was thegnland T.R.E. but was
afterwards turned into reeveland: and therefore the king's
legates say that the land and the rent from it are being
secretly withdrawn from the king.' On the other hand,

for the greater part of the information it preserves, no source or authority is given. The facts are just there, and we are left to wonder how such a vast collection was gathered together and committed to writing in an orderly manner in the course of a few months.

Apart from their historical value, the narrative entries in the Survey throw light on the varying procedure of the separate circuits, for they are found to differ widely in character and frequency from county to county. Some counties abound in vivid passages of this kind, while others confine themselves to an almost unrelieved statement of bare statistics. Again, in some, there is repeated reference to both the county and the hundred giving evidence: in others only to one or the other. Any attempt to summarize the evidence must take account of the fact that we have the full returns for only two complete circuits and part of another, viz. the East Anglian, the south-western, and Cambridgeshire. For the remainder we have only the summaries in Domesday Book, Vol. I, which for all we know omitted much that was in the originals. This possibility remains, but it is reassuring to find that the shortened form of the returns for Cambridgeshire and the five south-western counties in Vol. I do seem, in fact, to have preserved nearly every mention of shire or hundred in their fuller originals.

The commissioners' terms of reference describe the procedure as an inquisition of lands (*inquisitio terrarum*) to be made: 'by oath of the sheriff of the shire, and of all the barons and their Frenchmen and of the whole hundred, the priest, the reeve, six villagers of each village'. Of the priest, the reeve, and the six villagers, whose first appearance in our history this seems to be, one hears something but not much. Villagers (*villani*) say (*dicunt*) of land in Sussex they once used to hold that there was no hall there and that it did not pay any geld:[1] while at Mendlesham

---

[1] Vol. I, f. 27 a 2.

(Suffolk) the 'men of that village' (*homines illius ville*) gave testimony in conflict with that of the hundred jury.[1] Elsewhere in Suffolk five *villani* of the royal manor of Bramford[2] support a claim of Roger the sheriff against the evidence of the hundred of Ipswich. But, in general, the evidence of villagers, however often demanded, is rarely quoted in the text of the Survey.

At the opposite end of the social scale, the evidence of individuals—the sheriff, the tenants-in-chief, and their men (*homines*) or sub-tenants—is constantly recorded. The form of these entries implies that the great men were present in court and testify verbally (*dicit, dicens, contradicit*, &c.). But in what court? It was the opinion of Horace Round that the commissioners made a circuit through the hundreds, which gave their testimony by juries of eight 'medium' landowners, half French and half English. But since they clearly held meetings of the county court, it seems more likely that Maitland[3] was right in suggesting that they did 'no more than their successors the justices-in-eyre were wont to do, that is, they held in the shire-town a moot which was attended by (1) the magnates of the shire who spoke for the shire, (2) a jury from every hundred, and (3) a deputation of *villani* from every township'. The point is one of such importance as to justify a rapid summary of shire and hundred attestation in every shire: and this, while supporting Maitland's conclusion, also throws new light on the procedure in the various circuits.

We may begin with the evidence of East Anglia where the evidence of the hundred is much more prominent than that of the county. In Norfolk we read that the hundred or the 'men of the hundred' testify (*testatur, testantur*) or

---

[1] Vol. II, f. 285 b.   [2] Vol. II, f. 393 a.

[3] *Domesday and Beyond*, p. 11, n. 1, quoting the Yorkshire and Lincolnshire *clamores* (vol. I, f. 375) where we find successive entries beginning with (*a*) *scyra testatur*, (*b*) *Westreding testatur*, (*c*) *testatur wapentac*. See below, pp. 73, 78.

says (*dicit*) something on more than fifty occasions, while the evidence of the county is nowhere mentioned. Similarly in Suffolk there are more than forty attestations by the hundred and none by the county, while in Essex the county speaks half a dozen times, and the hundred about forty. When to this evidence we add the very numerous instances of evidence given by the sheriffs and the individual barons, we arrive at a total of recorded testimony far higher than that for any other circuit. Bearing in mind that any mention of testimony in Domesday Book normally implies some conflict of evidence, we get a clear impression that the East Anglian commissioners found unusual difficulties in arriving at the facts, due, it may be surmised, to the very large number of small freemen and socmen in this area.

The evidence of the circuits bordering on East Anglia repeats the pattern of East Anglia though with much smaller numbers. We read of both hundred and county bearing witness, and the predominance of hundredal evidence is maintained. Thus in the circuit which included the counties of Middlesex, Hertford, Buckingham, Cambridge, and Bedford, three counties mention only hundredal testimony, while Hertford and Bedfordshire[1] also mention the shire. In the south-coast circuit, with which Domesday Book begins, only the testimony of the hundred is mentioned in Kent, Surrey, and Sussex, and that rarely, while county evidence is frequent in Hants and Berkshire as is also that of the hundred. Postponing for a moment the Danelaw evidence, we may next consider circuits IV and V in Stephenson's list. These two circuits, which comprise a group of midland and Welsh-border counties, have one surprising feature in common; viz. that neither contains a single mention of the evidence given by the hundred. Indeed, No. IV[2] has only four references to

---

[1] Only a single mention of the shire against more than a dozen of the hundred.
[2] Oxford, Northampton, Leicester, and Warwick.

evidence given by the county, and only two or three to
evidence given by individual tenants-in-chief. In circuit
V,[1] especially in Gloucester and Worcester, we meet with
frequent testimony from the county in various forms:
the county, the whole county, the men of the county, the
best men of the county, *inquisiti* say or affirm or testify;
but the hundred[2] is conspicuous by its absence. This can
hardly be a matter of chance; and it points to a rather
different procedure from that followed in the eastern
circuits. The same phenomenon is met with in the south-
western circuit, which, apart from a few references to the
'thegns of the shire', and a single reference to the hundred
in Devonshire,[3] makes no reference to the testimony of
either hundred or county. This, moreover, is a crucial
instance, since we have the full returns in Exon Domesday
as well as the epitomes in Vol. I of Domesday Book. The
poor repute of the hundred in the south-west is best
attested by the fact that the returns in neither form contain any of those hundredal rubrications found in varying
completeness in the counties of every other circuit.

It remains, before we consider the significance of these
differences, to look at circuit VI,[4] which contains the
Danelaw counties, and adjoins that eastern region in which
the testimony of the hundred so strongly predominates.
This circuit conforms to the eastern pattern to the extent
that, where the text of Domesday mentions the giving of
testimony, the reference is always to the hundred or the
wapentake or simply 'the men who made oath'. These
references are, however, highly infrequent—one in Derby,

---

[1] Gloucester, Worcester, Hereford, Stafford, Shropshire, Cheshire.

[2] There is a single exception in Gloucestershire (vol. I, f. 165 b 2), where the
village of Wenric is assigned to Bernitone hundred *judicio hominum eiusdem
hundredi*.

[3] Exon Domesday, p. 277 (D.B., vol. I, f. 107 a 1). In both Devon and
Cornwall the commissioners seem to have relied neither on the hundred or
county as such, but on the testimony of the thegns, i.e. the English.

[4] Huntingdon, Derby, Nottingham, Rutland, York, Lincoln.

one in Yorkshire, one in Nottingham and Rutland, three in Huntingdon, and three or four in Lincolnshire. This at first sight is surprising in so 'free' a region, but the explanation is quickly forthcoming, at least for three of the counties concerned. For Huntingdon, Yorkshire, and Lincolnshire we have in each case an appendix of *Clamores*, which seems to collect and group together the evidence gathered regarding claims and clamours in the course of the Survey. These are broadly comparable with the appendixes of *Invasiones* in the three East Anglian counties and the lists of *Terre occupate*[1] in Exon Domesday. A hint of the purpose of these lists is given us by the heading of the Lincolnshire appendix: 'Clamores quae sunt in Sudtreding Lincoliae et concordia eorum per homines qui juraverunt', which suggests that the commissioners regarded their mission as one of 'healing and settling' rather than as a formal judicial eyre.[2] However that may be, these lists, which are lengthy, record impartially the evidence of hundreds, wapentakes, ridings as well as that of the shire. Moreover, the evidence of these different bodies is often combined. 'The men of the wapentake testify with the consent of the whole riding'; 'the wapentake and the county say that ...'; 'the wapentake and the riding say...'; 'the men of Hoiland say'; 'North Riding and the whole county testify'. The cumulative evidence of these *clamores*, as Maitland noticed, brings powerful support to the view that the commissioners held their sessions in a fixed place, presumably the county town, at which men from smaller administrative divisions as well as individuals attended to give evidence. To suppose that the evidence of different bodies on different occasions and in various places was elaborately harmonized 'afterwards' is unnecessarily to complicate the problem, and the *clamores* have every appearance of

---

[1] Omitted in the shortened version in vol. I of Domesday Book.

[2] The fact that one of the Lincolnshire *clamores* is specifically reserved for the king suggests that the rest were regarded as settled.

being extracts either from a single record, or notes made from a single series of joint meetings. They are very brief and informal; for they were partly intended to lighten the text, and were partly evidence for statements made as to 'matters of fact' in the text itself. They would be of little value without the preceding Domesday text; indeed they sometimes mention places and people, all trace of whom has disappeared from the record which they are meant to annotate. It is, therefore, reasonable to assume that they were made as appendixes to the original returns from which the text of these counties in Vol. I was compiled, and that they were retained when the epitomes were made. Why there are no similar notes for Derbyshire and Nottinghamshire, which it seems likely belonged to the same circuit, is unexplained.

Such, in brief summary, is the evidence supplied by the text of Domesday Book, Vols. I and II, regarding the procedure followed by the commissioners appointed to the various circuits, which suggests some tentative conclusions. And, first, it brings further confirmation, if such is needed, that the statement of procedure prefixed to the Inquisitio Eliensis was indeed a copy of what it has so far been assumed to be, and called 'the terms of reference of the commissioners in all circuits'. This conclusion was rendered probable long ago by Maitland, who minutely analysed the questions set out in this document against the answers given to them in Domesday Book,[1] and brilliantly illustrated the manner in which the too elaborate and cumbrous questionnaire was variously applied in practice on the various circuits by men who 'were easing their task and enabling themselves to obtain answers in the place of silence'.[2] Equally, or even more conclusive evidence,

---

[1] *Domesday Book and Beyond*. Essay III: The Hide.

[2] Op. cit., p. 423. He perhaps makes too heavy weather about his B formula regarding the number of teams for which there was land, which he describes as 'unasked for information' (p. 420). But surely it is the answer to 'si potest plus haberi quam habeatur' of the terms of reference (above, p. 60).

we have now seen, is supplied by Domesday Book regarding the machinery employed for answering these questions and the persons from whom it was obtained. The instructions as to procedure were treated in the same elastic manner, and we get a clear impression that with a fine disregard for red tape, the facts were supplied by almost anyone who had the required knowledge. Facts about York city are set out *ut plures dicunt*, in Lincolnshire *homines patriae et Wapentake nesciunt*; even the charters are made to speak (*sicut dicunt cartae de ecclesia*).[1] Yet, great as are the regional variations, there is ample overall proof of the systematic and painstaking effort to arrive at the truth by sworn evidence, in just the way set out in their terms of reference.

Secondly, we have to take account of the striking contrast between the eastern counties and those of the midlands, west, and south-west in regard to testimony. Broadly speaking,[2] the text of Domesday preserves a far greater bulk of recorded evidence, whether by individuals, counties, or hundreds, for East Anglia and the Danelaw counties than for the rest of England, the two extremes being marked by circuits VII (East Anglia) and II (the south-west) respectively. Thirdly, the recorded evidence of the hundred, which in the east shows a high preponderance over that of the county, diminishes as one goes west, and in circuits II, IV, and V virtually disappears.

These differences are too pronounced and too uniform to be explained as either accidental or due to varying degrees of compression in the compilation of the shortened versions in Domesday Book of the original returns. A rather different interpretation or application of the terms of reference between east and west must underlie them:

[1] Vol. I, f. 175 b 2.

[2] There are certain exceptions. In the first circuit, much more personal testimony is recorded for Hampshire and Berkshire than for the other counties; and in circuit VI very little is recorded for Nottinghamshire and Derbyshire.

and it is not fanciful to suppose that the procedure of the commissioners became in practice more authoritarian, aristocratic, and truly feudal in the midland and western circuits. The force of public opinion was different and did not call for the same nice balance of statement where evidence conflicted. Minds were evidently made up quickly and results categorically stated. A remarkable entry in Exon Domesday (p. 165), under the abbot of Tavistock's fee, confirms this conclusion. Of the manor of Werrington it is said:

> The abbot's predecessor held this manor, and the abbot was seised of it when King William sent his barons to inquire into the lands of England. He was disseised by them because the English testified that it did not belong to the Abbey on the day King Edward was alive and dead.

The manor accordingly appears under the royal demesne both in Exon and the summary in Domesday Book. Here, then, is proof that the procedure on this circuit was, as in the east, based on the testimony of hundred juries; but, the 'climate of opinion' being different, the western commissioners not only acted decisively but felt no obligation even to record objections.[1]

It is a far cry from this summary procedure of the west and south-west to the attitude of mind disclosed by the Inquisitio Comitatus Cantabrigiensis. The almost total absence of any record of the evidence of the hundred in the west and south-west, together with the omission of rubrics in Exon Domesday, and the faulty rubrication of other western counties alone render it extremely doubtful whether the written record of these circuits ever passed through an I.C.C. phase, for it is almost unthinkable that either Exon Domesday, or the abbreviated version in Vol. I, would have omitted all geographical identification of place-names if this information had at any stage been

---

[1] H. P. R. Finberg, *Tavistock Abbey*, p. 10. On this passage Mr. Finberg justly comments: 'How many other changes of ownership lie concealed under the terse formulas of the official record?'

put in writing. With all these considerations in mind, the absence of any substantial record of hundredal testimony in the west and south-west raises this doubt to the likely hypothesis that in the south-west circuit certainly, and not improbably in others, the written record from the very first took the same feudal and personal form which we find in Domesday Book, Vol. I. There was nothing to prevent the geographical inquiry by hundreds being converted, as it proceeded, into a written return under tenants-in-chief, which all contemporary sources agree was the purpose of the whole operation, and, if and where this was done, the hundredal juries would tend to be regarded as mere channels of information, record, if any, being confined to the more important evidence given by the county.

Between the object of the Survey, which was a series of descriptions of the fees of the tenants-in-chief, and the hundredal procedure adopted to attain it there was at first sight a certain incompatibility, the reasons for which were historical. From the very moment of the Conquest the feudal organization of England became a Norman assumption. The 'fee', the 'honour', the 'barony'—all new terms—governed the thinking of the ruling class, and it was left to the administrators to fit them into the complex O.E. system. Thus the circuit returns, as well as the final record (Vol. I of Domesday Book), inevitably followed a personal arrangement—the land of the king (*Terra Regis*) followed by the land of each tenant-in-chief. But this result was only reached by means of a complicated administrative process. The chief problems which faced the circuit commissioners may conveniently be listed as follows:

1. To distinguish between those who held in chief of the Crown, and the much larger body of mesne tenants.
2. To settle, as far as possible, the innumerable disputes regarding the ownership of estates both T.R.E.

and *modo* (1086), and to list the lands wrongfully occupied (*terrae occupatae*), and the invasions of Crown and other property.

3. To identify every estate, great and small, and to ensure that it was included in their Survey.

4. To compile detailed manorial descriptions of these estates.

The first three of these tasks were dealt with in the only possible way, viz. by the verdicts of a jury from each hundred, given in the county court in the presence of the landowners and their tenants. All our contemporary texts bear witness to the contentious character of these formal sessions, which must have consumed the greater part of the commissioners' time. Even so, very many claims were merely noted and their settlement left to the future. With regard to the fourth problem the case was very different. The manorial economy of each estate—the land in demesne and the *terra villanorum*, the ploughs, the villeins, the bordars, the cottars, the mills, the woods, the pastures, the very beasts—was a purely feudal and personal question, one which concerned the owner alone. It was also the most difficult, for it is highly unlikely that the larger owners themselves knew the answers to the formidable list of questions asked by the commissioners. There is evidence too that they resented such minute interrogation. The collection and arrangement of this immense body of statistics in a short time was the central problem of the commissioners. In the last resort the information could only come from the actual staff of each estate, and it was far too bulky to be handled in court. Since the unit of record was the single estate, great or small, the commissioners required some person to answer directly regarding its working economy. Scattered through the pages of Domesday Book there are repeated references to imperfect *descriptions* of estates owing to the failure of someone to furnish particulars. Thus, in Berningham[1] (co. Norfolk) we read of 28 acres which are in the king's hand because 'there was no one who rendered account' (*compotum*). In Gloucestershire it is said of two manors of Earl Hugh[2] that 'there was no one to answer (*responderet*) for these lands, but by the men of the county they are valued at £8': and of the hide and half virgate which the earl of Mortain held in Hankham[3] (co. Sussex) more briefly *inde nullum responsum*. From these and similar references it is clear that the commissioners relied, not upon juries, but upon individuals with exact local knowledge for the manorial details of each property. Who then were these men without whose co-operation a full *description* was impossible? Light upon this question is thrown by the curious entry regarding Woodchester[4] in Gloucestershire, which concludes: 'Concerning this manor no one rendered an account to the commissioners (*legatis*), nor did any of them (*aliquis eorum*) attend this description (*descriptionem*).' Here, then, we have evidence that someone had to be present in court to answer any queries that arose regarding each estate as it was recorded. But a distinction is drawn between this duty of attendance and the obligation to render an account (*rationem, compotum*), and to me it suggests a picture of the sitting tenants of each property conveying information to the commissioners' clerks, as it were, in the office and behind the scenes. This is borne out by an entry regarding the bishop of Hereford[5] which says, 'in all there are in the bishopric 300 hides, though concerning 33 hides, the bishop's men (*homines episcopi*) gave no account (*rationem*)'. This entry can hardly be a record of the 'hundredal' proceedings of the Inquest. It points rather to the activities, in this case, of the bishop's feudal tenants supplying details out of court to the commissioners' staff.

[1] D.B., vol. II, f. 279 b.   [2] D.B. vol. I, f. 166 b 1.
[3] Ibid., f. 22 a 2.   [4] Ibid., f. 164 a 2.   [5] Ibid., f. 182 b 2.

Thus in court the commissioners followed a summary, systematic procedure by hundreds, while simultaneously behind the scenes the information was regrouped and greatly expanded according to the feudal divisions of the fee and the honour. A local representative of each estate supplied the facts of manorial organization, and he or another was required to attend the formal session of the Inquest at which the manor was recorded and checked off. This machinery is taken for granted in our records, except when it broke down by someone's failure to attend the Inquest or to furnish the facts. These occasional lapses are the only direct evidence of a *de facto* distinction between the facts dealt with in court and those amassed, as it were, out of court. It is, however, indirectly confirmed by the whole text of Domesday Book which almost never[1] records any dispute regarding the manorial *descriptions* (no. 4). In this instance, too, the argument from silence is a valid one, for it is precisely from the many scores of disputes recorded in the Survey that we must form our picture of the actual court proceedings. In Hampshire, for instance, we meet with the phrase: 'concerning the hides they gave no account (*rationem*)': or 'they did not know' (or 'they did not tell us') the number of hides.[2] From these instances we can safely infer that the question 'How many hides?' was one asked in court in order to identify the estate in question. In contrast with these unanswered questions, we repeatedly encounter the phrase *Terra est . . .*, followed by a blank space.[3] These suggest that the number of ploughs for which there was land was often a matter of manorial economy, supplied out of court, and so in many scores of manors went unrecorded to the bitter end.

[1] Very occasionally a detail comes in for special comment, when the manorial agent was hazy about the facts, e.g. vol. I, f. 187a2: 'Silva est ibi magna, sed quantitas non fuit dicta.'

[2] D.B., vol. I, f. 38b1; 39a2.

[3] *Passim* in Kent, and very often in the other counties of this circuit. It is also found farther west, e.g. in Staffordshire and Northamptonshire.

All this has a bearing upon the question of those preliminary written returns which scholars have assumed, rather than proved, to have been sent in to the commissioners by the tenants-in-chief. They may well have done so: we do not really know. But even if they did it is useless to look for evidence of them in Domesday Book where the fiefs have been laboriously built up from the descriptions of individual manors, originally arranged in 'hundredal' order, and then regrouped under the names of their owners. Everywhere in Domesday Book there are traces of this original hundredal order, much interfered with and often breaking down entirely owing to the rearrangement behind the scenes of the skeleton information tendered in court. The true baronial returns of the Inquest in fact were not mere documents sent in by the tenants-in-chief, but live individuals who supplied their information in person to the commissioners' clerks. The final result was a *breve* or list of manors, fully described, of each tenant-in-chief, who, perhaps, agreed the record at a formal session of the Inquest.[1]

Considerations of this kind suggest a new and different picture of what actually occurred at the formal sessions of the Inquest. No assembly, however well informed, could have struggled in court with such immense documents as Vol. II of Domesday Book or Exon Domesday. Like all other 'blue books' these were largely a product of collation, rearrangement, and above all of expansion, hammered out between sessions of the court. The work of the commissioners in court, described above, was to identify each estate, to fix its ownership, and thus to produce a skeleton list of manors. There is good reason to believe[2] that in court they were chiefly, if not wholly, concerned with the basic facts—the name of the property and its owner, its hidage (*T.R.E.* and *modo*), its annual value, and its

---

[1] D.B., vol. II, f. 276 b, where Robert Malet speaks of the day on which he was *inbreviatus*.   [2] See below, pp. 117–22, 148.

ploughing capacity. The rest of their time was taken up with the endless disputes regarding title, and unjust seizure of lands. On this framework the clerks hung the voluminous mass of detail, which amazed contemporaries as it still amazes us. It could never have been compiled in court: but equally it could never have been compiled from written returns from the tenants-in-chief. In fact, as we have seen, it was the result of the testimony—partly, no doubt, in writing, partly viva voce—given by the sitting tenants and their manorial staff to the 'backroom' staff of the circuit commissioners.

It is difficult for us today to realize the chaotic state of tenure in 1086, and therefore to appreciate just how great an achievement Domesday Book was. Its elaborate statistics must have been as valuable to the magnates as they were to the Crown: for it is safe to say that neither king nor barons had such a systematic record of their lands when it began. The fundamental point to grasp is that it was compiled not from the top downwards, but from the bottom upwards. For this reason the search for 'original returns' by the barons is something of an *ignis fatuus* at this early date, though they were common enough later. For instance, many years ago Mr. Charles Johnson called attention to the fact that some of the smaller fiefs in Little Domesday are marked in the margin with the letters *f, n, fr, nfr*, and suggested that these indicated that the tenants-in-chief concerned either did or did not make a written return to the commissioners.[1] Such, I feel sure, is the purpose of these notes, but they are obviously *post factum* additions, made casually and occasionally. Moreover, as similar notes are also found in Great Domesday,[2] it seems clear that they refer to an inquiry made some years after the Domesday Inquest.[3]

[1] *V.C.H. Norfolk*, vol. ii, p. 2. ? *n* = nichil: *nfr* = non fecit returnum.
[2] e.g. in Nottingham and Yorkshire.
[3] In a review of the *Shropshire V.C.H.*, vol. i, Baring explained the fact that

Another indication of written returns has been thought to occur in Somersetshire where Round called attention to two descriptions of a manor, one under the royal demesne, and one under the name of the holder, which differed radically from one another regarding the valuation, the number of ploughs, and the name of the previous holder. Round[1] suggested that the Survey was done in two stages, a 'return' for the royal demesne (? *breve regis*) and a separate 'return' for the rest of the county. This suggestion has lately been developed by Professor Hoyt[2] in an article on the *terrae occupatae* of Cornwall. These lists, which are roughly analogous to those of *invasiones super regem* in East Anglia and the *clamores* of Yorkshire, Lincolnshire, and Huntingdonshire, are preserved in Exon Domesday for three of the five south-western counties, viz. Cornwall, Devonshire, and Somerset. Professor Hoyt maintains that the *terrae occupatae* are a 'wholly distinct and separate document' from the contents of Exon, and that behind them lay 'not only the Domesday Survey, or administrative inquest, but also a collection of *written* documents which were, I believe, nothing else than the original returns of the inquest'. By 'original returns' Professor Hoyt here means not the documents returned to Winchester by the Commissioners, but feudal 'returns' of their fees sent in *to* the commissioners by the separate tenants-in-chief.

Professor Hoyt's conclusions, if accepted, would, of course, settle the question of written returns sent in by the magnates once and for all: but for several reasons it is in

---

the manors of the earl's demesne are arranged in a different order of hundreds from that followed in the other fiefs on the supposition that a return was made by the earl's own officers. More recently Mr. Sawyer (*E.H.R.* lxx (1955), p. 183) has pointed out that in the Worcestershire Domesday there is a consistent hundredal order in almost all the fiefs except that of the Church of Worcester.

[1] *V.C.H. Somerset*, vol. i, pp. 426–7.

[2] 'The Terrae Occupatae of Cornwall and the Exon Domesday', *Traditio*, ix (1953), pp. 155–99. Cf. below, p. 122.

my judgement unacceptable. In the first place he over-simplifies the conditions of the problem by dividing the possible sources of information in Exon into just two contrasted categories, viz. the verdict of the hundred juries and the written returns of the magnates and of the royal demesne. But this is, in fact, to assume in advance the result one is seeking to prove. Secondly, Professor Hoyt misunderstands the meaning of the term *breve regis*, mentioned in the Inquisitio Comitatus Cantabrigiensis. So far from being 'a separate and distinct feudal return which concerned part of the *terra regis*', the term *breve regis* includes the whole of the king's lands in Cambridgeshire. Thirdly, it is really going too far to describe the *terrae occupatae* as 'a wholly distinct and separate document from the rest of Exon'. There is a manifest and integral connexion between the *terrae occupatae* lists and the manorial descriptions in Exon.

Yet, although we still await proof that *feudal* returns were sent in to the Domesday commissioners, Professor Hoyt has done good service in calling attention to the protracted and complex nature of the Survey. We have in Exon Domesday traces of the activities of two successive bodies of commissioners: and evidence that their duties included some sort of inquiry into the collection of geld in that year. We have also evidence in the marginal notes and the interlineations, of attempts to embody fresh information into the findings of the commission at a relatively late stage in their composition. My own examination of the *terrae occupatae*, for what it is worth, suggests three distinct stages:

(*a*) The *terrae occupatae* were first abstracted from the full findings on the royal demesne and listed.

(*b*) They were next, or simultaneously, abstracted from the manorial descriptions of the lands of the tenants-in-chief.

(*c*) Some further inquiry brought new facts to light[1] which were duly recorded in the *terrae occupatae* lists in Exon, and some of them on the margins or even in the text of the volume.

We see, in short, the rough copy of the results of a most involved administrative operation, the full details of which can only be guessed at. From this collection there is evidence that a fair copy was made embodying such additions, and producing a volume not unlike Vol. II of Domesday Book.

Such is the evidence, or at least some of the evidence, for the use of written returns made by the barons to the circuit commissioners: and the impression it leaves, it must be confessed, is somewhat confused. In both volumes of Domesday Book the Inquest is formally recorded as an oral and verbal operation carried out in open court: but few scholars have been prepared to accept Domesday Book at its face value. The tenants-in-chief were under obligation to render an account of their lands, and someone was supposed to be present at the Inquest who could answer for the facts regarding each separate manor. So much we know, and common sense requires us to assume that the vast array of facts must have been somehow committed to writing before the actual court sessions began. Whether the information was tendered in writing in advance, or gathered on the spot from the great men's stewards and bailiffs who attended the Inquest, is a somewhat unreal question. Moreover, we cannot separate the question of written returns, which must have listed the manors under the names of their owners, from that of the procedure followed by the commissioners, which was geographical and by hundreds. There was thus a certain incompatibility between the object of the Inquest and the

---

[1] Cf. *Exon Domesday*, f. 383 b: 'preter has terras additas quas superius commemoravi est adhuc addita 1 hida terrae quae vocatur Ulftona'; and f. 521.

only possible means by which it could be achieved. To this question we shall therefore return in discussing the In-quisitio Comitatus Cantabrigiensis, from which alone we can hope to gain first-hand information regarding the exact procedure followed by the circuit commissioners.

VII

THE GELD INQUISITION

BOUND up in Exon Domesday is a series of geld accounts written in Latin, which record the amount of money paid into the king's treasury at Winchester by the counties of the south-western circuit. There is a separate account for each of the five counties, while for Wiltshire we have in addition two other versions made rather later than the rest. The latest of the Wiltshire accounts is on parchment of smaller size than the other quires of the volume, though possibly written by a scribe whose writing appears elsewhere in the book. The other six accounts are clearly an integral part of its materials written by the same scribes, uniform in size and shape with the rest. Domesday scholars, assuming that all the Domesday returns were made in the form of rolls, commonly speak of these accounts as 'geld rolls'. This description of them is never found in Exon Domesday itself, which does in one place seem to refer to them as the *inquisitio geldi*, and the form of the accounts justifies this description, for they are clearly based on a sworn inquisition and one of them, the latest Wiltshire account, actually refers to the activities of two successive bodies of commissioners, 'Bishop William and his fellows (*et socii*)' and 'Walter and his fellows'. We may reasonably identify William with the bishop of Durham, who, according to a famous entry in Exon Domesday,[1] was ordered to inscribe *in brevibus suis* a royal grant to Winchester, and who, for this reason, is generally supposed to have acted as a royal commissioner on the south-west circuit.

[1] p. 163.

These unique survivals of William I's administration at work on the humdrum task of ordinary business are of fascinating interest to the historian. Within each county the accounts are set out hundred by hundred, showing how much money has been collected from each and, in some cases, giving a gross total of receipts at the end of the document. We hear of money paid to those whose duty it was to carry the money to Winchester, and of expenses incurred for purchasing money-bags, and for paying the scribe who wrote the accounts. In each hundred there were apparently four local collectors, variously referred to as 'fegadri', 'hundremanni', 'collectores geldi', and 'congregatores geldi'; and these officials are stated, here and there, to have 'failed to account' ('non poterant reddere nobis rationem') or to have 'given pledges before the king's barons' ('vadiaverunt foris ante barones regis'). At some stage, then, in its collection, this geld, which had been levied at the rate of six shillings on the hide, had involved an *inquisitio*; and the surviving accounts record successive attempts of central officials to check the renders made by the local men and to collect the arrears. The form of the account can be illustrated by quoting in translation the record of a single hundred, that of Stanford in Wiltshire.

In Staford [Stanford A] hundred there are 105 hides. Of these the barons have in demesne 19½ hides, of which the abbess of Wilton has 10 hides: Richard Puingant 5 hides and 3 virgates: Aiulf 3 hides and 3 virgates. And for 85½ hides have been rendered to the king £25. 3s. 0d. (A, B, and C). The collectors retained 10s. (B and C). [But those who collected the money retained 10s. which have now been rendered. A.]

The account begins with the number of hides in the hundred, followed by a statement of the amount of baronial demesne, which was exempt from payment: the subtraction of the demesne from the total then gives the amount of money actually received, unless, as sometimes happens, though not in this instance, some defaulters have failed to pay. The letters A, B, and C in the above extract, which is quoted from Professor Darlington's recent edition,[1] refer to the three versions of the roll, of which C is the earliest and A the latest. In his commentary on this passage the editor notes that in Domesday Book Richard Puingant's estate, now Trow Farm in Alvediston, credits the holder with 3 virgates less demesne and Aiulf, the sheriff, with 1 virgate more than the figure named above. When we reflect that the hundreds in these counties are systematically omitted both in Domesday Book itself and in the fuller returns in Exon, which have not even survived for Wiltshire, we can understand how laborious and how uncertain is the task of identifying in Domesday Book the holdings mentioned in the geld accounts. Indeed, it is very often impossible, and the whole process is one of so many certain identifications and, after that, a much larger number of more or less probable conjectures. Each scholar who has studied these accounts, W. H. Jones, Mr. Welldon Finn, and Professor Darlington, has his own 'table' of reconstruction.

In what year was this geld taken? The Anglo-Saxon Chronicle mentions the collection of a geld at the same rate in 1083–4, and Professor Darlington, following a long line of scholars, believes that these accounts refer to it. This traditional association of the geld accounts with the year 1083–4—two years before the Survey—was first given an ordered exposition by the Rev. R. W. Eyton, who in his *Key to Domesday* (1878) sought to prove from the united evidence of the accounts and the Dorset Domesday that 'the method and exactitude of its mensuration was such that we could reconstruct the precise acreage of the Domesday estates and parishes'. On the threshold of his inquiries Eyton was met by the difficulty that the figures for demesne in the geld rolls frequently differed from those preserved in the full returns in Exon and in

[1] *V.C.H. Wilts.*, vol. ii, p. 205.

the abstracts, when given, in Domesday Book. These repeated differences, which were really fatal to his whole
theory of 'exact mensuration', he sought to explain away
by the assumption that they were due to changes effected
in the two years' gap between 1084 and 1086. In his
later Somerset volume (1880) he summed up as follows:

Adding now the internal evidence of Domesday to that of the
Inquisicio we shall see that, between the completion of the (Geld)
inquest (Easter 1084), and the completion of Domesday (Easter
1086), changes, neither more nor fewer, took place than such as
may reasonably and credibly be bespoken for an interval of two
years or less.[1]

With misplaced ingenuity, Eyton used this small time
gap as a sort of *deus ex machina* to resolve all discrepancies and prove theories which have long since been
abandoned. In a field in which certainty was so restricted,
the possibilities for hypothesis were almost infinite, and
for Eyton the two years which he claimed separated the
two documents were a blessing in disguise. If the two
were contemporary and so mutually interdependent, his
whole edifice would have fallen like a house of cards. He
was thus led to reject the definite and weighty judgement
of Ellis, who in his Introduction to Domesday Book, a
generation before, had written: 'Certain it is that the
Record itself bears evidence that the tax was raised at the
time of the Survey: that it was connected with it: and
that, at least in the western counties, it was collected by
the same commissioners.' In attempting to decide between
these alternative dates, one has first to note the remarkable
fact that Round, who attacked the work of Eyton almost
as though he had been Edward Augustus Freeman himself, nevertheless, in this solitary instance took over
Eyton's conclusion unchanged. 'I am tempted to believe',
he wrote in 1886, 'that these geld rolls, in the form in

[1] *Domesday Studies: Somerset*, p. 3.

which we now have them, were completed at Winchester
after the close of Easter 1084 by the body which was the
germ of the future Exchequer.'[1]

It would be a mistake to underrate the weight of the
evidence in favour of this conclusion at the time when
Round wrote. The Anglo-Saxon Chronicle records a six-
shilling geld in 1083–4: and the great master, Bishop
Stubbs, had recently declared that this was the first imposition of the tax since its abolition in 1051. There was
no clear mention of the collection of geld under the year
1086, and a geld in that year would have accorded ill with
the universally accepted view of the Domesday Survey as
a 'fact-finding inquiry undertaken with a view to its just
and equitable reassessment'. There was some force too in
Eyton's argument that in 1084 Easter fell only six days
later than Lady Day, and the geld accounts speak of
arrears paid up at Easter and Lady Day indifferently.
And, above all, there were the undoubted discrepancies
between the facts and figures recorded in the geld accounts
and those in Domesday Book. To Round the arguments
appeared conclusive and Ellis's categorical assertion that
the accounts belonged to 1086, of which he gave no
proof, was forgotten. With the stamp of Round's approval
Eyton's view was henceforth unquestioned, largely because there seemed to be no other way of explaining the
factual discrepancies between the two records.

None the less there can be no doubt that Ellis was right
and Eyton was wrong. The geld rolls, in the form in
which we have them, are not earlier than the Domesday
Survey, and this fact could have been demonstrated even
in 1886 had anyone troubled to follow up Ellis's assertion.
The evidence, which is minute and complicated, has already
appeared in the *English Historical Review*[2] and is here
reprinted in the Appendix, and it is conclusive. Moreover,

---

[1] *Domesday Studies* (ed. P. E. Dove, 1888), vol. i, p. 91.
[2] lxv (1950), pp. 1–17. Below, p. 223.

it is supported by the simple fact that five out of the six accounts are in the same scripts as the full returns to the Survey, which form nine-tenths of Exon Domesday. Further confirmation comes from the evidence of Robert of Hereford, which was unknown when Eyton and Round wrote. And, finally, the differences in form and language between the geld accounts in Exon and the single surviving Northampton geld roll of earlier date are alone sufficient to prove that the former were the record of an exceptional administrative activity. This evidence must first be reviewed in more detail, after which it will remain to explain the differences between the statistics supplied by our two records.

We may begin with a summary of the evidence in the Appendix, the cumulative effect of which may be conveniently grouped under two heads.

I. First, there are a number of entries in the geld accounts which seem to be based on information derived from the original returns of 1086. Thus the Dorset geld account appears to distinguish between the cases in which the tax has not been received for this year (*hoc anno*) and those in which the king has never (*nunquam*) had his geld, because the land has been concealed (*celatum*). Since the facts are set out in the Domesday returns, we are forced to conclude either that in these instances the geld accounts are indebted to the records of the Survey, or that the lands 'discovered' in 1084 were rediscovered in 1086. In Wiltshire, similarly, we read in Domesday Book of land 'that has not paid geld since King William came into England', and this entry appears virtually *verbatim* in the geld accounts. Here, again, we must choose between two alternatives; either the geld accounts are indebted to the Domesday returns or vice versa. But, since the Domesday text gives us details of these tenures not found in the geld accounts, this indebtedness to the original returns is fully demonstrated.

II. Secondly, we have here the decisive evidence regarding Manasses the cook who, beyond question, died during the taking of the Domesday Survey. From the fact that Manasses is treated as still alive in the Dorset geld account and in Dorset Domesday, and as dead in both Somerset Domesday and Somerset geld account, it follows that these geld accounts, in the form in which we have them, were not drawn up in 1084 but in 1086. Since these facts were published, Mr. Mason[1] has brought to light a second tenant-in-chief, who is proved to have died in the course of the Survey by exactly the same correspondence of the Domesday evidence with that of the relevant geld account. This is Serlo de Burci, a much more important man than Manasses: and these two examples, together with the probable, though not quite certain, case of Odin the Chamberlain, rule out the possibility of explaining the facts away as verbal errors, or as due to the inconsistency of Domesday documents. This additional evidence brought forward by Mr. Mason completes the proof that the geld accounts belong, not to 1084, but to the year of the Survey, to which they are indebted for some of their information. There is still room for speculation as to the precise connexion of the *inquisitio geldi* with the Domesday Survey in these counties; but it is no longer possible to doubt that a six-shilling geld was being collected in the summer of 1086, and the persistent differences between the facts in the geld accounts and those

---

[1] *E.H.R.* lxix (1954), pp. 283–9. Mr. Mason has omitted to mention an extraordinary, indeed a unique, clause in Exon Domesday in the passage which records the claim of the son of Odin the Chamberlain to West Chelborough, then held by a tenant of William de Moyon: 'Has iii hidas calumpniatur filius Odonis Camerarii. Rex vero iussit ut rectum inde habeat' (p. 43). The personal intervention of the king is perhaps the best indication of an unexpected situation, due apparently to the sudden death of Odin. Nor is it an accident that one of these disputed hides is recorded both in Exon Domesday (p. 43) and in the Dorset geld account (p. 21) as having not paid the geld: decisive proof, surely, of the indebtedness of the geld account to the activities of the Domesday commissioners.

recorded in Exon Domesday can no longer be advanced as an argument for the earlier date.

We have next to consider the palaeographical evidence. There are, as we have seen, three copies of the Wiltshire accounts, all different, of which C is the earliest, and A the latest, the last being on smaller-sized parchment and in a hand which cannot certainly be identified with any of the four or five regular scripts in which the remaining six are written. All these geld accounts are, in Eyton's words, 'replete with coeval corrections and interlineations' which, together with certain positive statements, show that the accounts are still incomplete, and that part of the levy had still to be collected. In short, the view that they are copies of a geld over and done with, which might be of use to the Domesday commissioners—implicit in the attribution to 1084—is plainly untenable. They are manifestly an integral part of the same operation as the rest of the contents of Exon which certainly belong to the year 1086. Then, as we have also seen, they refer to the *consecutive* operations of two bodies of commissioners, Bishop William and his fellows (*socii*) and Walter and his fellows: 'et super eos qui collegerunt geldum recuperaverunt Walterus et socii eius V sol. et III den. exceptis VIII sol. et IX den., quos invenerunt episcopus et socii eius.'[1] These references recall Robert of Hereford's statement that on the Domesday Survey a second body of investigators (*inquisitores*) followed the first, charged with the task of denouncing, if necessary, the findings of the first. Clearly, then, there was behind these accounts an *inquisitio geldi* the activities of which are closely related to those. of the Domesday Survey. There is certainly no question of two successive panels of Domesday *legati*; and one may too easily conclude that Robert of Hereford confused the Domesday Inquest with the annual collection of the geld. It looks rather as though the two did in fact become

[1] *Exon Domesday*, p. 3.

mixed up. Perhaps the first body of inquisitors were the Domesday commissioners and the second a special Treasury panel to collect the arrears of the tax.

Further evidence in favour of the later date emerges from a comparison of the form and scope of these geld accounts, which differ profoundly from the only earlier surviving example, the Northamptonshire geld roll. At first sight it bears a general resemblance to the geld accounts in Exon Domesday: for it is set out hundred by hundred, and within the hundred records the number of hides at which it was assessed, the total number of hides on which geld was paid and the total of those which paid nothing either because they were baronial demesne or were 'waste'. The document, which is in O.E., began thus:

> To Sutton Hundred belong 100 hides as was the case in King Edward's time and of these 21 hides and two-thirds of a hide paid geld and 40 hides are in demesne and 10 hides are the king's own food-rent land and 28 hides and one-third of a hide are waste.[1]

Sometimes it mentions defaulters by name:

> To Spelhoe Hundred belong 90 hides, and of these 20 hides and half a hide are occupied and have paid geld and 25 hides are borough-land, and from 10 hides belonging to Abington—Richard's land—not a penny has been received, and from 6 hides belonging to Moulton—William's land—not a penny has been received, and 28 hides and a half are waste.

These typical extracts, however, reveal a more simple administrative process than that shown in the Exon geld accounts. There is no trace of any *inquisitio*, no mention of any commissioners; and it suggests that the collection of geld was at this date a routine operation, based on traditional figures and carried through without any close scrutiny of the facts. This impression is borne out by

---

[1] A. J. Robertson, *Anglo-Saxon Charters*, pp. 231, 235.

the use of the vernacular, which was the appropriate medium for the local collectors, the *congregatores geldi*. The Northamptonshire document, in short, appears as the typical and ordinary form of these documents, while the elaborate Latin accounts in Exon stand out as the record of some exceptional, even unprecedented, inquiry. This was apparently a separate *inquisitio geldi* carried out by the same commissioners as drew up the Domesday returns for these five counties. This, as we have seen, was the view put forward by Sir Henry Ellis, the original editor of Exon Domesday, and his conclusion, long forgotten and abandoned, is strikingly confirmed by the new evidence of Robert of Hereford, which after mentioning that two distinct and consecutive panels of commissioners were sent out, significantly adds that 'the land was vexed by many calamities arising from the collection of the royal money' (*ex congregatione regalis pecuniae*). Such forthright language can refer to nothing less than the collection of a geld and a heavy one at that. We are thus driven to conclude that the taking of the Survey coincided with still another six-shilling geld and that the south-western circuit, though not necessarily the others, checked the collection by an additional *inquisitio geldi*.

We have thus been led to infer from the joint testimony of the geld accounts in Exon Domesday and the statements of Bishop Robert of Hereford that successive oppressive six-shilling gelds were collected in the years 1084 and 1086. This is a hard conclusion for conservative minds, still only half emancipated from the standpoint of Bishop Stubbs that the geld of 1084, being the first to be levied since its abolition in 1051, revealed the need for a thorough overhaul of its assessment. The notion of geld as a more or less occasional tax in the Conqueror's reign hinges on the Chronicle, and historians are still loath to believe in any levy of geld not mentioned in the Chronicle. For this attitude there is no justification. In a famous paper read at the Domesday Commemoration in 1886 Round[1] first set out the known facts and these point to a very different conclusion.

Our information regarding the geld is intermittent and confused until we reach the Pipe Roll of 1129–30, when it appears as an annual levy at the rate of two shillings on the hide. We also know, of course, that it was being levied annually when it was abandoned by Edward the Confessor in 1051. The discontinuance of the geld was still remembered in the Conqueror's reign, and explains, I think, why the geld is not normally referred to in Domesday Book as an annual custom (*consuetudo*). We read, for example, that in Hereford, Edgar the Staller held a tenement (*occupatum quondam*) and seven houses, which rendered 'no custom except the king's geld when it used to be collected (*colligebatur*)'. But, if it was never formally reimposed by King William, there is no doubt about its collection. Apart from that of 1083–4, the Chronicle mentions only the geld of 1066–7 and that of the following winter; but its silence is more than counterbalanced by the other evidence. Round called attention to a Herefordshire entry in Domesday Book, from which we learn that William I remitted the geld to Mariadoc, and, after him, to his son Grifin. In Hertfordshire we read of the sheriff taking into the king's hand the land of a socman who had not paid geld;[2] while in the geld accounts in Exon Domesday we repeatedly meet with the formula 'non habuit rex geldum hoc anno'. There is, finally, the clinching statement in Domesday Book, that in the borough of Stafford 'rex habet de omnibus geldum per annum'.[3] I see no reason to question the evidence of this passage, which appears hitherto to have eluded notice, or to doubt that under

---

[1] *Domesday Studies*, vol. i, pp. 87 sq.

[2] D.B., vol. I, f. 141 a. See also D.B., vol. II, f. 117 b. A number of Norwich burgesses had fled the town. Several reasons are given, one being the geld (*partim propter geltum regis*).

[3] Ibid., f. 246 a 1.

William I geld became once more what it had been before
1051, and what it was later, an annual levy, which excited
notice only when charged at two or three times the usual
rate. That each collection of an annual custom involved
an annual *inquisitio geldi* is out of the question, and the
structure of the Northamptonshire geld roll doubtless
reflects the normal procedure. The geld rolls of 1084—
had they survived—would have been of much the same
form.

How, then, are we to explain those statistical differences
between the figures of the geld accounts and those of
Domesday Book? The patient and accurate topographical
researches of Eyton, which first brought these to light,
and which then seemed decisive evidence in favour of the
year 1084, have recently been brought to their logical
conclusion by Professor Darlington, and his analysis of
the Wiltshire accounts is so minute and exact as almost
to make possible a statistical estimate of agreement and
difference between the two sets of figures. Using Professor Darlington's convenient translation, let us look a
little more closely at the differences which have induced
scholars to prefer Eyton to Ellis.

The typical hundred quoted above, that of Stanford,[1]
supplies two typical instances of varying figures for exempt demesne. The differences are not in themselves
large, nor consistent in tendency. In one instance the
Domesday figure is larger, in the other smaller, than that
of the geld account. They could be easily explained as
scribal errors were it not that just such small variations
recur again and again in these lists. For Wiltshire there
are not less than forty certain, or at least probable, examples of this phenomenon. This is a very large number
when we bear in mind the endless cases in which no
comparison is possible since Domesday Book omits to
record the extent of the demesne. Without claiming to be

[1] Above, p. 88.

a statistician, one is tempted to suspect a consistent tendency to slight variation between the respective figures.
Quite often they agree: quite often, probably more often,
they tend to differ, if only slightly. At Kingston Deverill,
for example, the totals are respectively, 3½ hides less
3 acres and 3½ hides and half a virgate, while at Yatesbury
there is the difference of a single virgate between the two
estimates. And instances could be multiplied indefinitely.
Are we to suppose that these great barons added or sub-
tracted acres, virgates, and half hides to and from their
demesnes with such regular frequency? Are not all these
slight differences more than we want or can reasonably
postulate for so small an interval as two years? And would
we not be happier to find a greater proportion of larger
and more radical alterations in the demesne?

In addition there are other and more notable differences
inexplicable by the hypothesis of a ten years' time-lag, let
alone a mere two years. Thus, for instance, in Westbury
hundred the geld accounts mention 7 carucates of land, in
Dole hundred 3, in Elstub hundred 8, and in Melksham
hundred 13 which paid no geld and of which no trace is
found in Domesday Book. How, we may ask, could 31
carucates of land have disappeared between 1084 and
1086? In the same category lie differences in the attribution of ownership T.R.E., as, for instance, in Swan-
borough hundred, where Domesday Book names Gytha
as the holder of Rushall in 1066, while the geld accounts
state that it belonged to Harold. Similar differences can
be seen in Rowborough and Cawdon hundreds. Or,
again, take Whorwellsdown hundred[1] where the editor
decides that the hundred must have contained 92 hides,
though the geld account tells only of 78. There is constant
difficulty, too, in harmonizing the figures of the two documents respecting the extent of royal demesne: and finally
there are cases in which, though the figures agree, land is

[1] *V.C.H. Wilts.*, vol. ii, p. 188.

exempt in the geld account, which, by the evidence of Domesday Book, should have paid its quota. Without descending to a long list of particular instances, one is led to conclude that so many *types* of differences are incapable of explanation by the hypothesis of a mere two years' interval, while those of the first category, the extent of the demesne, which are theoretically susceptible of such explanation, are of all the most suspect.

Such, briefly summarized, are the discrepancies between the figures of the Wiltshire geld accounts and those of Domesday Book. The instances in which they differ regarding the extent of demesne, as Professor Darlington himself says, are 'innumerable', and he adds:

These discrepancies must imply either that the collectors of 1084 were given different information from that supplied to the Domesday commissioners or that the demesnes had actually changed in extent between the completion of the one record and the other.[1]

Professor Darlington prefers the second alternative; but it is obvious that the very thoroughness of his researches has destroyed his case. It was fundamental to Eyton's argument that 'changes neither more nor fewer took place than such as may reasonably and credibly be bespoken for an interval of two years or less'. The discovery of 'innumerable' alterations of demesne—not to mention the vanished hides and carucates—destroys the whole argument, and Eyton's hypothesis collapses from sheer *embarras de richesse*.

The facts, then, require another explanation of these differences: nor is it far to seek. The tendency towards a slight but constant variation between the figures for demesne in Domesday Book and the geld accounts, and the larger and arbitrary, yet more occasional, differences regarding hides and carucates are precisely what we should

[1] *V.C.H. Wilts.*, vol. ii, p. 176.

expect to find when the records of a traditional tax, collected for twenty years, without the special procedure of inquisition, by local collectors, using rule-of-thumb methods, are set against the figures disclosed by the stringent and searching Domesday Survey.

VIII

EXON DOMESDAY

In his Introduction to the text of Somerset Domesday Round was careful to remind his readers that the record of the Survey

was made Hundred by Hundred and that the original rolls in which the Survey was contained were lost at an early date. Even in the Exon Domesday their contents are entirely rearranged, while in Domesday Book they are rearranged in yet another system and also reduced by omitting certain details throughout.

It has already been pointed out above that this hypothesis —however plausible in other circuits—breaks down completely when faced by the evidence of Exon Domesday. The fortunate survival of this huge manuscript enables us to sketch with some confidence the broad outline of procedure on the south-western circuit, and the resulting picture is wholly at variance with Round's words. Broadly speaking the process was as follows. The commissioners or legates—as elsewhere—proceeded by sworn inquests, the jurors of the hundred systematically answering the questions put to them by the commissions. This evidence may even have been first committed to writing in the form of 'hundred rolls' arranged topographically, though this is extremely unlikely: but in the final record of their findings, that is to say the original return of the commissioners sent to Winchester, the information was already arranged by fiefs, exactly as we find it in Vol. I of Domesday Book. The actual volume (or quires) sent to Winchester became superfluous when the contents in a shortened form had been entered in Domesday Book, and has not been preserved.

We have, however, in Exon Domesday, along with much other material, an earlier draft of the return, made apparently by the commissioners at Exeter, and left behind them in the cathedral when the contents had been transferred, in revised form, to their final return to the Treasury at Winchester. The most cursory study of Exon Domesday fully supports this reconstruction, which finds strong corroboration in the text of Little Domesday (i.e. Vol. II). This volume seems to be the actual 'original returns' of the East Anglian circuit made to Winchester. Like Exon Domesday it contains the full findings of the commission, including the details of the livestock: but, unlike it, has been preserved in the Treasury because—for some reason —its contents (in shortened form) were never transferred to Domesday Book, Vol. I.

Such, it is here maintained, is the nature of Exon Domesday, and it remains, by looking more closely at the evidence to show that the abbreviated record of the south-western counties in Domesday Book is indeed derived— though at one remove[1]—from Exon Domesday.

For the historian of administration the Exon Domesday is the most informative surviving document of the Domesday Inquest. Though now a bound volume of more than 500 folios, it was to its compilers simply a collection of quires or quaternions recording the relevant information collected by the *legati* in their itinerary of the five south-western counties. Large as it is, the surviving quires are no more than a fragment of the total collection of materials from which this circuit compiled its 'original returns' to the Inquest. In Exon Domesday we can watch the commissioners at work, giving form and shape to a vast collection of facts: and, if only we could read its secrets, it would answer all our questions. The intermediate and

---

[1] For the proof that a fair copy was made locally and became the local return of the south-west circuit see below, p. 105–13.

tentative nature of Exon Domesday has not been grasped by historians who have treated it as a finished, engrossed record, in fact as an alternative form of Domesday Book.

Yet though just a collection of materials, it is a *single* collection, made on quires of uniform size, by a small number of scribes whose distinctive scripts, and no others, recur throughout. Here again Exon has been misunderstood by ignoring the evidence of the original. The view, held since Eyton, that the 'geld rolls' in Exon belonged to 1084 and therefore 'had nothing to do' with its other contents is really disproved by an examination of the manuscript. There can be no doubt that the *inquisitio geldi* was carried out, as Ellis said long ago, by the *legati* of this circuit, since it is an integral part of the manuscript. Apart from the 'geld rolls', the chief contents of this miscellaneous collection fall into three groups.

Firstly, an elaborate description, manor by manor, of the lands of the king and of his tenants-in-chief, separately listed for each county under the names of the men who held them. Four-fifths of the volume is taken up with the manorial descriptions, and, even so, a great deal has been lost. For instance, only one Wiltshire manor is described: much of Dorset is missing, as well as parts of Devonshire and Somerset.

Secondly, long lists of *terrae occupatae* for three of the five counties, viz. Somerset, Devon, and Cornwall. These records of unjust seisins are of a highly miscellaneous character. No attempt is made to separate the lands of the king from those of his tenants-in-chief, and many entries are substantially repeated. The record of *terrae occupatae* was still incomplete when the volume was compiled. The scribes repeatedly add brief notices of such *terrae occupatae* at the end of a baronial fief, and not infrequently these entries are interlined, or added in a more cramped hand wherever there is a vacant space.

Thirdly, there are a number of miscellaneous summaries

of the total extent and value of the lands held in each
county by certain tenants-in-chief, and notably of the
abbey of Glastonbury.[1] It is not clear for what purpose
these summaries were made, but merely to list the contents of this astonishing *mélange* is to realize that Exon
Domesday was the record of the full findings of the south-
western commissioners, of which only a fraction (in an
abbreviated form) was deemed worthy of perpetual preservation in Domesday Book. '

The difficulty of demonstrating the indebtedness of
Domesday Book to Exon Domesday lies in its very earli-
ness or primitiveness. Although more than 90 per cent.
of the abbreviated text is demonstrably derived from
Exon,[2] many changes clearly were made in the final return, and have left their mark on Vol. I of Domesday.
In a few cases the latter even supplies a fact not found in
Exon, but in general the differences lie in the order in
which the lists of manors appear under the separate fiefs,
in the grouping of the minor tenants-in-chief, and the
classification of the royal demesne. The significance of
these changes is plain enough. We can trace in Exon the
efforts of the commissioners, having gathered the facts,
to arrange them satisfactorily, and not seldom it is clear
from the shortened Domesday text that improvements
must have been made in the fair copy of the original
returns sent to Winchester. These improvements are most
striking in the feudal groupings of lands and of the
tenants-in-chief who held them. The task of arranging
and classifying men and lands—the cardinal problem of
the whole Survey—had to be hammered out slowly, and
by comparing the lists in the two documents, we can see
how it was done.

For Devonshire, from which we take our examples,

---

[1] ff. 173, 527, 530.
[2] Baring, 'The Exeter Domesday', *E.H.R.* xxvii (1912), pp. 309–18; R.
Welldon Finn, 'The Immediate Sources of the Exchequer Domesday', *Bulletin
of the J.R.L.* xl (1957), pp. 47–78.

Exon Domesday contains thirty headings, scattered impartially through the volume from f. 63 to f. 465. Many, indeed most of these, are substantially the same as those in Domesday Book, Vol. I. Thus, for example, the *Terra Abbatis Glastingheberiensis in Devensira* of Exon (f. 161) is virtually repeated in Domesday Book as *Terra aecclesiae Glastingberiensis*. There are, however, certain differences between the two, which can be usefully grouped under three heads:

I. The royal demesne. Exon lists the manors of the royal demesne under three separate headings, viz.

Dominicatus regis ad regnum pertinens in Devenscira (f. 83);

Dominicatus regis in Devenesira (f. 93);

Terra Mahillis Reginae in Devenesira (f. 108).

In Vol. I of Domesday the lands under these three titles are brought together (as always) under the single rubric *Terra Regis*. But within this inclusive grouping Domesday Book divides the manors into no less than five groups. Of these the first retains the Exon heading on f. 83, and reads 'Haec XIX maneria fuerunt in dominio regis Edwardi et pertinent ad regem', while those illogically grouped in Exon under the other two headings are neatly sorted out under five subheadings, viz. the lands held by 'Edded regina', 'Ghida mater comitis Heraldi', 'comes Heraldus', 'Lewinus comes', and 'Brictric et post regina Mathildis'. Thus the first fumbling attempts to group the material are later arranged in a more satisfactory pattern by the compilers of Domesday Book.

II. On f. 388 of Exon the lands of Goscelmus and of Walter de Clavile are grouped under a single heading— 'Terrae Goscelmi et Walteri in Devenesira'. This impossible arrangement is corrected in Domesday Book, Vol. I, where each man's lands are separately listed under his name. But we are fortunately able to see why the lands of two important men were so strangely conjoined in Exon, for the first entry is that of the manor 'Fereordin', which was held conjointly by Walter and Goscelm. The scribe accordingly wrote a joint rubric and after that the lands of each were added indifferently as the information was collected. Once again, then, Domesday improves on its exemplar.

III. Still more odd is the grouping of the thegns and knights of the county in Exon which distinguishes

Terrae Francorum militum in Devenesira,
Terrae servientium regis in Devenesira,
Terrae Anglorum tegnorum in Devenesira.

Here is confusion indeed at which Round long ago poked fun, for in Somerset the commissioners made a further heading of 'French thegns'! The Anglo-Saxon thegns, as Round pointed out, were the only true thegns; and, by the time we reach the shortened Domesday version, these experimental groupings were superseded by the simple and correct heading of 'the King's thegns'. The list of French knights is also broken up into separate *breves* for each tenant-in-chief, and the title *terrae servientium regis* retained for the smaller men. These changes were made partly no doubt, in the new recension of Exon which became the 'return' of the circuit to Winchester, and partly by the king's scribes who compiled Domesday Book. But historians failed to grasp either the fact or the nature of the whole evolution. The local commissioners, faced with a mass of names, did their best; and then consecutively the local revisers, and the king's scribes at the centre, standing as it were on their shoulders, arrived at the nomenclature and the grouping which we find in Domesday Book.

Domesday Book and Exon Domesday are thus not alternative or competing groupings of the Inquest material, as Round believed, but stages in the evolution of the final record.[1] His mistake arose in part at least from the assumption that the 'original returns' made by the circuits were 'rolls', and that they were then made into 'books' by the central government.[2] There are, however, two consistent and systematic differences between the Exon text and that of Domesday which taken together make it clear that the two records were produced by two separate and wholly distinct bodies of clerks, viz. those of the commissioners of the south-western circuit, and the king's clerks at Winchester respectively.

I. Exon Domesday, though not the final, is very far from being the first draft of the commission's findings. Written records must lie behind it: for the information has already been carefully digested and the description of each manor presents facts in invariable order and with unvarying formulas. Clearly, enormous labour had already been devoted to the ordering and presentation of the material. The facts supplied correspond very closely with the instructions given to the commissioners (above, p. 60) and each description is an answer to an identical set of questions. There is, however, no suggestion in these entries that the record is being abbreviated from a larger body of facts. The information is written in leisurely and even 'wordy' formulas, and the very script is far less contracted than in Domesday Book. The opening clause of thousands of such entries runs thus: 'X habet mansionem que vocatur Y quam tenuit Z die qua rex Edwardus fuit vivus et mortuus et reddidit geldum pro A hidis.' The full details of the land held in demesne and that of the villeins follow, and the extent of pasture and woodland is fully described by length and breadth.

[1] Even the Domesday text was not definitive, and we later encounter a still smaller volume, the abbreviation of Domesday Book made by the clerks of the king's *curia*. See below, p. 213.

[2] See Round's Introduction to Somerset Domesday in the *V.C.H.* (vol. i). The process of clarification here illustrated from Devonshire is equally apparent in the other counties of this circuit.

All this is in striking contrast to the presentation of the material in Domesday Book, or, as we shall see, in the I.C.C., where expert abbreviation has reduced the formulas to the briefest possible wording and the script almost to medieval shorthand. In short, it is borne in on the reader that Exon presents the full original findings of the commission set out in the form in which they were first committed to writing. It is well nigh impossible to suppose that Exon Domesday represents a rearrangement of the same material already supplied, perhaps at greater length, in a series of hundred rolls. The immense labour of such a task, we are justified in concluding, would have driven the scribes to a far more compressed form of presenting this material.

II. A still more conclusive indication that Exon and Vol. I of Domesday Book are of wholly different provenance is afforded by the changes of nomenclature and formulas which are made by the latter. For the opening formula quoted above Domesday Book substitutes 'X tenet Y (a place). Z tenuit T.R.E. Et geldebat pro A hidis.' The word *mansio* disappears or, where required, is altered to *manerium*: and 'T(empore) R(egis) E(dwardi)' replaces 'the day on which King Edward was alive and dead'. The word *acra* (acre) takes the place of *ager* and *silva* that of *nemus*. The object of these, and many more similar word-changes, is to eradicate, so far as could be, provincialism and to bring the abbreviated versions into line with those of the other counties in Domesday Book, and must have been the work of central scribes employing a technique of their own which probably differed more or less from that of any particular circuit.

In this connexion Mr. Welldon Finn has recently made a discovery of great interest.[1] It has been remarked above that the script of Vol. I of Domesday Book is not

---

[1] 'The Evolution of Successive Versions of Domesday Book', *E.H.R.* lxvi (1951), p. 561.

found either in Little Domesday or in Exon Domesday.
This statement is not strictly accurate, for two small fiefs
in Exon are written in the unmistakable script of Vol. I
of Domesday Book, and employ the formulas appropriate
to it.[1] They relate to manors held by the bishop of Bayeux
and Robert FitzGerold, which lie, according to Eyton,
in Horethorne hundred, and seem to be first attempts at
abbreviating the full descriptions made by the south-
western commissioners, and so converting them into the
form in which they now occur in Vol. I of Domesday
Book. Yet, although they omit details of the livestock on
demesne, and much else, they are not copied from the
entries in Vol. I for they still preserve facts there omitted,
and differ slightly in wording. How can we explain the
presence of these two lone entries by the compiler of
Vol. I, a Winchester clerk, among the full local material
of the south-western circuit?

So far as the bishop of Bayeux is concerned the answer
is not in doubt. His Somerset lands consisted of the single
manor of Templecombe, which was actually held by a
sub-tenant called Samson the chaplain, and this is fully
described in Exon under the rubric *French Thegns in
Somerset* (p. 432): 'Samson capellanus habet i mansionem
quae vocatur Coma quam tenuit Livinus Comes die qua
rex Edwardus fuit vivus et mortuus et redd[idit] gildum
pro viii hidis.' The entry continues with a detailed description of the ploughs, villeins, bordars, serfs, animals
(very elaborately set out), and so on, ending with the value
of the manor and some details of a second estate called
Turnietta which had been added to it.

The local commissioners, having subsequently discovered both that the term 'French thegns' was a misnomer and that Samson was only a sub-tenant, in their
final circuit return substituted the heading 'King's thegns'

---

[1] *Exon Domesday*, pp. 142, 408. Each entry occurs on an otherwise blank leaf:
but they are an integral part of the manuscript and not later additions.

and correctly assigned Templecombe to the bishop of
Bayeux, the tenant-in-chief. Accordingly, we find in Vol. I
of Domesday Book a brief epitome of the full description
in Exon beginning: 'Episcopus Baiocensis tenet Come et
Sanson de eo. Lewinus comes tenuit T.R.E. et geldabat
pro VIII hidis'.[1] These were normal changes to which
there are countless parallels. But Mr. Finn called attention
to the extraordinary fact that this entry in Vol. I is already
found, with trifling differences of wording, on p. 432 of
Exon Domesday and written by the scribe of Vol. I.

The other example of the script of Vol. I of Domesday
found in the Exon volume is that describing the fee of
Robert FitzGerold in Somersetshire.[2] He held two manors,
and the wording in both volumes is very nearly the same.
There is, however, one very significant difference which
proves that behind the abbreviated version of Robert's
lands in Somerset there must have been a full description
couched in the local formulas and containing details of the
livestock, though it is not preserved in Exon Domesday.
For the Exon entry still preserves a record of the land
held *in dominio*, which was a normal feature of the full
description, generally dropped, as in this case, in the
shorter text of Vol. I of Domesday Book. It is perhaps significant that the name of Robert's second manor, which
gelded for 10 hides, is omitted in both manuscripts, the
scribe leaving a blank space in each case. Vital omissions
of this kind are exceedingly rare in Exon Domesday,
and the interest of the central scribe may be connected
with this odd omission. The fact that the deficiency is not
made good in Vol. I at least proves that the shorter version was based exclusively on Exon. The occurrence of
these two insertions in Exon Domesday does not, I think,
justify the view that Exon Domesday was itself the final
return made to Winchester, if only because they are a
little fuller than the corresponding entries in Domesday

[1] D.B., vol. I, f. 87 b 2.   [2] Ibid., f. 97 a 1: *Exon*, p. 408.

Book, Vol. I. But they do suggest that advice and criticism were sought by the compilers of the circuit return from the central office at Winchester. They also bring out vividly the difference in form and technique between the compilation of Vol. I and Exon Domesday. Moreover, they prove—and this is of great importance—that Exon Domesday and Great Domesday are contemporary; and this fact, in conjunction with the discovery that the geld accounts belong to 1086, makes it practically certain that both Great Domesday and Exon, as well as Little Domesday, were all completed by the death of William the Conqueror in 1087. They also throw some new and welcome light on the palaeography of Vol. I of Domesday Book. Despite minor variations of carefulness, size, and spacing, the script of this volume is marked by a unity of style so sustained as to suggest that the whole volume is the work of a single scribe. Now the two entries in Exon Domesday are quite certainly written in the script of Great Domesday; and this in turn suggests that we should hesitate to accept as the work of the royal scribes at Winchester the strongly contrasting though miscellaneous scripts of both Exon and Little Domesday. These indications that Exon Domesday is the draft return of the south-western circuit are strengthened and confirmed, when set beside the parallel evidence of Domesday Book, Vol. II. The outstanding characteristic of the Exon Domesday is its basic similarity to Domesday Book, Vol. II, and the common contrast they present to Domesday Book, Vol. I. The miscellaneous scripts in which they are written are quite unlike the curial script of Vol. I; and, while differing from one another in detail, they yet provide a common contrast in shape and style to that volume. There are also the 'provincial' differences, as we may call them, that distinguish Little Domesday and Exon both from one another, and collectively from Vol. I. In Little Domesday, for example, in the lists of tenants-in-chief prefixed to the text of Norfolk and Suffolk, the names of great lay magnates precede those of ecclesiastical tenants-in-chief: and we find a distinction between manors *de regno* and *de regione*, which are apparently correlative to the *mansiones de comitatu* and the *dominicatus regis ad regnum pertinens* in Exon. Nor must we forget that the *terrae occupatae* of Exon Domesday find their parallel in the *invasiones super regem* of the East Anglian volume. So many common differences strengthen the argument that neither Exon nor Little Domesday was compiled by the king's clerks at Winchester, but both were the work of the circuit commissioners. We are driven to conclude that Exon was the draft of the original returns made by the *legati* for the south-west circuit, which, like all the other returns, was rendered superfluous by the compilation of the summaries in Vol. I of Domesday Book made by the curial clerks at Winchester. The contents of Little Domesday, the original return of the East Anglian circuit, were never abbreviated nor included in Vol. I of Domesday Book: and to this accident alone it owes its survival. So Exon Domesday, when superseded by the revised or 'fair copy', was left behind in Exeter, while Little Domesday—*faute de mieux* —was unevenly yoked to the larger volume of Great Domesday made at Winchester.

This view of Exon Domesday, at once simple and consistent with the whole of the material, has never been shaken by either evidence or argument. It has been ignored or dismissed in favour of an hypothesis, which however plausible for eastern England, is certainly untenable for the south-western circuit.

No direct comparison between Exon Domesday and Little Domesday is possible (any more than between Exon and Vol. I of Domesday) since they belong to different *stages* in the compilation of the original returns. Behind Little Domesday Book we know there was an earlier recension. But both, as compilations of circuits, do present a common contrast to Vol. I of Domesday Book. There is, however, one large and baffling difference between them that remains unexplained. In Little Domesday, the hundreds in which the various manors lay are carefully and systematically shown by rubrics in the text: and by these hundreds they can be identified with great certainty. On the other hand, in both Exon Domesday and in Domesday Book, Vol. I (for those counties), no attempt is anywhere made to record the hundreds in which the various estates were situated. Moreover, the five counties of the south-west are the only ones in the whole of Domesday Book where no effort is made to indicate the hundreds. What is the explanation of the omission of the hundreds in the south-west? To a certain extent the answer to this question must be a matter of guesswork; but it is safe to say that the absence of the hundreds is bound up with the relatively low repute in which the hundred was held in the west and south-west of England as compared with the east. The more authoritarian society of western England relied chiefly on the evidence supplied by the barons and other holders of land, whose conflicting claims were harmonized by the evidence of the thegns or the English. The formal procedure here, as everywhere, was by hundreds and villages, but the hundredal juries had not the same standing as in the east, and this lower rating, observable in the whole of western England, was in the south-west carried to its logical conclusion by the total omission of hundredal rubrics. It was evidently deemed sufficient that the owners of the lands knew in which hundreds they lay. We may reasonably suppose that hard words were used by the central government on being offered a vast array of wholly unidentified manors, and this may well explain the visit of the Winchester compiler whose handwriting is found in Exon Domesday. But it was too late to do anything about it when the error was discovered; the final return bore no

hundred rubrics, and for this reason there are none in the
abbreviation made in Vol. I of Domesday Book. In my
opinion, the absence of hundredal rubrics in the shortened
Domesday account of these five counties—a solitary exception in the whole of England—proves to demonstration that the original returns made by the circuit were not
a series of hundred rolls, while it is scarcely less certain
that the information was from the very first committed
to writing by the circuit commissioners in the form in
which it is now found both in Exon and Domesday Book,
Vol. I.

   If, then, there were no preliminary 'hundred rolls', how
exactly was Exon Domesday compiled? In attempting an
answer to this question we must bear in mind that Exon
is no more than a rearranged—and perhaps expanded—
fair copy of still earlier written records.[1] The form and the
scope of these documents are alike unknown to us; nor is
there any apparent significance in the erratic alternation
of the various set-hands of its numerous copyists. The
earliest stages of the Inquest are, in short, hidden from us:
and it would be dangerous even to guess at them since
Exon is no more than a fragment of a much larger collection of materials. What, however, we can say with some
confidence is that in Exon Domesday the clerks were
grouping or regrouping the earlier records in a new way.
The written sources from which they drew were already
arranged county by county, and fief by fief. In Exon the
scribes seem to be making a single consecutive record of
each tenant-in-chief's lands in all the counties of the south-
west circuit. Thus on f. 47 we find, one after the other, a
list of the *Terra Willelmi de Moione in Wiltesira* and then

   [1] This is apparent from occasional repetitions, e.g. the Devonshire manor of
Touretona is twice fully described in identical terms under different headings
on ff. 98 and 110. See R. Welldon Finn, 'The Exeter Domesday and its Con-
struction' (*Bulletin of J.R.L.* xli (1959), p. 384). I have drawn freely upon Mr.
Welldon Finn's unrivalled knowledge of Exon Domesday, as also from his 'The
Immediate Sources of the Exchequer Domesday' (ibid. xl (1957), pp. 47–78).

of the *Terra Willelmi de Moione in Dorseta*. Similarly on
f. 371 we find the *Terra Aluredi Hispaniensis in Devenesira* and on the verso of the same leaf the *Terra Aluredi de
Hispania in Somerseta*.[1] This curious grouping has been
destroyed by the order of the sheets in the modern binding. As originally written these materials were primarily
a record of the lands and wealth of the royal demesne and
of the tenants-in-chief consecutively in all five counties.
Could it be that the commissioners had not yet realized
that the final return required at headquarters in Winchester was one in which each county was, so to speak, 'complete in itself'? It may even be that this explains why the
still later version of Exon which became the original return to Winchester was made. In this connexion, it is
worth noting that on f. 531 of Exon Domesday there are
summaries of the total fiefs of the earl of Mortain and
several other tenants in chief. The note on the earl, for
example, runs as follows:

The count of Mortain has in Wiltshire, Dorset, Devon and Cornwall 623 manors (*mansiones*), comprising 833 hides, less 2½ virgates.
The land is sufficient for 2480 ploughs; its value (*appreciata*) is
£1409 less 6s. and 10d. Of these hides the Earl has in demesne 200
less 2 which are worth to him £400 and one silver mark per
annum: and his men have 655 hides, less half a virgate, which are
worth (*valent*) £1000 less 6s. and 10d.

Summaries of this kind would seem to be the logical purpose and outcome of the original arrangement of the
material in Exon Domesday, and though only a few
survive (f. 531) they may well have been made for all
tenants-in-chief.[2]

[1] For other examples see Exon Domesday, ff. 83 and 86 b; 108 and 111 b; 136
and 136 b; 161 and 173 b; 177 and 180 b; 334 b; 473 and 473 b, and many
more.
[2] Precisely similar summaries for the lands of Picot the sheriff and other great
feudatories in the county of Cambridge and Hertfordshire are found in the
Inquisitio Eliensis which for these counties was based on the full Inquest proceedings of the third circuit. See p. 137.

Thus, the very grouping of the material in Exon shows
that the primary interest of the commissioners in the
south-west was not with the assessment or collection of
geld but with the total wealth and lands of the king and
his tenants-in-chief. This abiding purpose of the Inquest
is to some extent disguised by the artificial arrangement of
the final circuit return, which was dictated by the O.E.
financial system. Since each shire accounted separately to
the treasury at Winchester, the fiefs of the great men were
returned in separate county bundles each complete in itself. In short, we must never forget that from start to finish
the Domesday Inquest was concerned not with taxation
in the abstract but with the wealth of persons, the 'men
of any account' in England, the tenants-in-chief.

The unusual grouping of the fiefs in Exon Domesday
is just another reminder of how little we know about the
evolution of the circuit returns in their early stages. It
does not, however, affect the value of the evidence it supplies regarding the actual Inquest procedure, whose broad
outlines have already been sketched above (pp. 77–80).
There a distinction was drawn between the proceedings in
court and the gathering of information which took place
out of court. In court the commissioners everywhere identified and listed each estate methodically by hundreds, and
their skeleton lists[1] when rearranged under the owners'
names, were worked up with full manorial descriptions
by the detailed evidence handed in by local representatives of each estate. This general picture is strikingly
confirmed by a number of so-called but wrongly called
'duplicate' entries in Exon Domesday. Of these the most
illuminating series relates to the royal manor of Winnianton in Cornwall, which at the time of the Conquest
had been held by Harold. It contained 15 hides, of which

---

[1] We do not know whether skeleton lists, which would have been well within
the competence of sheriffs and hundred bailiffs, were provided in advance, or
only made in the course of the Inquest sessions.

4 were held in demesne, while the remaining 11 had by
1086 passed into the possession of the count of Mortain.
In the time of Edward the Confessor, these 11 hides
had been divided between seventeen thegns who, with
this land, we are told, could not be separated from the
king's demesne manor of Winnianton.[1] Of the twenty-
odd estates held by these seventeen thegns we have two
very different accounts in Exon, one under the *Terra Regis*
in Cornwall (ff. 99 sqq.) and the other under the fee of the
count (*Terra Comitis*, ff. 224 sqq.). The first point to note is
that it is no accident that they are twice recorded. They
are mentioned under the royal demesne since, as we have
seen, they were an integral part of the royal manor of
Winnianton: and they are included in the fee of the earl
because he had seized or occupied them and in 1086 held
them in chief. The fact is plainly stated on f. 508 under
the heading *Terrae occupatae*, where we read:

From the manor of Winnianton have been taken away (*ablatae*)
22 [*sic*] manors which 17 thegns held on the day when king Edward
was alive and dead, who could not be separated from this manor.
The men of the earl of Mortain hold these manors from him, and
they are worth *per annum* £9–8s.

Let us next compare the two lists, taking as a typical
example the estate of Guihummarus at Tricoi. First on
f. 99 b under *Terra Regis*:

And Guihummarus [*has*] 1 manor (*mansionem*) which is called
Tricoi, and it paid geld for 1 hide in the time of King Edward.
Eight ploughs can till it and it is worth by the year 30d. and when
the Earl received it it was worth 40s.

Then on f. 226 under *Terrae comitis*:

The Earl has one manor which is called Trecut, in which is
1 hide of land: and it used to pay geld for two parts of 1 virgate.

---

[1] Exon Domesday, f. 99: 'qui non poterant separari a praescripta mansione et
reddebant consuetudinem in eadem mansione'.

Eight ploughs can till it. Unihumarus holds it of the Earl. There
he has in demesne two parts of 1 virgate, and the villagers (*villani*)
have the other land (*aliam terram*). There Unihumarus has 2 villagers and 4 bordars and 1 slave and one wagon-load (*quadragena-*
riam) and a half of pasture and it is worth 30*d.* and when the Earl
received it 40*s.* and this [estate] is of the king's demesne manor
which is called Winnetona.

The first entry (f. 99), it will be seen, tells us:

1. The name of the actual holder of the land.
2. The hidage T.R.E.
3. The number of ploughs required to till it.
4. Its value in 1086 and when the earl received it.

The substance of these four entries is repeated on f. 226
and to them is added:

1. The actual geld it paid.
2. The land held in demesne and that held by the
   villagers.
3. The account of the villeins, bordars, slaves, and
   pasture on the estate.

This analysis of these two accounts for Tricoi is, broadly
speaking,[1] equally applicable to the rest of the estates,
and it is obvious that the two lists are not duplicates.
They must have come from different sources. Yet they
have much in common, and, as it were, the same things
in common. Such consistent agreement and disagreement
suggests that the first list (f. 99) preserves the basic facts
recorded at the formal sessions of the Inquest, while the
second (f. 226) includes further manorial detail supplied
out of court to the commissioners by the actual tenant of

---

[1] In a few cases there are slight differences in the T.R.E. value: while for the
1-hide estate of Rentis, held of the earl by Ulward, the details of the manorial
stock, &c. (no. 3), are found on both lists. The apparent exception is perhaps
explained by the assumption that the earl who himself held in demesne a small
estate of 1 virgate at Rentis, or more probably his officials, supplied these details
for the sub-manor. But even at Rentis the actual geld paid (1) and the division
between demesne and *terra villanorum* (2) are only found on f. 225 b.

each estate, either directly or indirectly through the earl to whose fee they belonged.

If this hypothesis is correct the procedure with regard to the manor of Winnianton was, more or less, as follows. The basic facts regarding both the 4 hides held in demesne and the twenty-odd thegn lands held in 1086 of the Crown by the count of Mortain were recorded at the actual Inquest under the *Terra Regis*. This skeleton document, we may suppose, was subsequently worked up into the full description as we have it on f. 99 by the addition of items 1, 2, and 3 above for the 4 hides held in demesne. The full descriptions of the thegn lands were the responsibility of the count of Mortain, and these are duly found under his *breve* (*Terra Comitis*) on ff. 224 sqq. There the order in which the estates appear is different from the list on f. 99, and several of them seem to have been omitted. The two lists then in this final form are independent, but since they have an identical skeleton basis,[1] we are forced to conclude that they are the result of two consecutive operations. That the first of these was the actual Inquest is intrinsically probable, and is strongly supported by evidence from the county of Kent which is dealt with below.[2] Just how the second operation by which the vital particulars recorded at the Inquest were expanded into the full descriptions found under the earl's *breve* is not so clear. In the last resort, so much detailed information about these tiny estates can only have come from the men who cultivated them, and it is reasonable to suppose that these minute particulars were furnished directly by the subtenants out of court, and after the formal sessions of the Inquest.

In keeping with the above interpretation is the evidence supplied by another pair of so-called duplicate entries to

---

[1] e.g. the estimate of the number of ploughs required to till each estate is identical in every case.

[2] Chapter X, p. 149 below.

which Mr. Welldon Finn has called attention.[1] The manor
of Newton St. Cyres, which is fully described on f. 483,
is there said to be held in chief by a certain Domnus
who had formerly held it of Edward the Confessor. It is
clear, however, from the entry that there was some doubt
as to the legality of his tenure for the entry explains that
Domnus held the land of King Edward 'et modo dicit se
eam tenere de Willelmo rege'. We are therefore not surprised to read on f. 117 under the *breve* of the bishop of
Exeter:

> The bishop has/claims[2] 1 manor which is called Newton which
> Domnus holds, and it paid geld for 3 hides. Concerning this manor
> bishop Osbern showed his charters which testify that his church
> was seised thereof before the reign of King Edward and he further
> says that in the times of King William he lodged a plea about the
> manor and proved by the testimony of Frenchmen that it was his.
> And it is worth £3.

Both entries clearly derive from the actual court proceedings of the Inquest, when Domnus, the sitting tenant,
made his claim to hold in chief of King William, and the
bishop, showing his charters, put forward his counter-
claim. And since the question remained unsettled, a note
was made of his claim under the list of the bishop's lands,
but the full description of the manor was, as always in
such cases, supplied by the actual tenant, Domnus. But the
important point here is that the court proceedings seem
to have dealt only with the basic facts—the name of the
manor, the hidage, the value, and above all (though in this
case it could not be settled) to whom the manor lawfully
belonged. From this bare statement the full description

---

[1] 'The Exeter Domesday and its Construction' (*Bulletin of J.R.L.* xli (1959),
p. 385. Once again the two entries are not duplicates, nor is it quite accurate to
say that the 'manor was twice described'. Though twice mentioned, the only
descriptio is on f. 483. The matter apparently remained unsettled and both entries
are retained in Domesday Book, Vol. I (ff. 101 b 2 and 118 a 2).

[2] *Has* is interlined above *claims*.

on f. 486 was later worked up from information supplied
by Domnus.[1]

[1] For another example see R. W. Eyton's *Analysis of Somerset Domesday*,
vol. i, p. 178, where the three entries regarding the church of St. Andrew in
Ilchester are printed in full. The procedure outlined above also explains an instance
of 'double entries' regarding a hide at Torrels Preston (co. Somerset) stolen by
the earl of Mortain from the royal manor of King's Brompton (see *V.C.H.
Somerset*, i. 425–6, referred to above, p. 83). These differ considerably as to the
facts, and the version given under the Mortain fee is preferable to that of the
Terra Regis. Cf. below, p. 228.

IX

THE INQUISITIO COMITATUS CANTABRIGIENSIS AND THE INQUISITIO ELIENSIS

I N turning from the Exon Domesday to the Inquisitio Comitatus Cantabrigiensis we pass from the evidence which historians have ignored to the single document on which the old hypothesis of the making of Domesday Book rests. It was described by Round with pardonable exaggeration as 'the true key to the Domesday Survey', for its publication in 1876 opened out new and illuminating lines of research. Not unnaturally it took the learned world by storm: and in particular it led in Round's capable hands to our first clear understanding of the nature and assessment of the land tax or geld. As so often in the history of learning a great discovery was pushed a little too far; and as we have seen, the evidence of Exon Domesday makes unacceptable the view that the original returns of *all* circuits were arranged geographically as a series of hundred rolls. But the I.C.C. certainly suggested a prima facie case for believing that the original returns of the Cambridge circuit (no. III) were in geographical form, and it is this possibility which must next be examined.

The very existence of the document is proof, not merely of the procedure followed by the commissioners, but of the hard fact that in this circuit the evidence of the juries and all other sworn evidence was committed to writing in the form in which it was tendered to the commissioners. Moreover, the written record made of the names of each hundredal jury strongly suggests that the record was made in court during the hearing. So far all can agree: but it does not necessarily follow that the final 'original return' sent in by the circuit was arranged in the same form as the preliminary written record. The procedure followed in court was dictated by the ancient administrative organization of the country: but the written record could equally well be made either as we find it in the I.C.C. or as in Exon Domesday; or it could be made first geographically and then rearranged before the original return to Winchester was sent in. Thus the narrow question to be answered is simply this. Granted that the first written record of the Cambridge circuit was made in the form of hundred rolls, was this arrangement retained in the final return, or was the material rearranged before dispatch, according to the form followed by Exon Domesday, Little Domesday, and (in epitome) in Vol. I of Domesday Book? This issue is a simple one, but its solution, inevitably technical and complex, is made still more difficult by the fact that the text of the I.C.C. comes from a late-twelfth-century manuscript which belonged to the abbey of Ely. In examining Domesday Book and Exon Domesday one enjoys the advantages that attend the study of public and official documents which are both original and contemporary. All these are lost when we turn to the single surviving manuscript of the I.C.C. Though written in a careful hand it is exceedingly inaccurate, which suggests that the Ely scribe found his exemplar so highly abbreviated as often to be indecipherable. These deficiencies in the material both complicate the argument and detract from the certainty of the conclusions it suggests.

Let us then begin by examining the I.C.C. afresh,[1] freeing our minds so far as may be from all preconceptions as to either its origin or its purpose. It is a unique fragment: nothing comparable survives from any other circuit.

[1] Both documents were elaborately analysed by Round in *Feudal England*, pp. 6–27.

Moreover, it covers only one county, Cambridgeshire; and even that is imperfect since the last leaves of the manuscript are missing. Either it is a fortuitous survival of what must have been at the time a huge mass of similar documents, or a jealously preserved copy of a document recognized as extraordinary when it was first made. Judged by the plentiful survival in monastic cartularies of Domesday material in Domesday form, the second alternative seems preferable. It begins with the names of the eight jurors for Staploe hundred. Then follow detailed descriptions of the manor or manors of every village in that hundred. The first hundred thus complete, we arrive at the list of jurors for Staine hundred, followed by the manorial descriptions of the constituent villages: and so on, through seven more hundreds till the manuscript breaks off unfinished in the middle of Northstow hundred. The descriptions of the separate estates are recorded in the I.C.C. very much as we have them in Vol. I of Domesday Book, where, however, they are considerably shortened by the omission of the stock on demesne, of the names of the socmen and a good many other details. Our first impression is that the script of the manuscript is more than usually abbreviated and, as has been said, that this explains some at least of its many inaccuracies. Next one notes a tendency to economy of words in the descriptions. Thus the very first entry begins 'In hoc hundreto Nicholaus Kenet de Willelmo de Warenne pro 111 hidis et dimidia se defendit T.R.E. et modo pro 11 hidis et dimidia . . .', and the second 'In hoc hundredo Ormarus de Comite Alano Belincgesham. pro 111 hidis et dimidia se defendit . . .'. Only on turning to Domesday Book (Cambridgeshire) do we grasp that Nicholas holds (*tenet*) Kennet from William of Warenne and Ordmar Badlingham from Earl Allan. In addition to this omission of key words, suggestive of men writing under pressure, is a certain variety and uncertainty in the formulas used and the order in which they occur. This tendency is more marked in Staploe and the earlier hundreds, the formulas becoming more stereotyped as we advance. It could even be that the scribes were evolving their technique as they went along. Slight irregularities of this kind have been rather ignored in the past on the assumption that they are merely deviations of a scribe from the original returns, where everything was in proper order. But to argue thus is really to assume what we are trying to prove, and we must take our document as we find it. The manuscript of the I.C.C. was made by an accomplished scribe: and it is so carefully written and rubricated as to suggest that these variations were part and parcel of his exemplar. If so, these little irregularities are at least compatible with the view that we have in the I.C.C., not some partial copy of a fuller original, but a careful copy of a document made hastily in court, or based on notes so made, and therefore so heavily abbreviated as to have puzzled later copyists. The possibility is then already in our minds that we have in the I.C.C. the Survey record for Cambridge in its earliest form, substantially complete but still lacking a good many details.

How, it may be asked, does the I.C.C. compare with the record for Cambridgeshire in Vol. I of Domesday Book? The places, of course, are arranged geographically under hundreds instead of under the names of tenants: and the information is rather fuller. Otherwise, where manor and village are identical, there is little difference between the two: and this is admirably shown in Hamilton's edition which presents the two records in parallel columns. But in those cases—and they are a majority—in which the village is broken up into two or more estates (manors) belonging to different owners, the I.C.C. re-groups the separate village holdings which, of course, are widely separated in Domesday Book. The entry for Burwell, for instance, omitting the manorial statistics, can be analysed as follows:

In hoc hundredo [Staploe] Burwelle pro XV hidis se
  defendit et modo pro X.

Et de his XV hidis tenet abbas de Ramesio			10. h. 1. v.
,, ,, ,, Alanus de comite Alano			2½. h.
,, ,, ,, Gaufridus			1. h. 1. v.
,, ,, tenent moniales de Chatriz			½. h.
,, ,, tenent Harduuinus de Scalariis			½. h.
		Total	15. h.

In this way the I.C.C. laid bare for the first time the
whole system of village assessment for taxation and defence. It also revealed a serious discrepancy between the
hidage figures of the I.C.C. and the Cambridgeshire
Domesday. In Cambridgeshire, as in some other counties,
royal favour or the action of sheriffs had by 1086 greatly
reduced the number of hides charged on particular villages, and many examples of such 'beneficial' hidation are
recorded for Cambridgeshire. Thus, for example, the
I.C.C. tells us that the assessment of Burwell had been
reduced from 15 hides to 10. But, when we turn to
Domesday Book, the total obligation of the five separate
manors, which make up the village, adds up, not as we
should expect to 10, but to the old T.R.E. figure of 15.
Examination proves that the reduction of hidage set out
in the I.C.C. is only recorded in Domesday Book for
'unitary' villages, which formed a single manor. Where
the village was divided into two or more manors, then,
the Domesday figures are incorrect, and such villages in
Cambridgeshire are a majority. The error is all the more
serious since in several of the Cambridgeshire hundreds
there had taken place an all-round reduction of hidage of
a quarter or a fifth—another and significant fact only revealed by the I.C.C.

The failure of Domesday Book to record the reduction
of assessment in the fragmented villages of Cambridgeshire is inherent in the plan of the volume. A reduction by

a quarter or a fifth throughout the whole hundred involved impossible arithmetical calculations for the subdivided estates, set out in hides, half-hides, virgates, and acres. It is none the less an odd and disturbing phenomenon, and, if such reduction of hidage in whole hundreds was of frequent occurrence in other counties, the errors in Domesday hidage would run into three and even into four figures. Domesday historians have glossed over this curious discrepancy between the I.C.C. and Domesday Book, which at least shows how uninterested the authorities were in the current hidage obligation and therefore in the assessment or reassessment of the geld. The interest of the king's officers lay rather in the collection of geld and in 'uncovering' concealed hides which ought to pay. Yet one cannot but wonder why the careful clerks who compiled Domesday Book with such meticulousness allowed these wholesale errors to pass into their final record. Is not the answer that these reductions of hidage were not recorded in the original return sent to Winchester? They were, in fact, unknown to the central government because in the original return of this circuit the information was already rearranged as we find it in Domesday Book.

One other extraordinary feature of the I.C.C. calls for explanation; the more so as its significance has been largely ignored. The Cambridgeshire portion of Domesday Book begins on f. 189 with the *Terra Regis*, the king's land; and the first nine items are the ancient manors of the royal demesne, divided between six different hundreds. These nine manors, and no others, are not described in the I.C.C. Indeed, only two of them are even mentioned, viz. Soham and Kingston, and mentioned only because they were parts of what I have called above fragmented villages. The I.C.C. entry for Soham begins 'In hoc hundredo (Staploe) Saham pro XI hidis et dimidia T.R.E. se defendit et modo facit. De his XI hidis habet rex IX hidas et dimidiam VI acras minus *in brevi suo.*' The particulars of the royal manors are omitted, and we have only the detailed survey of the remaining 1½ hides (which formed two estates) much as we get them in Domesday Book. In exactly the same way the reader is referred later in the I.C.C. to the king's *breve* for a full description of the royal manor at Kingston. The other ancient manors are omitted without comment (though often found in fragmented villages);[1] but it is clear from the references to Soham and Kingston that the manors of ancient demesne were never included in the I.C.C. For the survey of the royal manors of ancient demesne we are thus wholly dependent on Vol. I of Domesday Book.

The meaning of the word *breve* in this connexion is not in doubt. In Domesday Book each tenant-in-chief's manors are listed, county by county, under his name and this list is referred to as his *breve* or schedule. Thus the king's *breve* refers to the *Terra Regis* or royal demesne, and the *breve* of Roger Bigot, say, to the list of his lands in the county where the reference is found. It was J. H. Round who discovered this and drew attention to the fact that this usage occurs both in Great Domesday and in Little Domesday.[2] To these instances we have now to add the use of this technicality in the I.C.C. Its compilers were able to cite a *breve regis* or classified list which contained the full description of the manors of ancient demesne. They were, in short, already thinking of the original returns arranged as in Domesday Book itself, under the names respectively of the king and his barons.

---

[1] With the result that in some villages the total number of hides mentioned in the I.C.C. does not tally with the sum of the separate holdings. For instance, Haslingfield (p. 72) is said to defend itself for 20 hides, though the separate estates only add up to 12 hides and 3 virgates. The remaining 7 hides and 1 virgate belonged to the royal manor there (D.B., vol. I, f. 189 b 2). So too at Wilbraham (p. 15) and Comberton (p. 69). Such omissions suggest strongly that the I.C.C. is a hasty record of the actual court proceedings.

[2] *Feudal England*, p. 136.

The significance of this usage in the I.C.C. is not easily exaggerated. Obviously, it is incorrect, even in thought, to divide the Domesday Inquest into stages; first a written record by hundreds and villages (the I.C.C.) and then, as a later operation, the conversion of this information into a return by owners and fees. The two operations proceeded *pari passu* and the *breves*[1] of the royal demesne and the tenants-in-chief were compiled either earlier than or simultaneously with the taking of sworn evidence in court. From first to last the commissioners thought in terms of owners and of manors, though their procedure had to follow the age-long administrative divisions of the hundred and the village. For each tenant-in-chief a moment came when he appeared before the king's commissioners. His *breve* was scrutinized and formally entered in the local return. Robert Malet,[2] a great Norfolk landowner, whose fee is duly entered in Little Domesday, actually refers to this occasion as 'the day on which he was enrolled' (*dies qua fuit inbreviatus*). Logically, we have reached the point at which we must choose between the naïve conception of the Survey as a furious scribbling down of statistics tendered verbally in court on the one hand, and, on the other, the more realistic view of the commissioners checking over in court from sworn evidence manorial descriptions already committed to writing by the 'back-room boys'. In fact, we can be perfectly sure that, as in any modern court of inquiry, what actually occurred was a compromise between these logical but unhistorical alternatives. Much of the agenda must have been written down before the proceedings began in court, and this nucleus was no doubt altered and added to during the proceedings.

The I.C.C., then, is not a copy of the 'original return' for circuit III, for it omits the royal manors of ancient demesne, and that this is a deliberate omission is shown

---

[1] *Breves* as the plural of *breve* occurs in Little Domesday, f. 409 b.
[2] D.B., vol. II, f. 276 b. Cf. above, p. 81.

by the two references to the king's *breve* in its text. But, though not itself the original return, nor even a partial copy, there is no doubt that it formed the basis of that return, which, however much altered by being regrouped under owners instead of places, was certainly derived from it. The proof of this lies in a most curious error on f. 189 b 2 of Cambridgeshire Domesday under the heading *Terra Regis* (i.e. the king's *breve*). There we read: 'In Saham habet rex W. VI hid. 7 XL acras in breve suo'. The entry makes nonsense as we have it, since a full description of the royal manor of Soham appears higher up as the first entry under *Terra Regis*, but there can be no doubt that it derives ultimately from the reference to the king's *breve* regarding Soham quoted above. We can only suppose that the details of the manors of royal demesne, already set out in writing, when the hundredal juries appeared in court to give their verdicts, were 'taken as read' and immediately set down in strict hundredal order, as the first nine entries of the *Terra Regis*.[1] Its particulars were omitted from the I.C.C., which, however, accounted for all the rest of the land of Cambridgeshire. From the I.C.C. was made out, no doubt, a first draft of the original return of the circuit, arranged as *breves* under the names of owners. This, in turn, after further amendment was sent to Winchester, where the abbreviated version found in Domesday Book was made from it. In no other way can we account for the persistence of the error by which a clerk who was drawing up the *breve regis*[2] from the I.C.C. mistakenly extracted this reference.

The conclusion to which we are led is, then, that the

---

[1] The same practice was apparently followed in Buckinghamshire (f. 143) and Bedfordshire (f. 209); but in Hertfordshire (f. 132), where the king's lands had all belonged to Harold the royal manors were included in a first draft resembling the I.C.C.

[2] The *breve regis* or *terra regis* of the circuit return contained full descriptions of the royal manors of ancient demesne, followed by particulars of other lands in the king's hand extracted from the I.C.C.

I.C.C. is a careful copy of the first written record of the Cambridge circuit, made in court or from notes taken in court: and that this geographical record was *at once* converted into a return arranged under the names of owners, first the king, and then the several tenants-in-chief. The references to the *breve regis* in the I.C.C. are fatal to the whole conception of the original returns as pictured by Round and Maitland. The I.C.C. was no more than a preliminary draft of what was to be, through addition and revision, the local return to Winchester, but already it envisaged the information as arranged under owners, and had made a beginning with the first *titulus* of the return— the *Terra Regis*. From the I.C.C. was constructed the rest of the *Terra Regis* and lists of the separate fees, new facts being added from time to time and corrections made. We can say confidently that some such process occurred since there are plain indications in the I.C.C. that the surviving record in Domesday Book simply could not have been constructed directly from it, or indeed from any record so arranged.

These may be summarized as follows:

I. The case of the village of Shingay[1] in the hundred of Armingford. From the I.C.C. we discover that between 1066 and 1086 the hidage had been uniformly lowered throughout the hundred by a fifth, so that Shingay, which had defended itself for 5 hides in the time of King Edward, now answered for only 4. We also learn that it was the only example in the whole hundred of manor and vill being coterminous: in every other case the villages are divided between two or more owners. It follows from this that the current hidage obligation of every one of the manors of these multiple villages is erroneously recorded in Domesday Book, the fractions of the obligation on the component manors adding up to the original T.R.E. total. In Croyden, for instance, where the obligation had been reduced from 10 to 8 hides, the half-dozen estates

[1] I.C.C., p. 59.

into which it was divided still added up to the higher figure. What of Shingay? As it is a unitary vill we should expect Domesday Book to record the reductions according to its usual practice; but in fact Shingay is still credited in 1086 with 5 hides. The failure to record the reduction can be explained away as an oversight, but it is much more probable that the reduction of the hidage was a fact brought to light by the evidence of the hundred jury of Armingford, and that the higher figure has passed into Domesday Book direct from the preliminary draft which had uniformly recorded the higher assessment for every village in the hundred.

II. In several cases the I.C.C. fails to put at the head of its entry the name of the owner of the manor. Thus on p. 27 the village of Hinton is said to have defended itself both T.R.E. and now for 7 hides, but it is only from the shortened text in Domesday Book that we learn that Hinton was held by Earl Allan. Surely the inference to be drawn from these cases is that the I.C.C. was drawn up from a long list of manors, set out as in Exon Domesday, Little Domesday, and Great Domesday under the names of the tenants-in-chief: for in such a list there would be no need to repeat the owner's name in each entry. We have confirmation that this is what happened on p. 49 where we read: 'In hoc hundredo Stapleford pro X hidis se defendit et modo. *Et has X hi. tenet abbas de Eli.*' The clumsy insertion of the words printed in italics suggests that the scribe, expecting a multiple vill, and that therefore the entry would continue *et de his X hidis tenet*, all but omitted the name of the owner.[1] Such a unitary village would normally begin 'Abbas de Eli tenet Stapleford. Pro X hidis . . .'.

III. Still more decisive evidence is found in those instances in which Domesday Book and the I.C.C. give

[1] See also Horningsea (p. 28), Hauxton (p. 47), Gransden (p. 88), and Willingham (p. 92). All belonged to the abbey of Ely.

different names to the same manor. Thus in Wetherly hundred the I.C.C. records in successive entries the details of Comberton[1] (divided into three manors) and Barton, likewise divided into three manors. But one of the component manors of Comberton, held by William de Cahainges, appears in Domesday Book as Barton. Again, Foxton[2] in Thriplow hundred was assessed at 10 hides divided in 1086 into three separate estates, of which the third and smallest appears in Domesday Book as in Fowlmere. Similarly on p. 87, a manor of 3 hides and 1 virgate held by the abbot of Ely is shown as a component of the village of Toft in the I.C.C., while in Domesday Book it is called Hardwick. Finally, we may cite the villages of Burch and Westley[3] which conjointly defended themselves for 10 hides whose five component manors are then described. Four of these appear in Domesday Book under the name of Westlai, the fifth is called Burch and is responsible for half the hidage. In none of these cases could the compilers of Domesday have discovered this information from the I.C.C. It could only have come from a copy of the returns set out as lists of manors. In short, Domesday Book was compiled from a much fuller original, already arranged under owners, and not as a series of hundred rolls.

From this long discussion, then, three inferences may be drawn:

I. That the information collected by the Survey in Cambridgeshire was already grouped under the royal demesne and the names of the individual tenants-in-chief when the I.C.C. was made up.

II. That the Cambridgeshire summary of the original returns found in Vol. I of Domesday Book contains facts which could not have been drawn from the I.C.C. or, indeed, from any document arranged in that way.

---

[1] I.C.C., p. 68.　　　　　　　　　　　　　　[2] I.C.C., p. 45.
[3] I.C.C., p. 19: Borough Green and Westley Waterless.

III. The likelihood—we cannot put it higher—that the I.C.C. was actually written down in court, or more probably written up from the full descriptions of each manor (the *breves*) already available, helped out by notes of additions and amendments made by the hundredal jurors, the sheriff, and other oral testimony to the commissioners. It is no longer possible to regard the I.C.C. as an imperfect transcript of some much larger original returns drawn up in the same way. Contrariwise, there is every reason to suppose that the I.C.C., its errors apart, is a complete copy of its exemplar; and if so, that the descriptions of the royal manors of ancient demesne were never recorded in I.C.C. form, presumably because the 'descriptions' were accepted *in toto* without amendment. With this large exception the I.C.C. appears to be a record of the 'court proceedings'. Difficult as it is to argue from a late transcript, there are strong indications that the I.C.C. was written down in much the same way as the early *Curia Regis Rolls* a century later. What has been referred to above[1] as 'its extreme economy of words' may well be due to its hasty compilation. There is, moreover, a certain variation and looseness in its formulas[2] which is in keeping with a document made from oral proceedings. Finally the palaeography[3] suggests that the careful scribe who wrote the only surviving text was troubled by the abbreviations of the document before him, where he found many words so reduced as to make him uncertain what was intended.

These conclusions, suggested simply by an analysis of

---

[1] Above, p. 125.

[2] e.g. the omission (noted above, p. 133) of the names of owners; and the failure to record the existence of all but two (Soham and Kingston) of the royal manors of ancient demesne. The uniformity and precision of the 'descriptions' of the Cambridgeshire royal manors even as abbreviated in Domesday Book contrasts markedly with the varied terminology of the other estates.

[3] e.g. t = terra; p = postea; re = regis; o = oves; h = hoc; pc = pecunia; ho = homo, which the scribes of Tiberius A. vi read as *honor*.

the I.C.C., can be cross-checked and tested, as it were, by
the evidence of another document from Ely, with which
it has long been associated. This is the so-called Inquisitio
Eliensis, for the title has no contemporary authority,
printed in the Record Edition of Domesday Book, and
reprinted in 1876 with the I.C.C. in a more scholarly
way. The I.E., once thought to be a return to a writ of
William the Conqueror,[1] is now generally regarded as a
sort of private Domesday Book of the abbey of Ely, made
contemporaneously from the original returns, though now
surviving only in three twelfth-century Ely manuscripts
whose texts are a good deal better than that of the I.C.C.[2]
The estates of the church of Ely were scattered over six
counties which fell in three different circuits, viz. Essex,
Norfolk, and Suffolk in circuit VII; Cambridgeshire and
Hertfordshire in circuit III; and Huntingdonshire in
circuit VI. In the I.E. all the Ely lands are listed county
by county, hundred by hundred, and manor by manor.
The source of these extracts was for each circuit the
full findings of the commissioners, a fact attested by the
systematic inclusion of the stock—pigs, sheep, oxen—
on the manorial demesnes as well as a great deal else
omitted from the shortened versions for Cambridge, Hertford, and Huntingdon in Vol. I of Domesday Book,
though of course still found in Little Domesday for the
East Anglian counties. The I.E. begins with the 'terms of
reference' of the commissioners (above, p. 60), followed

---

[1] Edward Miller, 'The Ely Land Pleas in the reign of William I', *E.H.R.* lxii
(1947), p. 452. Round's view is disproved by a charter of Henry I which
mentions the presence of Bishop Walchelin and the bishop of Coutances at the
Kentford plea in 1080 (Bentham, *History of Ely*, appendix xvii).

[2] Mr. Salzman, who describes the I.E. as 'a careful piece of work', called
attention to what at first sight seems to be a serious blunder regarding the hidage
of Trumpington (*V.C.H. Cambridge*, vol. i, p. 338). But in fact the passage in
question relates correctly to the next entry concerning Whaddon, and the
apparent error is due merely to misplacing by the twelfth-century copyist. The
entry is of great interest, as it is one of several which prove that the I.E., or more
probably its direct source, was compiled from the I.C.C. exactly as we have it.

by the names of the 'men who swore' in each of the hundreds of Cambridgeshire and in those hundreds of Hertfordshire in which the church of Ely held lands. The descriptions of the manors are then set out in order, county by county, as follows: Cambridgeshire (pp. 101–20); Hertfordshire (pp. 124–5); Essex (pp. 125–30); Norfolk (pp. 130–41); Suffolk (pp. 141–66); Huntingdonshire (pp. 166–7). Pages 120–4 contain a summary of the lands held by the abbey in each of these counties, together with an estimate of their value, e.g. on p. 121: 'De toto quod habemus in tota scira Grantebrigge £318–3–0.' Separate summaries are then given of the extent of the 'thegn' lands, the 'soc' lands, the lands of the knights, as well as of the individual holdings of Picot, the sheriff, Hardwin d'Escalers, and Guy de Raimbercurt, who all had lands in Cambridgeshire on which the church of Ely had claims. A note of the abbey's possessions in the borough of Cambridge is also added and the degree to which the revenue of the lands have improved (*emendatas*) in the hands of Abbot Symeon is carefully recorded. After Cambridgeshire has been dealt with, the details of lands in other circuits follow, the compiler listing, not merely lands actually held by Ely, but those held by lay barons which the church of Ely claimed. The county totals of Hertfordshire and Norfolk are repeated on pp. 126 and 136 respectively. It should also be noted that the order of counties followed by the compiler bears out the suggestion made above that the Ely lands belonged to three distinct circuits, viz. no. III (Cambridge and Hertford), no. VII (Essex, Norfolk, and Suffolk), and no. VI (Huntingdon).

What, then, were the immediate sources of the intricate compilation summarized above? The answer to this question is of crucial importance since the Ely lands belonged to three different circuits, for each of which the compilers had at their disposal the full, unabbreviated findings of the

Survey. But before we tackle the main problem, a preliminary question obtrudes itself to which no satisfactory
answer has as yet been found, viz. why does the I.E. record
the names of only the jurors who swore in the hundreds
of Cambridgeshire and Hertfordshire? In Huntingdon
and the three counties of East Anglia—beyond all question—similar juries gave evidence. Why were their names
omitted? The most probable explanation surely is that in
the third circuit alone were the full findings of the commissioners recorded in writing by hundreds. In the other
two circuits, though the procedure was still by the sworn
evidence of hundredal juries, the evidence from the outset
was recorded under the names of the tenants-in-chief who
held the lands. The I.E. was too formal and serious a
document to have omitted the names had they ever been
committed to writing. From this conclusion the only
escape is the improbable supposition that the I.E. was
compiled from documents which belonged to two separate
stages in time in the making of Domesday Book. And, in
fact, scholars have hitherto been driven to this unlikely
hypothesis. The I.E. was drawn, it is said, from the
original returns in the form of hundred rolls for Cambridgeshire and Hertfordshire (circuit III) and from
Little Domesday for East Anglia. As for the Huntingdon
lands no satisfactory explanation has ever been found.[1]

So poor a conclusion springs from a failure to distinguish the true 'original returns' to Winchester from
the complicated, and to some extent contradictory, process which produced them. Everywhere the commissioners
proceeded by hundredal juries, but in the third circuit
alone perhaps was a written record attempted of their
proceedings in this form. The answer, then, to our main

---

[1] The ingenious solution proposed by Mr. Lennard (*E.H.R.* lxi (1946),
p. 257) would have been acceptable if the writ of William I there quoted belonged to the year 1086, but the evidence suggests that it refers to the meeting
at Kentford and was issued some years before the Survey.

question is that for each of the three circuits involved the
I.E. was compiled from the local, or circuit, or (if you
like) the 'original return', arranged under the names of
the holders of land, but that in the third circuit alone had
this local return been preceded by a preliminary record,
viz. the I.C.C. That this is the correct answer is shown
by a significant difference in the I.E. itself between the
methods used for recording the Cambridgeshire lands and
those of East Anglia. In Cambridgeshire the Ely lands
are recorded hundred by hundred in a single list which
includes both the lands which were actually in Ely's possession in 1086, and those which they claimed as theirs,
though in the possession of others. This was made possible and easy just because for this county the monks had
at hand not only the local circuit return, arranged under
holders of the land, but also the I.C.C. where the information was set out geographically—village by village—
under the successive hundreds. For East Anglia, they had
only Little Domesday, or more precisely the first draft
of Little Domesday, which we are justified in thinking
bore some general likeness to Exon Domesday for the
south-west.[1] It was Round himself who first pointed this
out; for after analysing the Cambridge section, he remarks:

With Essex, we enter at once on a different system. This portion,
which extends from p. 125 to p. 130 (l. 8), is arranged not by
hundreds, but by fiefs. It first gives the lands actually held by the
Abbey (as coming first in Domesday), and then those of which
laymen were in possession. To the latter section are prefixed the
words: 'Has terras calumpniatur abbas de Ely secundum breves
regis.'[2]

He then proceeds to examine both Norfolk and Suffolk
where the same method is followed. The change of procedure on the part of the Ely compiler is explained by

---

[1] The argument applies equally to Huntingdon, for which they had only a
draft of the circuit return (no. VI).
[2] *Feudal England*, p. 137.

the absence of any such written record as the I.C.C. for East Anglia, where the lands claimed by the abbey had to be sought under the *breves* of the individuals actually in possession of them. That the actual document from which the Ely compiler worked was only a preliminary draft of Little Domesday is made certain not only by the inclusion of Burgh Apton (co. Norfolk) in the I.E. which is absent from Little Domesday, but from the wide differences in detail and treatment between it and the I.E. for the county of Suffolk. That the I.E. was directly derived from Little Domesday, as we have it, is ruled out by a collation of the two documents. In making the fair copy of the draft local return the compilers of Little Domesday must have tidied up the arrangement of the Ely fief in a radical manner, and the differences between the two documents for Suffolk[1] are in marked contrast with the close agreement displayed in the other two counties of this circuit.

No direct collation, then, of the I.E. and Little Domesday[2] is possible, since the I.E. was made up from the draft return of which Little Domesday is a much-amended fair copy. And to this it may be added that it is unprofitable to attempt a close comparison of the I.E. with the I.C.C., which was after all only a first stage in the compilation of a return for circuit III roughly analogous to Little Domesday. Not only so, but we must never forget that nine-tenths of the information recorded about Ely in Domesday Book was supplied—in the last resort—by the monks of Ely themselves, and we are bound to suppose

---

[1] Cf. D.B., vol. II, ff. 381 b–388 b and *I.E.* (ed. Hamilton), pp. 141–66. The I.E. text omits a great many details found in Little Domesday, and adds some others. There are also wide differences in the order in which the places are named.

[2] Nor, of course, with Great Domesday, which besides omitting much of the detail given in the I.E., sometimes flatly contradicts its evidence: e.g. at Meldreth. The *I.E.*, p. 108, speaks of ten sokemen, eight of whom could not sell their land without the abbot's permission, while the remaining two could. In Domesday Book the figures are respectively one and nine (f. 199 b 2).

that they attended the Inquest with all their data already recorded in writing. Thus when we find in the I.E. lists of names of sokemen, which are not recorded in the I.C.C., valuations of holdings in shillings and pounds similarly unrecorded, and even occasional mentions of the evidence of the hundred not now found in the I.C.C. or in Vol. I of Domesday Book (which is an abbreviation of the local return), we can never be sure whether these facts, known to and recorded by the abbey before the Inquest was held, were ever actually recorded in writing at the Inquest.

We are thus finally led to the questions which logically precede all others, viz. when was the I.E. made and for what purpose? As to the date, it may now be taken as proved that it was based on documents made while the Inquest was actually being held, and therefore belongs to the year 1086. It is then well enough described as a 'private Domesday Book made by the monks of Ely for their own use'. It is certainly not, as Round believed, a return to a writ of William the Conqueror in 1086, though that hypothesis is correct in so far as it attributes its composition to that year. Indeed it may be that the I.E., in the form in which we have it, is a return demanded by Ranulf Flambard in 1093, when Abbot Symeon died and the possessions of the abbey were taken into the king's hands there to remain until the accession of Henry I. This would explain—what needs explaining—why a record so unique, so elaborate, and so formal is found at Ely alone among English religious houses. The whole form and structure of the I.E. is closely analogous to that found in the county summaries of the lands of Glastonbury in Exon Domesday.[1] There too the full descriptions of its manors are followed by a précis and analysis of their extent and value. Separate totals are also given for the lands of the Church and of its knights, and we read that the value of the land has increased (*emendata est*) under Abbot Turstin

[1] Exon Domesday, pp. 160–1, 490–1. Above, pp. 105, 116.

by £128. There are other summaries of the extent of the
lands of certain lay tenants in Exon Domesday, but only
in the Glastonbury instance is the improvement in value
recorded. In just the same way the I.E. records the total
lands of Picot and Hardwin, as well as the abbey lands,
but for them alone records the improvement in value.
Now at the time of the Domesday Inquest the abbey of
Glastonbury was in the king's hands, as the Norman
abbot had been sent back to Caen as a result of a famous
'incident' in which some of the monks had been killed.
It seems, then, reasonable to suppose that the I.E. is connected with either a forfeiture or a vacancy at Ely: and,
if so, the most likely moment for its compilation, as we
now have it, would be at the death of Abbot Symeon in
1093, when the abbey estates, as well as the books, ornaments, and vestments of the Church were seized by the
Crown. The Liber Eliensis[1] tells us that the estates
(*possessiones*) were listed and an inventory made of the
ornaments in its treasury. There would have been no
point in recording the increase in the value of the abbey
estates in 1086, when Abbot Symeon was still in the
saddle, but these facts would have been of vital importance
in 1093. It may then be that the I.E., originally compiled
in the very throes of the Inquest, was expanded[2] and
elaborated in 1093 into the imposing document it now is,
and a copy forwarded to the Treasury.

In concluding this discussion of two very different texts
we must stress once more the special difficulties arising
from the lateness of the manuscripts and their many corruptions. These prevent really close collation of the one
with the other, and for this very reason seem at first sight

---

[1] *Liber Eliensis* (1848), p. 282. Cf. p. 220: 'possessiones sicut Liber Terrarum
insinuat'.

[2] e.g. the reference in the I.E. (p. 122) to those who hold lands of the abbot
concessione et iussu regis Willelmi which is based on a royal writ to Ely (I.C.C.,
ed. Hamilton, no. V, p. xix.).

to support the hypothesis of a complete series of hundred
rolls behind them in which there were no errors and no
omissions. But a closer inspection justifies us in dismissing
these 'perfect' documents as a figment of the imagination.
In three separate circuits—nos. III, VI, VII—the evidence suggests that the local return sent to Winchester
was already arranged under the names of the holders of
land, just as we get it in Vol. I of Domesday Book. In two
of them, nos. VI and VII, there is no trace even of a preliminary record drawn up by hundreds and by villages.
For the third we have not an imaginary set of complete
hundred rolls but simply the Inquisitio Comitatus Cantabrigiensis, a preliminary and incomplete geographical
record, which never included the royal manors of ancient
demesne, but still, despite its corruptions, an actual document produced by the commissioners. As such it is apparently unique not only in these three circuits, but as
will appear below, in all the others. There may have been
others like it; the possibility cannot in all cases be ruled
out; but the evidence such as it is points with varying
strength against it. We may speculate as to how and why
the I.C.C. was made. It may, for instance, have sprung
from the fact that the hidage obligation in several Cambridge hundreds had been lowered by a definite per-
centage; but we do not know the reason and it is wiser not
to guess. The fundamental lesson conveyed by the I.C.C.
is simply that when, and even before, it was made the
commissioners were thinking of their material and already
had it arranged under *breves*, that is lists of manors belonging either to the Crown or to an individual tenant-in-
chief. Its evidence is reinforced by that of the Inquisitio
Eliensis which repeatedly refers to the *breve* of the abbot
of Ely (e.g. p. 123), and more generally to the *breves regis*
(p. 127), that is the various lists of the individual tenants.
Faced by these facts we have no option but to discard
the whole hypothesis of the original returns as a series of

hundred rolls; and secondly to identify Vol. II of Domesday Book as the local return of the East Anglian circuit, a conclusion borne out by the omission of the names of the hundredal jurors from the I.E. for all counties but those of Cambridgeshire and Hertfordshire.

It is important to bear in mind that the whole hypothesis of the original returns as a series of hundred rolls rests upon a misunderstanding of a single late text, the I.C.C., which in fact was a preliminary compilation from which the local return of the circuit was made. The reader of the I.C.C. who cares to pick out, hundred by hundred, the manors of a particular baron will normally find that the order of the entries within a hundred is the same as that in Domesday Book. The only argument for ever thinking of the original returns as a series of hundred rolls sprang from this fact. What it really proved was simply that the *procedure* of the commissioners was everywhere based on the old administrative divisions of the hundred and village. From this it was but a short step to the assumption that the original returns were everywhere the written record of facts given orally by the hundredal juries. The simplicity of this hypothesis made it attractive; but that eight small landholders should have at their fingers' ends the details of every acre of land in a hundred is out of the question. The juries at the Domesday Inquest were not unlike the juries at an *Inquisitio post mortem*, who checked and passed a return of the dead man's land, which must have been the joint compilation of the lord's steward and the king's escheator. The information given to the Domesday commissioners was certainly supplied by the stewards and bailiffs of the men who held the land; and the essential function of the hundredal juries was to register and, so far as possible, decide upon conflicting claims to ownership. The whole record was in circuit III committed to writing, but at once restored to its original form as a record of the fees of the several landowners. The local commissioners thus ended, as they began, with their information grouped under the names of the holders, who alone could supply it.

The text of the local return for the third circuit, in short, was evolved from the I.C.C. and much amended in the process. It was precisely the assumption that behind all our texts lay a 'perfect original' which marred J. H. Round's elaborate collation of the I.E., the I.C.C., and the Domesday text for Cambridgeshire.[1] More particularly, his comparison of four 'duplicate' entries on p. 18 and five more on p. 22 indicate, first, that both the I.E. and the Domesday text for Cambridgeshire were ultimately based upon the I.C.C., and secondly, that certain errors in the original' I.C.C., corrected in the I.E., persisted in the circuit return and so passed into Domesday Book. To these another and curious example may be added. On f. 200 a of Great Domesday we find one of those excessively rare marginal notes which reads, *Inquire quot villani*. The note refers to a statement in the text at Tadlow that the villeins and 13 bordars have 3 ploughs. On this Mr. Salzman, who brought the passage to light, comments: 'The I.C.C. (p. 52) shows that this should read: "2½ villeins and 13 bordars have 3 ploughs".'[2] But surely 'half a villein' is an even more monstrous birth than Maitland's famous 'half-ox' (*semibos*), and was too much for the Domesday abbreviator!

---

[1] *Feudal England*, pp. 6–27.
[2] *V.C.H. Cambs.*, vol. i, p. 392.

X

THE KENTISH DOCUMENTS

WE have next to consider the evidence of a different group of documents relating to the great churches of Kent, viz. Christchurch Cathedral,[1] St. Augustine's abbey[2] at Canterbury, and Rochester Cathedral.[3] Each of these preserved a description of their lands in Kent unquestionably derived from the sworn proceedings of the Inquest which nevertheless are very different from the final text preserved in Vol. I of Domesday Book. Take, for example, the record of the archbishop's manor of Northgate, which is found both in the Domesday Monachorum of Christchurch and in the *Excerpta* of St. Augustine's Abbey:

Excerpta[4]	*D.M.*	*D.B.*
In hundredo de Canterberia habet archiepiscopus manerium Norgate et est de cibo monachorum sanctae Trinitatis. Tempore regis Edwardi se defendit pro uno solino cui nunc subiacent c. burgenses xix minus qui reddunt ix lib. et vi den. de gablo et est appreciatum xvii lib.	Nordwda est manerium monachorum sanctae Trinitatis et est de cibo eorum et est de hundred de Cantuarberia et in tempore Edwardi regis se defendebat pro uno sull et ei subiacent c burgenses iii minus qui reddunt viii lib. et vi denarios de gablo et est appreciatum x et vii lib. Hoc manerium est de Hundred de Cantuarberia.	Ipse archiepiscopus tenet Nordeude. pro uno solin se defendit. *Terra est* . *In dominio i caruca et dimidia. Et vii villani cum xxvi bordariis habent ii carucas.* Huic M̃ pertinent in civitate Cantuaria c. burgenses iii minus reddentes viii lib. et iiii sol. *Ibi viii molendina de lxxi sol. xxiiii acrae prati. Silva xxx porcorum.* Inter totum valet et valuit xvii lib.
	(f. 6 b)	(D.B., vol. I, f. 5 a 1)

[1] *Domesday Monachorum*, ed. D. C. Douglas (R. Hist. Soc. 1944).

[2] *An Eleventh-Century Inquisition*, ed. A. Ballard (1920).

[3] Textus Roffensis, ed. T. Hearne, 1720, pp. 209–11. There is another copy in *Domesday Monachorum*, pp. 95–98.

[4] Ballard, op. cit., p. 12, who conveniently printed all three versions. The

The *Excerpta* and D.M. clearly have a common source, and both omit the manorial details included in D.B. and printed above in italics.

Beside these we may next set the description of Frindsbury which belonged to Rochester cathedral.

D.M.[1]	*D.B.*
Frendesberi est manerium episcopi rubitoniensis et in tempore E. regis se defendebat pro x sullinc et nunc pro vii et est appretiatum xxv libris. Et infra leugam de Tunebrige est inde tantum quod valet x solidos. Et etiam de Hallinges est tantum infra leugam eandem quod est appretiatum vii solidis.	Isdem episcopus tenet Frandesberie. Pro x solins se defendit T.R.E. et modo pro vii. *Terra est xv carucis. In dominio sunt v carucae et xl villani cum xxviii bordariis habent xi carucas. Ibi aecclesia et ix servi et unum molendinum de xii solidis et xl acrae prati. Silva v porcis.* T.R.E. et post valebat viii libras et modo xxv libras. Quod Ricardus tenet in sua leuua valet x solidos.

(D.B., vol. I, f. 5 b)

Here again the manorial detail is omitted and the *form* of the description is identical with that of Northgate.

Thus for all three churches we have in leisurely *formulas* a short account of their lands which records the name of the owner, the number of sulungs for which the manor answered and its value; and where the ownership has changed since 1066 the name of the owner T.R.E. is generally included. The editors of the D.M. and the *Excerpta* have concluded that these short descriptions derive from the original returns sent by the first circuit to Winchester, and that these returns, like the I.C.C., were arranged geographically by hundreds. But this view

Excerpta or Extracts relating to St. Augustine's retain the order of lasts and hundreds of the actual Inquest. The order of the material has been changed both in the Domesday Monachorum and in Domesday Book. See Ballard, pp. viii and xiv, and below, p. 152.

[1] *Domesday Monachorum*, p. 95.

requires us to believe that all three churches by an astonishing coincidence made exactly the same choice of material from the fuller description before them, now preserved in abbreviation in Vol. I of Domesday Book. May it not be that our three texts are extracted from a draft of the Inquest proceedings, which lacked the manorial details still preserved in part in Domesday Book? Such a view implies that in the first circuit the local return was compiled in two main stages: first the actual sworn Inquest, arranged by hundreds, which recorded the ownership, hidage, and value of each estate; and secondly the rearrangement of this material according to the names of their owners, and its enlargement by embodying the details of stock, ploughs, villeins, bordars, and so on, supplied by the actual tenants of each estate to the clerks of the commissioners. To some such view we are driven by the identical form and scope of our three documents: and there is fortunately strong evidence in its favour in the archbishop's manor of Stursete, a description of which is found in both D.M. and the *Excerpta*.[1] In Stursete, which answered for seven sulungs, some of this land was held by five sub-tenants, whose holdings are successively described in the D.M. and the *Excerpta*. As an example we may quote the description of the first two:

Et ex his supradictis vii sullinc habet Godefridus Dapifer unum sullinc de archiepiscopo Tenitune et est appreciatum C sol. Adhuc autem et Vitalis habet inde unum iugum terre de archiepiscopo et est appreciatum xx sol.

These are followed by the other three sub-tenures in identical form, and we are left to infer that these small holdings were independent units separately cultivated by their owners. From Domesday Book, however, we learn that this was not so. Four of the tenants farmed their

[1] Ballard, op. cit., pp. 12 and 13, where the three texts are printed side by side.

several holdings as a single unit with five and a half ploughs in demesne, and eight villeins with twenty-six bordars having two ploughs, &c., while the fifth, Hamo the sheriff, farmed his own half sulung separately with two ploughs, five bordars, &c. The total value of the two estates, as set out in Domesday Book, viz. £14, agrees with the total for the five separate holdings in D.M., but each document contains vital facts absent in the other. Domesday Book thus preserves the record of a later stage of the inquiry than that set out in D.M., for it describes the actual working economy of these sub-tenants in two separate farms by adding new information not contained in D.M., and omitting the size of the five separate holdings which together formed them. On this evidence we are justified in concluding that the original written record of the Inquest from which both the D.M. and the *Excerpta* were derived, recorded only the ownership, extent, and value of each holding. With the help of this brief, sworn record the commissioners rearranged their information under the names of the owners, and to this new record were added the innumerable details of the way in which they were actually organized and farmed. The final result was the circuit return, which was sent to Winchester, and there abbreviated to form the permanent record now found in Vol. I of Domesday Book.

From Kent, then, we have evidence of the Inquest procedure followed in the first circuit, which strikingly confirms that of Exon Domesday[1] (circuit II) and the more general evidence of Vol. I of Domesday Book[2] for other parts of England. From these converging streams of evidence it follows that in the short time allowed for the Inquest, the bulk of the information needed to give a full description of each estate was personally tendered out of court by individuals, rather than at its formal sessions. The function of these was to identify and list each separate

[1] Above, pp. 117–22.　　　[2] Above, pp. 40, 41, 77–80.

property and to cope with innumerable cases of 'invasion' and disputed title. The special interest of the Kentish document, henceforth called P.,[1] is that it preserves, however imperfectly, a copy of the restricted written record compiled at the formal sessions of the Inquest in its circuit (no. I). It is tempting to think that the Kentish procedure, or something like it, was widely followed, but it is unfortunately a unique survival. For the I.C.C. with which it invites comparison differs fundamentally by including the full manorial details of each estate. It is possible that something like P. lay behind the I.C.C. But the balance of the evidence rather favours the view that in the third circuit an attempt was made—perhaps unique—to review in court the whole of the evidence.

These conclusions regarding procedure are not without historical interest. The climate of opinion in the late eleventh century still favoured the spoken word and the living assembly rather than the written documents. The more closely too we examine our texts, the poorer seems the evidence for any systematic written returns to the commissioners from the great tenants-in-chief. It was, after all, the very essence of an Inquest (*inquisitio*) that the evidence should be personally vouched for by the individuals who knew the facts: and the final record of the Survey in Vol. I of Domesday Book, on every page, makes just this fundamental assumption. To this assumption Domesday Book owed its unquestioned authority for centuries to come. Yet the Domesday Inquest is a great turning-point in administrative history; for it marks the beginning of a transition from a predominantly oral and customary society to one based on archives and written documents, which, in its medieval phase, was hardly complete till the thirteenth century. A great many documents survive from the O.E. period, and their number would have probably been greater still but for the abrupt check

[1] The text is best preserved in the *Excerpta*.

upon the vernacular which resulted from the Norman Conquest. But these, in general, were of oral transactions of which they formed no essential part; and the Domesday Inquest appears as the first great step towards a *ius scriptum*, and a bureaucratic society which did its business on a documentary basis. To what extent those who supplied the facts to the circuit commissioners used written documents we shall never know; though the extraordinary fullness of the manorial descriptions suggests that their employment was considerable. But the evidence of the Domesday texts conclusively proves that for the commissioners documents were still not enough, and they had to be supported by the evidence and the presence of the men personally acquainted with the massive detail demanded. The true 'returns' of the barons to the commissioners were not, then, documents but, as has been said, the living men who supplied the facts. But this phase was soon to pass and within a century, as the Book of Fees shows, English administrative practice rested fairly and squarely on written returns made by the higher feudal class.

But what of the full circuit return of which P. was the basis? It is both striking and curious that no copy of that part which related to Rochester and the Canterbury churches has been preserved. Either they preferred the text of P., or perhaps more probably, only P., in the making of which they had all taken part, was available for copying. Later on, no doubt, copies of the much abbreviated text of the full return preserved in Vol. I or Domesday Book were obtained by the Kentish as by most of the great churches.

Of the actual making of the full circuit return we can still learn something from a comparison of the shortened text in Domesday Book for Kent with that of the *Excerpta* and to a lesser extent from the Textus Roffensis and the Domesday Monachorum. Adolphus Ballard, who edited the *Excerpta*, pointed out that the order of the Kentish hundreds in Domesday Book is very different from that of the *Excerpta*, and printed the two lists in parallel columns.[1] At first sight the differences are so great as to suggest that in one document or the other the order had become hopelessly confused, but in fact this is not so, for a closer examination shows that the unit of inquiry was not the hundred but the lest, last, or lathe. In Domesday Book the county of Kent[2] is divided into five full lasts, and two half-lasts; and these in turn are each subdivided into a large number of small and rather shifting hundreds. The commissioners proceeded systematically by lasts, and in fact the only outstanding difference between the order of the hundreds lies in the inversion of the order of the two great lasts of Wyewarlest and Borowarlest.

Excerpta	D.B.
Sutton (half last)	Sutton
Aylesford	Aylesford
Milton (half last)	Milton
Wyewarlest	Borowarlest
Borowarlest	Wyewarlest
Limowarlest	Eastry
	Limowarlest

The last four of these are grouped together in Domesday Book as the four lasts of east Kent whose juries agree (*concordant*) on the king's laws (*leges regis*) in the county. The difference of order between the *Excerpta* and Domesday Book is thus probably due to the physical make-up of P. which apparently consisted of seven separate booklets or quires; and its only significance is that it affords an additional and strong proof that the *Excerpta* were derived directly from P. and not from the completed circuit return which was the source of Domesday Book. Further examination would probably show that within each last the sequence both of hundreds and of manors within the hundreds was normally identical in both documents.

[1] P. viii.   [2] *V.C.H. Kent*, vol. iii, pp. 3–5.

So much for the administrative structure of Kent, and the procedure of the Inquest. In addition a comparison of the *Excerpta* and Domesday Book brings out clearly that even while P. was being compiled by lasts, hundreds, and villages, the commissioners were simultaneously thinking in terms of their final objective, viz. a return of owners with a list of their lands. For when they came to the hundreds of Bewsborough and Cornilo in the last of Eastry, in which lay the prebends of the church of St. Martin[1] at Dover, they made an unbroken list of the whole of them, which, when filled out by the addition of manorial information, was transferred unchanged to the circuit return and so to Domesday Book, and which there still follows, as in the *Excerpta*, the account of Dover on the same folio. The prebends of St. Martin's were thus treated as an appendix to the very full account of the town of Dover, and since in Domesday Book this was transferred from its proper place and placed, together with Canterbury, at the head of the county, the description of the lands of St. Martin's actually precedes the schedule of landowners in Kent from which their name is omitted.

In this way, by comparing P. with the text of Domesday Book, we can trace in vague outline first the making of the circuit return sent to Winchester, and secondly the composition of Vol. I of Domesday Book for this circuit. As a final example of the information such a comparison brings to light we may take the manor of Badlesmere in Faversham hundred. From the *Excerpta* we learn that Badlesmere was held T.R.E. by Godrich Wisce, and is now (1086) held by Anfridus from Odo Bishop of Bayeux, and the entry concludes: 'Hoc idem manerium reclamant monachi sancti Augustini per cartam et sigillum regis Edwardi.'[2] Turning to Vol. I of Domesday Book we find Badlesmere entered, according to its invariable practice, under the fee of Odo, whose tenant Anfrid was in actual

---

[1] D.B., vol. I, f. 1 b.   [2] Ballard, op. cit., pp. 4, 5.

possession of it in 1086. No mention is made of Godrich Wisce's tenure T.R.E. This note is *added* at the close of the description: 'Hoc M̄ reclamat abbas Sancti Augustini quia habuit T.R.E. et hundred attestantur ei. Sed filius hominis dicit patrem suum se posse vertere ubi voluerit, et hoc non annuunt monachi.'[1] As it stands this note is unintelligible, but thanks to the *Excerpta* we can infer that the 'son of the man' (*filius hominis*) referred to is the son of Godrich Wisce. Even so his claim that his father could change his allegiance at will is a *non sequitur* in relation to what precedes it.

If now we turn to the fee of St. Augustine's in Domesday Book we find that it ends with this entry or postscript about Badlesmere (Bedensmere): 'Scyra testificatur quod Bedenesmere fuit S. Augustini T.R.E. et de illo qui eam tenebat habebat abbas sacam et socam'.[2] There can be no doubt as to what has happened. In the full entry in P. it was stated that Badlesmere was held T.R.E. by Godrich Wisce, but is now held by Anfrid of the bishop of Bayeux; that it is claimed by the abbot of St. Augustine's by the charter of King Edward the Confessor, and that the abbot had *sac and soc* over Godrich Wisce: that both the hundred and the shire bore out this claim, but that Godrich Wisce's son says his father was not under the abbot's *sac and soc*, but could go where he liked (*se posse vertere*).

When P. was converted from a geographical return to one arranged under owners the commissioners removed the chief testimony to the abbot's ownership, viz. that of the shire, to the abbot's *breve*, so that the evidence of the abbot's just claim should be put on record in his own *breve* or list of manors. This they did to facilitate future legal action by the abbot. In Yorkshire and Lincolnshire the entry would have been made in the appendix of *clamores*.

[1] D.B., vol. I, f. 10a2.   [2] Ibid., f. 12b2.

This little story suggests three definite comments.

1. That the Domesday Inquest was not a judicial eyre as the term was understood later, though it furnished evidence for endless future litigation.

2. That in this circuit, as doubtless elsewhere, the formal Inquest proceedings took place in the county court to which the hundredal juries were summoned. There was no touring of the hundreds by the commissioners.

3. The possibility that the son of Godrich Wisce was still the actual farmer and occupant of Badlesmere, though the manor had passed to Bishop Odo, who had inserted a mesne tenant, Anfrid, over the head of the Anglo-Saxon tenant. If this is indeed what happened, and if such a practice was common, it suggests that we can easily exaggerate the severity of the tenurial upheaval caused by the Conquest. Behind Norman sub-tenants, in short, there may have been a great many unrecorded Saxons who continued actually to farm the land.

XI

THE HUNDREDAL ORDER

IN the two preceding chapters we have examined the
chief surviving documents which illustrate the actual
process by which the circuit returns of the Survey
were compiled. For the third circuit the I.C.C. remains
as proof that for Cambridgeshire the circuit return was
preceded by a document, arranged geographically—hundred by hundred—which omitted the Crown manors of
ancient demesne, but was otherwise a record of the full
findings of the commissioners, including even the details
of the livestock. From Kent (circuit I) we have from
Christchurch Cathedral, St. Augustine's Abbey, and
Rochester extracts of an analogous record, which we have
called P., also arranged geographically by hundreds, but
more restricted in scope than the I.C.C. Apparently P. was
the direct source of the circuit return, the information
being first arranged under the names of the holders of
land, and then enlarged by the addition of the details of
the manorial economy of each separate estate. In two other
circuits, nos. II and VII, we have, though at different
stages, the full text of the circuit returns. For the remainder we have only the shortened text in Domesday Book,
Vol. I; but this, most fortunately, has much to tell us of
the process by which the circuit returns were put together.

Everywhere in Vol. I, except in the south-west (circuit II), the possessions of each landowner are listed and
rubricated according to the hundreds in which they
were situated, and not infrequently the separate fiefs still
show traces of a consistent order of hundreds. This 'hundredal order', which reflects the procedure followed in the
formal court activities of the Inquest, is not a constant

phenomenon; very often it has been disturbed, and sometimes it is barely, if at all, discernible.

Take, for example, the county of Cambridge, which we should expect *a priori* to reproduce consistently the order of the hundreds in the I.C.C. In the larger fiefs, such as Ely Abbey and Count Alan, there is a tendency —we cannot put it higher—towards a regular sequence of hundreds; but there are many exceptions, and in the smaller ones, like Ramsey Abbey and William of Warenne, it just breaks down. Clearly there is no great significance in the 'hundredal order' and we are left with the impression that the circuit return was compiled from fifteen separate documents—one for each hundred— which were all examined in the compilation of the individual *breves*, but without any special regard to their order. More significant than the 'hundredal order' is the village order. Within each hundred the villages are cited in the Cambridgeshire Domesday in an unvarying order, so that if a tenant-in-chief holds, say, three or four manors in the same hundred, they will be listed in his *breve* in the same sequence as in the I.C.C. This interesting discovery enables us to detect some serious blunders in the Cambridgeshire text of Domesday Book. For instance, on f. 195b 1 in Staine hundred under the fief of Earl Alan we read that Odo holds of the count 4 hides of which full particulars follow. The next entry states that Odo holds 1 hide of the count, of which once more the particulars follow. It would be a natural assumption that these two manors lay within Swaffham, the last place mentioned; but, thanks to the I.C.C., we know that they are manors in Wilbraham (the 4-hide one) and Quy (the 1-hide one), the two following villages in Staine hundred. In these and other cases,[1] it is clear that the clerk, intent on picking

---

[1] Another example will be found in f. 199b 1, where half a hide held by Reinald of Aubrey de Vere is located in Wilbraham but really belongs to Quy, the next village mentioned in the I.C.C.

out the relevant holdings from the confused I.C.C. text, has omitted the names of the villages. Less serious perhaps but more common is the attribution of manors to wrong hundreds;[1] and, thanks to the I.C.C., we can not only watch the clerks making their mistakes, but actually correct them.

It is beyond question that the mistakes arose when the I.C.C. was changed into a list of tenants with their manors; but they do not support the view that the shortened text in Domesday was made from the I.C.C. or any text so arranged. Contrariwise we can be confident that these errors were made by the clerks of circuit III in preparing their original returns. The mistakes occur in the final Domesday text simply because they were already in the original returns; and they are not corrected because the careful Domesday compilers (and abbreviators) had not the material with which to correct them. Similarly in all the counties of circuit I we often encounter *terra est* . . . and then a blank space, while in Oxfordshire the hundreds are mentioned in a very casual manner. These deficiencies were not made good in Vol. I of Domesday Book, for the same reason that alone in the whole of England the five counties of the south-west lack hundred rubrics, viz. because they had been left out of the original returns.

If, now, we turn to the county of Essex for which we have the full return, the difference is very striking. The twenty-one hundreds are most scrupulously recorded and the fiefs are described according to a clear order of hundreds beginning with Barstable and ending with Thurstable.[2] Most curious, too, and significant is the fact that two of them, Dengie and Uttlesford, each occur twice in the series. The careful preservation of a single hundred-order in the separate fiefs is most simply and probably explained by the Inquest procedure, which in this circuit

---

[1] e.g. f. 191 a 2, Whaddon (Armingford), and f. 195 b 2, Burch (Flendish).
[2] *V.C.H. Essex*, vol. i, p. 409.

recorded the facts from the very start under the names of
the landowners. Though the procedure was by hundreds
and villages, the record made was by tenants. In no other
way can we easily account for the two hundreds each commonly occurring twice in the same fee. The original record
set down day by day, under the owner's names, the lands
so far dealt with; and when—for some reason—a hundred
was recalled, the record of its testimony was added and the
hundred rubric repeated. This piecemeal method was at
times rather untidy. The fee of Eudo Dapifer,[1] for example, shows two references—widely separated—to lands in
Dengie and Uttlesford hundreds, as well as two references, also separated, to Rochford hundred, while an omitted entry in Dunmow hundred has been clumsily added
lower down with the words 'in supradicto hundredo de
Dommauua tenet etc.'. It was, however, more simple and
probably more accurate than that employed in Cambridgeshire. There the record of every hundred apparently formed
a separate document, from each of which the clerks extracted in meticulously correct order the particulars of
land owned by the tenant whose *breve* they were con-
structing. No doubt they divided the separate hundred
records between them, and it made no difference which
hundred was examined first, so long as all were searched.
The Cambridge procedure was neater, for there was no
repetition of the hundreds, but it had, as we have seen
above, its own dangers.

The whole question of the 'hundredal order' of the
fiefs in Domesday Book, to which Round[2] first called
attention, has recently been analysed by Mr. Sawyer.
He has shown that there are still traces of such a consistent hundredal order in at least seventeen counties,
against nine others that appear to lack such order. He
(wisely) omits from his examination the five counties of the

---

[1] D.B., vol. II, ff. 50, 51.
[2] *V.C.H. Essex*, vol. i, pp. 410, 411.

south-west which have no hundredal rubrics, and Derbyshire, Yorkshire, Lincolnshire, and concludes as follows:

It can therefore be argued that for over half the counties of D.B.
the material was at some stage arranged by hundreds. . . . If it is
correct to argue from a consistent hundredal order . . . for counties
so wide apart as Cheshire and Kent, Norfolk and Devon, we may
assume, until an alternative and convincing explanation is offered,
that similar returns were made for every county including those
where there seems to be no such consistent hundredal order.[1]

The inference, stated in such uncompromising form, is
irreconcilable with the crucial evidence of Essex, where the
consistent repetition of the hundreds of Dengie and Uttlesford in the separate fiefs proves to demonstration that the
circuit return was arranged from the first under the name
of the tenants. But in point of fact the whole question at
issue is an unreal one, and should never have been raised.
The traces of a consistent hundredal order reflect simply
the *procedure* followed in every circuit. The object of the
Inquest was a return of fiefs, made county by county,
under the names of their holders, but the procedure was,
and could only be, geographical by hundreds and villages. The commissioners had thus to reconcile the conflicting claims of the ancient administrative divisions of
England with the achievement of a feudal return by fiefs
and baronies, a return of tenants-in-chief. It must all have
been very difficult and very complicated, since the immemorial English tenures with their 'alods', 'socmen',
'freemen owing *sac and soc*', or commended to superiors,
were fundamentally at variance with the new French doc-
trine of 'nulle terre sans seigneur'. The simple, logical form
of Domesday Book and of the circuit returns from which it
was derived is thus the true measure of the revolution of
tenure brought about by the Norman Conquest. Domesday
Book is the formal written record of the introduction of
feudal tenure, and therefore of feudal law into England.

[1] *E.H.R.* lxx (1955), p. 181.

We make a false simplification if we assume that the
two volumes of Domesday Book and Exon Domesday,
which are all 'engrossed records', were made from still
earlier 'engrossed records' in a different form. Behind
them lies a mass of preliminary notes and drafts, made
before, during, and after the formal sittings of the Inquest.
Indeed, it may be taken as certain that nine-tenths of the
manorial statistics in the circuit returns were furnished—
probably out of court—by the tenants themselves or their
agents. The function of the hundred juries at the formal
sessions was apparently to approve and check the information variously assembled and to record all *invasiones*, *clamores*, *calumpniae*, and other clashes of individual interests:
also no doubt to guard against the concealment of lands,
stock, or other assets. The early stages of this vast assem-
blage are hidden from us, but for Cambridgeshire we have
in the I.C.C. a record of the actual Inquest proceedings,
which, however hasty and incomplete, is unique in its
fullness and elaboration. For Kent we have a much more
restricted record, in similar geographical form, of the
actual Inquest procedure in this circuit, and it is even
possible that the I.C.C. was worked up and elaborated
from just such a primary record in the Cambridge circuit.
On the other hand, in the East Anglian circuit and that of
the south-west there is every reason to think that the facts
were recorded from the outset under the names of the
tenants-in-chief. Procedure may even have varied from
county to county, for in Buckinghamshire, which belonged
to the same circuit as Cambridgeshire, the hundredal
order is so consistent in Domesday Book as to suggest
that there too the facts were recorded right away under
the tenants' names.[1] But however much the preliminary
records varied from county to county, the final circuit

---

[1] The preliminary written record also varied, perhaps, in the East Anglian
circuit where the exceptionally consistent order of hundreds which distinguishes
Essex and Norfolk is much less evident in Suffolk.

return was arranged, as Vol. II of Domesday Book and Exon Domesday are arranged, under the names of the tenants-in-chief. The task of the Winchester clerks was simply to make the final summary and abbreviation of these huge returns which is preserved in Vol. I of Domesday Book.

Our conclusion, then, is that the varying and unequal traces of a consistent 'hundredal order' still discernible in Vol. I of Domesday Book are due simply to the procedure followed at the Inquest; and do not justify the conclusion that at some stage in the preparation of the circuit returns the material was in all circuits written down geographically by hundreds. Mr. Sawyer's valuable analysis, however, convincingly illustrates the complexity of the problem and warns us against easy solutions. In no. I circuit, for example, Mr. Sawyer finds clear traces of an hundredal order only in the county of Kent, which suggests that no such document as P. was made for Sussex, Surrey, Hampshire, or Berkshire. Similarly in circuit III the I.C.C. was not improbably confined to Cambridgeshire and Hertfordshire.[1]

There remains one other angle of approach to the question, which is closely connected with that of the hundredal order, namely the duplicate entries which we encounter here and there in the text of Domesday Book. Most of these were brought to light by J. H. Round, and on them he laid great stress, for properly understood they have much to teach us. Of these the most significant, which occur in Essex,[2] were carefully analysed by Round, and we may briefly review them here. We note first that in the whole county, which runs to more than 100 folios and contains many hundreds of manorial descriptions, there are no more than four pairs of such duplicates. Moreover, half

---

[1] There are no instances of a reduction of hides, either for single manors or whole hundreds in the other three counties of this circuit.

[2] *V.C.H. Essex*, vol. i, pp. 410–11.

of them, that is two pairs, refer to land in Dengie hundred, which suggests that the second entry in each case was the record of a second meeting of that hundred. The third pair deal with land of Eudo Dapifer in Rochford hundred; and the last pair are found in the section devoted to 'Invasions' (*invasiones*).

Before we look at these a little more closely, it is worth observing that the very rarity of duplicate entries is itself a tribute to the care and accuracy shown in compiling Little Domesday. Furthermore, the term duplicate entries, which suggests mere repetition, is itself a misnomer.[1] In no instance can we suppose that any pair of these 'duplicates' are mere accidental repetitions drawn from a single written source. Contrariwise they differ so materially from one another on matters of fact that we can be sure there is some special reason to account for them. Nor is this hard to find in the two manors in Dengie hundred. The first of these relates to Fenne, a manor belonging to the fief of Geoffrey de Mandeville, and we can say with confidence that the later entry records a second meeting of that hundred, and gave a revised description of the manor, with new figures regarding its hides and the numbers of villeins. Exactly the same is true of the second manor, Hainctuna, in Dengie hundred, which belonged to Suain's fief. In this case the second meeting of the hundred corrected the name of Suain's tenant, and did not bother again to include a list of the livestock.

In our third case, the village of Hawkswell in Rochford hundred, the second entry as in the former cases corrects the first, by stating that Eudo Dapifer holds the manor in demesne, the first having assigned it to a sub-tenant called Pirot. It is in short a revised description, correcting the first, and appears to have been added, with one other entry at the end of Eudo's fief. For though the circuit return entered under each fief the relevant material as the actual

---

[1] Cf. above, p. 117.

Inquest proceeded, and therefore preserves a regular order of hundreds, there were slips to be remedied and occasional additions to be made.

The same moral is suggested by the fourth example, found among the *Invasions*. The first states:

> In Braintree 30 acres of land were held by three freemen in King Edward's time, and are worth 3 shillings. This land was seized by Ledmar of Hempstead and held as part of the fief of Richard (Fitz Gilbert): and Richard does not warrant it to him.[1]

The second:

> In Braintree 3 free men held, in King Edward's time, 30 acres which Letmar the reeve claimed as belonging to Richard's fief; but his men do not testify (in the reeve's favour). And he has given pledge concerning it. And it is worth 3 shillings.[2]

These two entries may profitably be taken as a test case. If, as Round thought, Little Domesday was a rearrangement of original returns to Winchester in the form of hundred rolls, we should have to suppose that these two entries were verbal variants of a single entry in the roll of the relevant hundred. This view, it seems to me, is ruled out by what Round himself described as 'the very considerable difference between the two accounts'; and they are better explained as two independent attempts at recording a decision made by the jurors of the hundred, and, if so, they are not derived from a common written original.

The evidence of the duplicate entries in Essex, in effect, underlines the difference in procedure between the circuit (no. III) which included Cambridgeshire, and that of Essex which appears to represent the more normal 'direct' circuit procedure. Nor need we feel surprised by such occasional instances of conflicting evidence in so complicated an inquiry and one carried out in such haste. Another pair of duplicate entries, printed elsewhere by Round,[3] shows large discrepancies between the estimate included

---

[1] *V.C.H. Essex*, vol. i, p. 570.   [2] Ibid., p. 573.
[3] *E.H.R.* xv (1900), p. 299.

under Newport in Essex for the berewick of Shelford
(Cambridge), and that given in the Cambridge return.
Still another pair in Somerset[1] give widely different
accounts of the manor of King's Brompton. Only when
the compiler of Great Domesday is abbreviating the full
local returns, as for instance in the duplicate entries for
the fief of Robert Hostiarius in Leicestershire,[2] do we
find behind the differences of order and phrasing such
close agreement on matters of fact as to suggest a common original. It is unhistorical to suppose a vast and perfect written record of the returns of which the surviving
documents are an imperfect survival. To argue, as Round
did, from the omission of the livestock in one of the
entries at Fenne, that its entry was optional throughout
the Essex survey, is unsound; but collectively these duplicate entries do suggest that the local compilers of Domesday were embarrassed by the vast body of facts laid before
them and were driven from the very first to omit much of
what they gathered. The line had to be drawn somewhere,
and not everyone drew it at the same place.[3]

---

[1] *V.C.H. Somerset*, vol. i, p. 426.

[2] D.B., vol. I, ff. 235 a 1, 237 a 1.

[3] In Huntingdonshire a written record was made of the number of slaves
(*Inquisitio Comitatus Cantabrigiensis*, ed. Hamilton, pp. 168–9), but they are
omitted from the Inquisitio Eliensis (pp. 166–7), and also from Domesday Book.
Mr. H. C. Darby, who first pointed this out, remarks: 'Can we be sure that
there were not some serfs even in the "free" county of Lincolnshire?', where
none are mentioned in Domesday Book. See *Domesday Geography of Eastern
England*, p. 331.

XII

THE ORIGINAL RETURNS

ROM a detailed examination of the basic official documents of the Domesday Inquest some simple and definite conclusions have emerged. There is no doubt, for instance, that Little Domesday is the original return—meaning the actual document sent to Winchester—of the East Anglian circuit (no. VII); and it is equally clear that Exon Domesday is an advanced draft of the original return for the south-west (no. II). These are important gains, but the analysis of the I.C.C. and the Canterbury document (P.), even while they have brought us close to the actual making of the Survey, have also complicated the argument. Each of these it was found was *not* derived from the original return, but preceded it. They were, in fact, attempts to represent in writing the actual proceedings in court, including the verdicts of the hundredal juries; but they also show that their compilers were already familiar with their material, arranged under the holders of land, i.e. as *breves*. The two statements seem to conflict; but, if so, it is because the actual making of the Inquest was more drawn out and of a complexity we have now no means of unravelling. The actual sessions of the commissioners must have been preceded by a gathering and writing down of the particulars recorded in the original returns. We may speculate as to how the 'back-room boys', as we say today, went to work; but it is certain that in the last resort the facts must have been derived from the bailiffs and stewards of tenants, and secondly that the vast array of statistics listed in either Little Domesday or Exon Domesday were not *first* written down in open court.

The bulk of the material must have been made ready in advance, and 'taken as read' at the official sessions. On the other hand, the activity of the hundredal juries, the sheriff, and the individual owners in court is beyond question, while of any *formal* written 'returns' of lands or fees by the barons there is virtually no evidence. It now remains to survey the circuit returns as a whole and to see what use was made of them by the king's clerks at Winchester. For two circuits we have the text of the original returns, and from these, helped out by the county summaries in Vol. I of Domesday Book, it should be possible to learn something of the original returns in the other circuits; and finally to examine a little more closely the final outcome of all this activity, the first volume of Domesday Book.

With regard to the circuits, though their existence is not in doubt, there is still some uncertainty both as to their number and to their arrangement. It is just possible that no. VI, despite the homogeneity in the treatment of all its counties, did in fact form two circuits; but our chief doubts concern nos. IV and V, which still remain somewhat speculative groupings. We have always to bear in mind that, although a circuit of four or five counties will tend to show traces of a single procedure, reflecting the disposition of the *legati* employed on it, the unit of inquiry and therefore of final record was not the circuit but the shire. The shires were ancient organizations, each with its distinctive history, and often very different from its nearest neighbour. It follows that in deciding the constitution of the circuits, we have to balance two factors, the inherent differences between counties and the tendency to uniformity imposed by the legates of each circuit.

We begin with the south-western counties for which alone we have both the original return and the shortened text in Domesday. The short text occupies 60 folios in vol. I, while the text of Exon Domesday fills more than

500, and a great deal of it is missing. Even allowing for the greater size of the page in the short text, it is obvious that the full returns have been drastically summarized. Some details of this process have been set out above; but a broader impression is best conveyed by quoting a whole entry from Exon, and after it the shortened text in Domesday Book. As an example, let us take from Exon Domesday (f. 173 b) the bishop of Winchester's manor of Pipeminster in Somerset:

> The bishop has 1 *mansio* which is called Pipeminster which Archbishop Stigand held on the day on which King Edward was alive and dead, and rendered geld for 15 hides. Twenty ploughs can plough these 15 hides. The bishop has five hides there and two ploughs on the demesne; and the villagers (*villani*) have 10 hides and 14 ploughs. There the bishop has 17 villagers and 8 bordars and four slaves and 1 swineherd and 1 rouncey and 20 pigs and 36 goats and 1 mill which renders 16 pence and 400 acres of wood (*nemoris*) and 6 acres of meadow and 400 acres of pasture (*pascue*). This renders £16 and when the bishop received it £13.

This is abbreviated in Great Domesday (f. 87 b) as follows:

> The said bishop holds Pipeminster. Archbishop Stigand held it and paid geld for 15 hides. There is land for 20 ploughs. Of it 5 hides are in demesne and there are 2 ploughs and 17 villagers and 8 bordars with 14 ploughs. There are 6 acres of meadow and 400 acres of pasture (*pasturae*) and as many acres of wood (*silvae*). It was worth £13: now £16.

These two extracts are illustrations, almost in fact the simplest possible, of a process which is repeated some thousands of times in the Domesday version of these counties. The stock on the manors—cattle, sheep, pigs, &c.—so carefully recorded in the original returns, is consistently omitted: so too are the details of all sub-tenants (when such exist), and these are often of great complexity. Clearly the interest of the king's clerks centres upon the tenants-in-chief, the men who *hold* the land, and the facts they value most are precisely those which are required by the 'terms of reference' which controlled the Inquest. Each of the entries quoted above is typical of the record from which it is taken, and one cannot but be impressed by the monotonous regularity with which Exon set out, in leisurely formulas, the full facts in an invariable order and in invariable terms. Equally striking are the skill and regularity with which the abbreviator has performed his difficult task. For Domesday Book, Vol. I, is no fair copy of first attempts and earlier drafts, but a précis made direct from the original returns. The not infrequent marginal additions, the irregular spacing of the entries, and the actual corrections which suggest this, are confirmed by a curious and revealing slip in the abbreviated text of Leicestershire. There the fief of Robert Hostiarius has been twice recorded, and the two entries differ so much in wording and in content as to put the matter beyond a doubt.[1]

After a few hours spent in collating the two texts, the reader gets the feel of the process of abbreviation, and is soon sufficiently expert, if he wishes, to forecast with precision the form each abbreviated entry will take. The abbreviator knows exactly what he wants, and what he extracts is set down with incomparable brevity. The contrast between the verbosity of the one record and the compression of the other is the final demonstration that in Exon we are indeed face to face with an advanced draft of the original return, for it is unthinkable that such wordiness could have been retained, if behind it lay the same information cast in the form of hundred rolls. The clerks at Winchester, as we have seen above,[2] in making this abbreviation of Exon for Vol. I of Domesday Book freely altered the formulas of the original, yet, in doing so, they

[1] D.B., vol. I, f. 235 a 1, and f. 237 a 1. Round, *Feudal England*, p. 26.
[2] Above, p. 109.

changed them in a consistent way and their shorter version preserves, though in other terms, the systematic and mechanical structure of Exon Domesday. On this evidence we may proceed to the hypothesis that, wherever Domesday Book presents its information in an unvarying form, it is working from original returns cast in the same sort of rigid mould as those of the south-west.

With this in mind let us examine the form of entry used in Hampshire, selecting once more an example from the bishop of Winchester's lands (D.B., vol. I, f. 40 a 1). 'Walchelinus episcopus Wintoniensis tenet in dominio Alresforde. De episcopatu est et fuit semper. T.R.E. se defendit pro LI hida (*sic*). Modo pro XLII hidis. Terra est XL carucis. . . .' The usual particulars regarding ploughs, villains, bordars, &c., follow together with a brief list of sub-tenants within the manor, and the entry concludes: 'Totum M̄ T.R.E. valebat £40 et post £20. Modo dominium episcopi £40: Roberti £4: Walteri 40s.: Durandi £11.' It will be seen from this entry that there are two striking differences in form between the Hampshire Domesday and that of Somerset, viz. that Hampshire gives *two* estimates of the geld (*T.R.E. et modo*), while Somerset gives but one, and three estimates of the value where Somerset gives only two. It is therefore of great interest to find that the entry is in these respects as typical of Hampshire as were the Somerset formulas, and *mutatis mutandis* is repeated many hundreds of times. If next we extend our examination to Kent, Sussex, and Berkshire we find that, while few manage as well as Hampshire to give three estimates of value, they all tend to give, with unvarying regularity, the two estimates of the hidage, using always the formula *defendit se pro*. The reason no doubt for this is that these counties, with Hampshire, seem to have formed a single circuit (no. I), and we may safely conclude that the original returns for the circuit consistently recorded the geld liability in hides both T.R.E. and *modo* for every manor. We may even go farther and conclude with some probability that the original returns for this circuit employed the *se defendit* formula found in Domesday Book. It seems to have been the normal formula in general use in south-eastern and southern England, and we have seen already that it was used in the I.C.C. for Cambridgeshire and Hertfordshire (circuit III).

Thus an examination of the shortened text in Vol. I of Domesday Book suggests that the return to Winchester made by the first circuit was elaborated with the same care and precision as that of the south-western counties. Though they differed somewhat in structure and terminology, the almost mechanical consistency with which the information is set out in Exon Domesday must have been equally characteristic of the full return of circuit I. Whether any preliminary document corresponding to P. was made in the south-west is simply unknown, but the same basic procedure of checking evidence supplied by the landowners against the testimony of hundredal juries underlies both; and it is clear that both were mainly composed by the commissioners' clerks, as it were behind the scenes. The formal court sessions, though vital, were in practice subsidiary to the immense toil of hammering so great a mass of detail into unvarying and rigid formulas, set out in a consistent order. The most striking difference between the two returns must have lain in the complete failure of Exon Domesday to record the hundreds in which the several estates lay. In this respect the south-western circuit was at odds with all the others; and the mere fact of the difference reminds us that the recording of the hundreds in Domesday is no more than an incidental survival of the procedure followed, and not in itself an object of the Survey.

We may next turn to the forms used in the third circuit which included Cambridgeshire, taking as an example the first manor listed in the *breve* of the bishop of Winchester (vol. I, 190 a 2). 'M̄. Walchelinus episcopus Wintoniensis tenet Mordune. Pro viii hidis se defendit. Terra est xvi carucis.'

The entry proceeds in much the same form as in Hampshire, but two things are notable about its opening formulas—the initial M̄ in the margin and the fact that (as in Exon Domesday) the geld obligation is only given for a single date, viz. T.R.E. But—and this is most curious—in Cambridgeshire we cannot say that this entry is typical. Take, for instance, the very next entry:

In Cloptune tenet isdem episcopus III hidas et dimidiam. Terra est V carucis. . . .

Hoc M̄ iacuit et iacet in dominio aecclesiae S. Petri Wintoniensis.

From these examples we see that the unchanging pattern of recording information found in both Hampshire and Somerset Domesday is not found in Cambridgeshire. There we have less-settled formulas, for while entries cast in the form of Abintone and Cloptune are the most common, we have, say, forty examples of the first (Mordune) in some cases with the hidage obligation recorded, unlike Mordune, both T.R.E. and *modo*. But this is not all. In all three cases quoted above one would naturally assume that the hidage obligation was the same both T.R.E. and *modo*, and in all three cases we should be wrong, for the hidage of the whole Armingford hundred had, by 1086, been reduced by one-fifth, so that the 1086 figure was in fact less by one-fifth than that given. Careful examination, in fact, reveals a slight but persistent difference between the recording of the geld obligation in the Domesday of the circuit which included Hampshire and that employed in Cambridgeshire and the other counties—Buckinghamshire, Hertfordshire, Middlesex, and Bedfordshire of circuit no. III. It is therefore reasonable to conclude that

between the original returns of the first circuit, and those
of the third there must have been some difference of *form*
which explains the varying practice of the Winchester
clerks who made the précis of both circuits in Vol. I of
Domesday Book. Can we discover what the difference was?

The answer is supplied by the I.C.C., where, as we
have seen, the lands are described geographically by
hundreds, and the hidage obligation of each *village* is
recorded in precisely the same way as each manor is in the
first circuit. In Cambridgeshire the great majority of villages were divided into several manors, and in the I.C.C.
the opening statement that the village of X *se defendit* for
so many hides is followed by a description of each constituent manor, beginning with the words 'and of these X
hides' so and so *tenet V hidas* or *habet X hidas*. The I.C.C.,
of course, like P. for circuit I, was only a preliminary compilation, and its material was recast locally by the commissioners to form the circuit return. But it was a much
more elaborate document than P., embodying the whole
mass of manorial statistics, including the full details of
the livestock on each manor, and its conversion into the
circuit return involved a great deal of extra labour which
was cut out by the system followed in Kent. The commissioners' clerks who recopied and rearranged the I.C.C.
tended to reproduce the varying formulas of their exemplar. Thus the I.C.C. explains the varying and uncertain
practice of the Domesday clerks in dealing with the original returns of this circuit. Wherever there was more than
one manor in a village, the odds are that the simple *tenet
X hidas* formula will be employed in Domesday Book;
where manor and vill coincide will be found *se defendebat
T.R.E. et modo*. There are exceptions, of course, and there
are mistakes. Nor must we forget Round's warning that
the Domesday clerks had little idea of verbal fidelity and
revelled in paraphrase. None the less, a careful study
of Hamilton's edition of the I.C.C., which sets the

Domesday entries alongside the geographically arranged text, shows decisively that in this matter the abbreviators followed with remarkable fidelity the formulas used in their original.

From the examination of circuits I, II, and III it follows that the circuit returns of nos. I and II differ from III in the regularity and fixity of their formulas. Much the same is true of the other circuits, all of which present their material in Vol. I of Domesday Book with a regularity of phrase in strong contrast with that of no. III. Two of these (nos. VI and VII) begin all entries with the name of the place: in X, Y holds . . . . The remainder begin with the name of the tenant: Y holds X; and this is done with such consistency as to suggest that in circuit III alone was the circuit return preceded by any such full written record of the labours of the commissioners as the I.C.C. A more restricted record of the actual court proceedings on the lines of P. may well have been made in other circuits, but in all circuits, save no. III, the insertion of the manorial statistics was subsequent to the actual sworn Inquest. The addition of this great volume of detail which must have constituted the heaviest task of the circuit commissioners was—apart from circuit III—everywhere only made when the material was arranged in its final form as the *breves* of individual owners.

We have next to consider the fourth and fifth circuits in Stephenson's list, comprising the counties of the midlands and the Welsh border. So far as concerns the geld the two are very much alike, for in both we tend to get a single reckoning of the number of hides or carucates. So and so holds such and such a place: there are so many hides. We hear little of reduction of the T.R.E. obligation in 1086 (*modo*), but a good deal about inland and hides which have never gelded. Moreover, there is real doubt in this area as to the number and composition of the circuits. That Worcestershire and Herefordshire formed

parts of a single circuit may be taken as certain; and
Oxfordshire and Northamptonshire, no doubt, were both
in the same circuit; but a general resemblance between
the treatment of all these counties is accompanied by
certain peculiarities in each one, and this division into
circuits still remains pure guesswork. More significant
than the formulas used in the description of the counties
is the striking fact, already noticed, that all the counties
grouped in circuits IV and V together with those of the
south-west (no. II) make no reference to evidence given
by the hundred. To this rule there is but a single exception in Gloucestershire, where a hundred is recorded as
affirming that a place once in another hundred is now included within its own boundaries.[1] The exception is a
salutary warning not to conclude from the silence of the
shortened text in Vol. I of Domesday Book that the commissioners made no use of the hundreds in these counties.
Indeed, in some of these counties there is clear evidence
in the sequence of the hundredal rubrics that procedure
here as elsewhere was systematically based on the hundred.
Of the sixth circuit it is possible to speak more definitely
than of nos. IV and V. This, according to Stephenson,
included the counties of Huntingdon, Derby, Nottingham, York, and Lincoln, all of which are characterized
by the use of a special formula recording the geld obligation, of which a typical example reads: 'M̄ In Sibestune
habebat Ulf II hides et dimidiam ad geldum.' As in circuit
no. III, there are frequent capital letters added in the
margin, which in circuit no. VI are both more systematic
and more complex (M̄. Ñ. B̄. S̄.) than in III. We can,
I think, infer from this variable intensity in the use of
these capitals in the two circuits, as well as from the total
absence of the practice in the other five circuits, that these
letters were already found in the original return sent to
Winchester. Add to this the *invariable* use of the *hidas*

[1] D.B., vol. I, f. 165 b.

or *carucatas ad geldum* formula, and the absence of any record for these counties of reduced geld assessment in 1086, and one is forced to conclude that the original returns for this circuit sent to Winchester were, like those of nos. II and VII, already cast in Domesday form, that is, as a record of separate estates under the names of the tenants-in-chief who held them. This conclusion is borne out by a slight but significant irregularity in the Domesday record of Nottinghamshire. The numbered table of tenants which precedes the text (f. 280 b) lists the earls before the archbishop and other ecclesiastics—an order found also in the two East Anglian counties in Little Domesday—but, except in this instance, nowhere in Great Domesday (Vol. I). This unique departure from correct procedure is no doubt a 'carry-over' from the original return from circuit no. VI, an analogous compilation to Little Domesday.[1] Here, as elsewhere, we are left in no doubt that the commissioners proceeded by wapentakes and/or hundreds in collecting their information, though in some of these counties the wapentakes in which the estates lay are very imperfectly recorded in Domesday Book. The actual procedure, in fact, in three of them, viz. Huntingdonshire, Yorkshire, and Lincolnshire, is vividly reflected in what we may call appendixes which list the testimony of county, hundred, wapentake, and riding in Yorkshire and Lincolnshire on disputed claims. To these no title is given in Huntingdonshire, but in Yorkshire and Lincolnshire they are called *clamores*, and those in Lincolnshire are described as being settled by the 'men who swore'; 'clamores quae sunt in Sudtreding Lincoliae et concordia eorum per homines qui iuraverunt'. The *clamores* must be clearly distinguished from the *invasiones super regem* in East Anglia, and the *terrae occupatae* of the south-west with which they have little in common. That they were made by the Winchester clerks who drew up Vol. I of Domesday

[1] See also p. 182.

Book is highly unlikely. Had this been so we should have expected similar lists not only in Derbyshire and Notting- ham, but in counties like Hampshire and Berkshire where we meet with very many entries *in the text* of precisely similar tenor. These appendixes were almost certainly in the original returns and because of their importance deemed sufficiently valuable to be preserved even in the shortened version of Domesday Book. But, if so, the original returns were also in their present shape, that is arranged under tenants, when they arrived at Winchester.

A last word needs to be said regarding the parts of Domesday Book which deal with Yorkshire and Lincoln- shire. These occupy the last eighty folios of Vol. I, and the two returns are so closely associated, almost inter- woven, as to suggest a query whether these two vast counties did not in fact form by themselves an extra cir- cuit. We get in order the text of Yorkshire, followed by that of Lincolnshire, and last of all in the volume a geo- graphical index and summary for Yorkshire. In this unique Domesday document we learn on good authority that some of the places mentioned in the summary do not occur in the Domesday text, and vice versa that places mentioned in the Yorkshire text are not found in the summary.[1] The conclusion, then, is almost certain that the summary already formed a part of the original returns, retained by the Winchester abbreviator because of its extreme usefulness in locating the hundreds and manors mentioned in the text. But, if the Yorkshire original returns were themselves a series of hundred rolls, such a summary would have been unnecessary. We may surely conclude that the Yorkshire original returns sent to Winchester—and, if so, those of Lincolnshire—were like

[1] I. S. Maxwell, 'The Geographical Identification of Domesday Vills', *Institute of British Geographers* (1952), *Papers and Transactions, 1950*, p. 100: 'It therefore appears certain that both the Text and the Summary were copied from the same source.' It would be interesting to compare the Summary with the Yorkshire *clamores*.

Little Domesday written in book form, as quaternions or quires, already arranged under the names of the tenants-in-chief.

There remains the East Anglian circuit (no. VII), whose original return became Vol. II of Domesday Book, or Little Domesday. The basic arguments for this view set out above, are:

1. The colophon to Little Domesday which states that it was made in 1086.

2. The close general similarity of Little Domesday and Exon Domesday and the common contrast they present to Vol. I. The two represent successive stages in the evolution of the original returns, and had Little Domesday ever been added—in shortened form—to Vol. I, we can form a shrewd idea of the changes that would have taken place. The distinction between manors *de regno* and *de regione* would have disappeared; the lists of *invasiones* would have been omitted, together with the catalogue of many hundreds of small socmen and their holdings; and the description of the city of Norwich would have been moved from its present position at the end of the *Terra Regis* to the opening folios of Norfolk.

That Little Domesday was ever preceded by a document analogous to the I.C.C., or P., is unlikely. The precise 'hundredal order' of the royal demesne and the separate fiefs in both Essex and Norfolk implies rather that the day-to-day proceedings of the Inquest were recorded not geographically by hundreds, but personally as *breves* of the tenants-in-chief. The very notion of a full record by hundreds of the commissioners' findings is pointless in East Anglia where the geld was levied according to special administrative divisions called 'leets', which incidentally are unrecorded in Little Domesday. Thus a return by hundreds would have been useless for reassessing the geld, and would only have saddled the clerks at

Winchester with the vast and useless toil of rearranging the material as we now have it.

Little Domesday is a fair copy of a local return which was analogous to Exon Domesday, and must have been the result of an immense preliminary work both in collecting the facts and ordering them and arranging them in writing. Much of this must have been done before the *legati* held their sessions and took their evidence, after which it would need considerable amendment and rewriting. That Little Domesday, as we have it, is essentially the production of clerks in an office is proved, as in Exon Domesday, by the order and monotonous regularity of the text. This is also suggested by the occasional use of direct speech, as on f. 2 b,'Postea recuperavimus dimidiam hidam quam tenuit i socman Haroldi', in the account of the royal demesne for Essex; or on f. 397 a, 'ut superius diximus' (Suffolk), where the scribe harks back to a previous entry.

The general survey of the Domesday circuits has brought to light clear evidence that local problems and local conditions necessitated considerable variations in the way each circuit went to work. These variations are reflected in the absence of uniformity which characterized the circuit returns. Yet behind all differences there was a single basic procedure by hundreds and by manors. Everywhere the Inquest was apparently conducted in the county court, and everywhere the information collected from individuals was checked both by personal testimony and the verdicts of hundredal juries. Everywhere, finally, the local circuit return was sent to Winchester arranged, as in Domesday Book, Vol. I, as *breves*, or lists of manors for each tenant-in-chief in each county. These governing considerations enable us to reconcile the general tendency towards an hundredal order in the presentation of the facts with the constant exceptions we encounter. Three main types of procedure in the actual making of the circuit returns have come to light, one in Kent (P.), one in Cambridgeshire (the I.C.C.), and one in Essex and Norfolk. Of these three the procedure used in the I.C.C. was apparently unique, for there is no trace of such a document in any other circuit. Elsewhere a restricted preliminary account of the Inquest, like P., may well have been made in several circuits, or indeed in nearly all, but in East Anglia it is difficult to escape the conclusion that no preliminary written records by hundreds preceded the circuit return, which still survives as Little Domesday.

It remains to summarize the known facts regarding the date of the two volumes of Domesday Book and of Exon Domesday. The thesis, set forth above, requires the assumption that all three were compiled before the Conqueror's death in 1087, and its arguments would be to some extent invalidated if any of the three were shown to belong to a later period. There is fortunately a formidable array of evidence in its favour, which is detailed below, at the cost of some repetition, as shortly as possible:

1. It is a natural and reasonable assumption that all 'work' on the Survey stopped on the Conqueror's death. In the eleventh century the king's peace died with him, and law and order were at an end until his successor was crowned. Nor was there any permanent nucleus of clerks to carry on the government. There is, as far as I know, no later precedent for centuries of a task of this kind being finished by the next sovereign. William II and Ranulph Flambard were as interested in the 'honours' of their subjects as the Conqueror himself, but we are specifically informed that their energies were directed towards a new and very different type of Survey.[1]

2. The colophon to Little Domesday states that 'this description' was made in 1086 not only through these counties but also through the others. Nothing has been so

[1] *Trans. R. Hist. Soc.*, 4th series, xvi (1933), pp. 106–8.

great a stumbling-block to Domesday scholarship as this famous colophon. It will not therefore be amiss to consider it here more closely; for what I have called 'the old hypothesis' regarding the making of Domesday Book really turns on the meaning we give to these words. Taken at their face value they relate to the text which precedes them and state that Little Domesday was actually compiled and written down in 1086. But such a conclusion was incompatible with the assumption that the *descriptio* of England sent to Winchester in 1086 was a great series of hundred rolls. The problem was treated by Round on pages 139–41 of his *Feudal England*. He wrote:

It seems to have been somewhat hastily concluded that because the Survey (*Descriptio Angliae*) took place in 1086, Domesday Book, which styles itself *Liber de Wintonia*, was completed in that year. The phrase '*per hos tres comitatus*' proves, surely, that '*descriptio*' refers to the Survey, not to the book.

To this remark the obvious answer is, first, that Great Domesday was finished, so far as it was finished, not in 1086, but before the Conqueror's death in 1087; and secondly, that Domesday Book does not style itself 'Liber de Wintonia'.[1] However, to justify his interpretation of the colophon Round asserted that Little Domesday was 'a first attempt at the codification of the returns' discarded in favour of Vol. I at some later date (unspecified) because of its many blunders and its 'unwieldy proportions'. As evidence of its 'inferior workmanship' he asserted that the opening words of the Suffolk survey, *Terra Regis de Regione*, were a blunder: the last two words should read *de regno* in line with the words 'Dominicatus regis ad regnum pertinens' in Exon Domesday. A further blunder, he added, was the 'muddled order' of the tenants-in-chief for Norfolk and Suffolk, where laymen precede the

---

[1] The words are taken from the description of the Bruce fee, a twelfth-century addition, f. 332 b.

Church. There is, however, no substance in any of the so-called proof, for, as Mr. Hoyt[1] has rightly pointed out, the occurrence of *de regno* and *de regione* in East Anglia, as of *de regno* and *de comitatu* in the south-west, is merely provincial usage discarded by the central scribes of Great Domesday. The same provincialism applies to the order of the tenants in Norfolk and Suffolk, and has in fact persisted in Great Domesday for the county of Nottingham.

Finally, in a footnote on p. 141, Round refers to 'a curious deleted list of church fiefs in Essex which has no business there'. To this matter he returned some years later in his Introduction to Essex Domesday in the *Victoria County History*.[2] By this time he had noticed that there were in Little Domesday *two* such deleted lists for Essex, the first county in the volume. They occur on the front or recto of the first leaf of the second and third gatherings, viz. f. 9 and f. 17. These 'extraordinary breaks right in the middle of the text' proved 'difficult to account for'; after the second (f. 17) there 'is no further break: the text proceeds continuously'. The explanation Round offered was that the compilers of Little Domesday first intended to make each gathering a *fasciculus* complete in itself, with its little index of fiefs on the first page. The difficulties encountered in compressing the fiefs named on f. 1 into an eight-leaf gathering induced a change of plan as the work proceeded, and reliance was then placed on the preliminary index which is now found at the head of each of the three counties. The hypothesis that Vol. II was an unsatisfactory attempt at codifying the returns, abandoned for the more succinct version in Vol. I, he maintained, explained and was supported by the abandoned experiment at the beginning of the county of Essex.

The logic of the reasoning is not easy to follow, but

---

[1] *The Royal Demesne*, p. 16. [2] Vol. i, p. 413.

this is no matter since the whole theory is a mare's nest. The idea of an experiment abandoned after two quires were written requires the further supposition that it was twice tried again and twice abandoned, for on f. 292 and on f. 372 in Suffolk there are further deleted lists of fiefs, each on the recto of the first leaf of its gathering! The lists were, of course, simply made by scribes beginning a new quire to make sure that their text followed the correct order of fiefs as set out in the preliminary schedule at the head of each county. So many mistakes in three pages from a scholar of Round's competence could only spring from a complete misunderstanding of the problem. Nevertheless, scholars have clung tenaciously to his interpretation of Little Domesday's colophon in order to salvage, as it were, his theory of the 'original returns'. It has been suggested in the *Victoria County History*[1] that the first stage in the compilation of Domesday Book was as late as 1100, and more recently Professor Douglas[2] has rallied to Round's defence. The word *descriptio*, he writes, 'refers to a survey, to a process of inquiry, and not to its final results'. Is this statement borne out by contemporary usage?

We may begin with the book of Abbot Baldwin's enfeoffments, a compilation of the reign of Henry I or earlier, which Professor Douglas himself has edited and published.[3] It begins as follows:

These are manors which Saint Edward had in his demesne. And these are the lands of his men which they held at the time when by the order of King William was made the description (*descriptio*) of all England according to the oaths which almost the whole of the inhabitants of that land swore. . . . The Saint and his men held these lands on the day the aforesaid king was alive and dead.

[1] *Norfolk*, vol. ii, p. 4.
[2] *Domesday Monachorum* (R. Hist. Soc. 1944), p. 24.
[3] *Feudal Documents from the Abbey of Bury St. Edmunds*, ed. D. C. Douglas, 1932, p. 3.

Then follow in substance the relevant portions, some-what rearranged, of Little Domesday. Here, surely, the *descriptio* or process of enrolment and writing down of the facts is assumed by the compiler as synonymous with and as comprehending its final result, and the word *descriptio* refers directly to the text that follows.

For our second example we turn to the Liber Eliensis,[1] which lists in detail the contents of the Ely treasury made by Ranulf Flambard in 1093, beginning thus: 'Descriptio autem rerum huiusmodi erat, viginti et vii cruces parvae et magnae . . .', and so continues the inventory for two pages. The list, in short, *is* also the *descriptio* and the *descriptio* is equivalent to its 'final result'!

A third and final example is found in the Chronicle of Jocelin of Brakelonde[2] in the passage where he relates the making of Abbot Samson's famous 'Kalendar'.

There was made, he says, by his (abbot Samson's) order a general description (*descriptio generalis*) by hundreds of the leets, suits, of hidages and foddercorn . . . so that within four years of his election no one could deceive him to the value of a single penny about the rents of his abbacy: for he had received from his predecessors only a small schedule (*schedulam parvam*).

Here again the 'survey' or writing down is equated with the 'final result', i.e. the final written record; and, as if to prove it, the very next sentence begins: '*This Book* he called his Kalendar.'

In face of these examples, chosen at random, it is im-possible to doubt that the colophon to Little Domesday alludes to the very *text* of which it forms the completion and therefore that Vol. II of Domesday Book was actually compiled in the course of the year 1086. There was indeed no other way at this early date (1086) of describing Little Domesday, since the *true* Domesday Book, i.e. Vol. I, was not yet written, and Little Domesday was itself.

---

[1] p. 282.
[2] *Memorials of St. Edmund's Abbey* (R.S.), vol. i, ed. T. Arnold, 1890, p. 234.

compiled by the East Anglian circuit. Even when Great
Domesday was compiled it was only slowly that men
forgot the local returns and that the summary in Vol. I
of Domesday Book acquired its later prestige as the book
of the Treasury and still later as Domesday Book.[1]

So much is certain; and we can with great probability
go even farther. Little Domesday was written in East
Anglia and sent in to Winchester unrubricated and un-
illuminated. It was only when these quires were bound
and the volume so made coupled, *faute de mieux* with the
still unfinished Great Domesday that an effort was made
to smarten it up. This involved the illumination of occasional capital letters, numbering in red the preliminary
lists of tenants-in-chief in each of the three counties,
adding these numbers in red against the fees of the tenants
through the text, and rubricated headings of the county
and the tenants' name at the head of the left and right
leaves respectively, and finally the addition of the rubric
or colophon discussed above. I deduce that this was done:

(*a*) from the fact that the names of the tenants in the
text of Little Domesday are written in black ink instead
of in red as in Great Domesday;

(*b*) from the occasional insertion in the text of the next
group of tenants whose fees had to be copied. It was difficult for the scribes to preserve the correct order of fees
from the still unnumbered schedules at the head of each
county; and when these interim lists had served their
purpose they were crossed out.

(*c*) from the awkward spacing of the names in the preliminary schedules in East Anglia, which left little room
for the insertion of the real figures.

Little Domesday, in short, was a last-minute makeshift
supplement to the still unfinished Vol. I.

3. It is also virtually certain that Exon Domesday also

---

[1] The slow growth of the fame of Domesday Book after William I's death is
traced in more detail below, Chapter XIV.

belongs to 1086. So long as the 'geld rolls' could be attributed to 1084 the date of Exon was open to question. But, since the 'geld rolls' are now known to belong to 1086, it is reasonable to assign the rest of the contents of Exon Domesday to the same year.

4. Mr. Welldon Finn's discovery of the very script of Vol. I of Domesday Book in Exon proves that the two compilations are strictly contemporary, and so implies that Domesday Book Vol. I is also prior to the Conqueror's death.

5. The records of the Survey are never referred to as rolls or as a roll until two or three generations after the Conquest. The contemporary designation was *descriptio Angliae*, the description of England, a term which emphasized its fundamental character as a recording of the facts *in writing*. To contemporaries the word *descriptio* included all to do with the Inquest, and most especially its records which *were* the description. The use and meaning of the word *descriptio* is both normal and unambiguous in the colophon to Little Domesday. The clerks who actually compiled it commonly referred to both the original returns and their abbreviation in Vol. I of Domesday Book as *breves*, that is lists of manors arranged under the names of the king, his archbishops, bishops, abbots, barons, and lesser landholders in chief. We have already examined the practice in Domesday Book and in the Inquisitio Eliensis, which refers to the *breve regis*, the *breve abbatis*, and more generally to the *breves regis qui facti sunt in vicecomitatibus*. This use lasted on in to the reign of William II, one of whose writs (1093–1100) refers to the land 'inbreviata in meis brevibus ad opus ecclesie Sancti Benedicti qui sunt in thesauro meo Wintonie'.[1] It actually cites the *breve* of St. Benet Hulme in Little Domesday (f. 216 b) where the details of men, meadow, and arable mentioned in this writ can still be verified.

[1] Davis, *Regesta*, vol. i, p. 138, no. lxxx.

6. Towards the end of the reign of Rufus—we may guess—these *breves*, which were in form loose quires or quaternions, were bound into a book; and the first mention therefore of Domesday, as we now know it, occurs in a royal writ (1096–1100) which cites it as the *liber regius*.[1]

7. Roger of Poitou, Rogerus Pictavensis, appears in both volumes of Domesday Book as a large landowner in many counties. There is, however, a difficulty: for in some of them the lands, though fully described, are said to be now in the king's hand. Thus in Essex his name is no. 46 in the prefatory table of tenants, and a full description of his lands is headed *Terra Rogeri Pictavensis*. In Suffolk also he is entered as a normal tenant, and in Vol. I similarly he appears in Nottinghamshire, and Lincolnshire, and in Hampshire (in the margin) as holding a single manor. Against this we have to set the counties of Chester (the lands between the Ribble and the Mersey), Yorkshire, Derbyshire, and (in Little Domesday) Norfolk, where his lands are said to be in the king's hand. Moreover, there are signs of uncertainty and hesitation in these shires. In Yorkshire, for instance, his name does not appear in the prefatory table of tenants, but a full description of his lands is added on a blank leaf at the end of the county (f. 332). In Norfolk his name appears in the table, but the list of his lands is headed *Terre que fuerunt Rogeri Pictavensis* (f. 243 a). Finally, in Derbyshire he is in the Table, and his lands are described as *Terra Rogeri Pictavensis*, but at the end of the fee is added 'Has terras habebat Rogerus Pictavensis, modo sunt in manu regis' (f. 273 b 1).

These conflicting entries, which still baffle Roger's biographers, at least throw light on the making of the Survey. They seem to show that Roger's lands were taken into the king's hands at a later date in the year 1086, when the original returns were everywhere all but completed. In some cases the text of a particular county was

---

[1] *E.H.R.* xxxv (1920), p. 389.

finished before the news reached the local commissioners; in others it arrived just in time to be noted. They also prove that Little Domesday (which we know was made in 1086) is contemporary with the original returns of the circuits abbreviated in Vol. I. More generally we can, I think, confidently attribute Exon and the two volumes of Domesday Book to William I's reign, and no later, since Roger rose very quickly to such high favour with his successor, that no such confusion would later have been possible.

XIII

THE MAKING OF DOMESDAY BOOK

WITH the original returns of the circuits before him, how did the Winchester compiler put together Vol. I of Domesday Book? His task was to produce a drastic abbreviation, not of hundred rolls, but of seven or more carefully drafted returns, already arranged under the names of the holders of land or tenants-in-chief. Somehow or other this huge mass of material had to be reduced to manageable proportions, and the result was a volume of under 400 folios. To effect the reduction much more than half of the hardly gathered information was simply omitted, and what was retained, recorded with far greater brevity than in the full returns. Still further space was saved by such thoroughgoing abbreviations of the actual script as to turn the final text wellnigh into a system of statistical shorthand. Nor, as we have seen, is Great Domesday a fair copy, but the actual manuscript in which the full materials are condensed. Such wholesale reduction, so systematically applied to so large a mass of material, is without precedent in the Middle Ages. The actual compilation of Domesday Book was, then, a very great achievement; and its preservation for nearly 900 years is due to the unflinching logic of its compiler. Because it was manageable in size, it was, and remained, useful; because it was useful, it was preserved.

With Exon Domesday and Little Domesday as models of the compiler's raw material, we can see pretty well how he went to work; for taken as a whole the thirty counties in the volume show a consistent pattern. First he assigned a quire, normally of eight leaves, to each county.

Sometimes a small county is disposed of in a smaller quire: sometimes a big one needs two or even more quires. Very occasionally two counties, e.g. York and Lincoln, are 'made up' together;[1] but normally each county begins on a new quire, so that before they were bound into a single volume, each county was individually accessible for reference. On the first leaf of the quire the compiler normally entered at its head the description of the chief borough (or boroughs), or city in the county, which, if we may judge from Little Domesday, were generally spread through the local return, or put at the end of royal demesne. Next he copied from the local return—still on the first leaf if there was room—the numbered list or index of tenants, to which he soon began to put the heading 'Hic annotantur tenentes terras in (say) Kent'. He then abbreviated from the quires before him the record of the successive fees, beginning with the *Terra Regis*. Each fee bore a rubricated heading, while the appropriate number in the list was added in the margin. In this way the prefatory list was keyed to the text, and the reader, who was generally a Treasury clerk,[2] would quickly find out the name he wanted from the list and turn the pages till he came to the entry in the text. Nothing could be more simple or quicker: yet modern students of Domesday Book have often called attention to the frequent discrepancies between the prefatory lists and the text to which they are meant to serve as a guide. Even so, it may be doubted whether scholars, working on particular counties, have realized how widespread and persistent these discrepancies are. They are not as a rule very serious. In every county

---

[1] Also Devon and Cornwall; Shropshire and Cheshire with the lands between Ribble and Mersey; Nottingham and Rutland. See below, p. 200.

[2] *Dialogus de Scaccario*, p. 63: 'The survey is made by counties, hundreds and hides. The king's name heads the list, followed by those of the nobles who hold of the King in chief, according to their order of dignity. The list is then numbered, and the matter in the actual text of the book relating to each tenant is easily found by the corresponding number.'

the prefatory list does serve as a guide, though often as an inexact one, to the text that follows. But on the natural assumption that there is a direct and immediate relation between the list and text, the odd thing is, surely, that they differ at all. Whether the prefatory list was written in after the text which follows it, or vice versa, one would expect a perfect correspondence between one and the other. In fact, we encounter a definite tendency towards slight variations, and these variations fall into well-marked groups. First, we have instances in which the same man is differently identified in the prefatory list and the text headings. Eudo Dapifer, for example, in Hertfordshire, Cambridgeshire, and Bedfordshire, is called Eudo son of Hubert in the text headings of these three counties, though uniformly described as Eudo Dapifer in the prefatory lists, and in the actual text. Secondly, there are numerous instances of tenants not mentioned in the prefatory lists whose fees are described in the text. Thus in Yorkshire the name of Goisfrid de Lawirce, in Dorset that of Alured of Spain, in Leicestershire that of Robert de Buci, and in Hertfordshire that of the abbot of Ramsey are omitted from the prefatory lists, though their fees are described in the text. Contrariwise, the Yorkshire list includes the abbot of York (no. IV), whose fee is not described in the text: while in Surrey, the fee of Rainald son of Erchenbald, no. XXXIII in the list, is assigned in the text to Alfred of Marlborough, whose mesne tenant Rainald was. There are, thirdly, several instances in which the grouping of the smaller tenants-in-chief at the end of the prefatory list is slightly varied in the text, as, for example, in Berkshire. To all these have to be added a large number of cases in which for various reasons the numbering of the fees in list and text disagree. In Leicestershire, for example, Earl Hugh's name is twice entered in the prefatory list and described in the text under the later number (XLIII): but in many instances (e.g. Wiltshire) the difference is due to the careless omission by the scribe of a marginal number in the text.

A close examination will reveal so many discrepancies between the prefatory lists and the text as to suggest, at first sight, that Great Domesday was a most slovenly compilation. But to anyone familiar with it, this impression is so much at variance with all our other evidence, that one hesitates to explain these differences as due to mere carelessness.[1] The mistakes are there; but why are they there? The only possible explanation lies in abandoning our assumption of a direct relation between the prefatory lists and the text which follows. May it not be that list and text are in fact distinct compilations which belong to successive stages of the Inquest? And if so are not these discrepancies or at least some of them significant and not mere blunders?

In the answer to these questions lies the final proof of the contention advanced in this book: for it can easily be shown that the prefatory lists were automatically copied by the scribe from the circuit returns made to Winchester, and that the discrepancies between these and the text arise, in the main, from the editorial revision and alteration which accompanied the main task of abbreviating the full text of the Inquest. What happened? The circuit returns were no unsorted mass of hundred rolls, as in the later days of Edward I, but careful, finished compilations. Turn to Essex, for example, and the correspondence between prefatory list and text is complete. Indeed, it is soon evident that the compilers of the text scrupulously followed the order of the list, for on ff. 9 and 19 they have copied from it the next group of fees to be successively

---

[1] Cf. Eyton, *The Somerset Domesday*, vol. i, p. 55: 'Except that the Index, or first Schedule of the Somerset Domesday (Exchequer version) indicates no distinctive chapter of the lands of the French Thanes, its sequence and method are faultless. But then this Index was not followed by the transcribing clerks: neither if it was made after the said clerks had finished their work, did it truly represent what they had done; it only represented what they ought to have done.'

dealt with in the text. The same exact correspondence is found in Norfolk and Suffolk, where on f. 372 we again meet with a list of fees to guide the compiler of the text. The circuit return was accurate because it was made directly from the geographically arranged evidence given by the hundreds. The text just could not be written until the precise order of the tenants-in-chief was fixed. In the case of Great Domesday the text was already before the compiler in its final order, and his main task lay in the process of abbreviation. He therefore first extracted particulars of the chief city or town in the county, and wrote them at the head of f. 1 of the county quire. Next, he copied the list of tenants-in-chief from the circuit return. Only then did he get down to abbreviating the text before him, the order of which he normally followed, subject to editorial changes and correction of errors in the text. It would have been an easy matter to alter the list of tenants he had already copied out at the head of the county to conform with the changes made in the text, but he simply did not bother to do it. Occasionally he amended the headings or the numbering of the fees in the text to correspond with the prefatory list, as in Somerset (f. 98 b), but never troubled to alter the lists so as to agree with changes made in the abbreviated text.[1] Herein lies the explanation of the repeated discrepancies in Great Domesday between list and text, many, if not most, of which are seen to be full of meaning for us and deserving of careful study.

[1] Eyton in his meticulous way elaborately analysed the many discrepancies between index and text in his books on Dorset and Somerset Domesday. He is wrong, I think, in saying that 'the Indices of Domesday, though in the Codex they precede the Survey, were engrossed after it' (*Key to Domesday: Dorset*, p. 74): for there is no single instance in Vol. I of an alteration to a preliminary index. The last operation was undoubtedly the rubrication of the names in the text and the numbering of them. This seems to have been done by the same man as wrote both index and text, and to have been carried out in the most perfunctory way. In both Dorset and Somerset the rubricated numbers in the text were 'fudged' to produce the same total for both index and text! Had the preliminary index been left to the end, it could have been accurately and quickly made from the completed text.

That this is what happened becomes clearer still when we examine the county summaries in connexion with the circuits to which they belong. The first circuit, for instance, shows on the whole a close correspondence between text and indexes for all the counties in it. There is, however, a tendency to slight variation in each of them. In Kent, Richard of Tonbridge in the index becomes Richard fitz Gilbert in the text. In the Sussex index Odo and Eldred are entered separately with the numbers XIV and XV, while in the text they are grouped together as no. XIV. In Surrey, the name of Rainald fitz Erchenbald in the index has been altered in the text to Alfred of Marlborough. In Hampshire, in the Isle of Wight, no. IX, 'Godric the priest and others', becomes 'lands of the king's thegns' in the text. Finally in Berkshire, Rainbald the priest of the index becomes Rainbald of Cirencester in the text, and no. LXIIII Stefanus filius Eirardi of the text is absent from the index, no doubt because the Winchester clerk included him with the other thegns who are there grouped as no. LXV. Thus in the first circuit a close general agreement is marred by slight variations which could hardly have occurred had there been any direct and immediate connexion between text and index at the moment when Great Domesday was compiled. Exactly the same tendency towards variation can be traced in the other circuits.

In the compiler's odd, but very human, failure fully to correlate the county indexes in Great Domesday with the text, we have, as it were incidentally, the final proof that the circuit returns to the great inquest were already arranged in exactly the way we find them in Vol. I of Domesday Book. More interesting, and even exciting, is the fact that we can now picture him at work and so appreciate both his difficulties and his achievement.[1]

---

[1] For the rest of this chapter see *Domesday Re-Bound* (Stationery Office, 1954), and more especially the valuable Appendix I showing the arrangement of sheets in gatherings.

Even if there were several scribes employed on Great
Domesday, the whole volume bears the stamp of a single
mind. The script, the style, and the overall pattern in
which the information is presented are constant throughout. Take, for example, the order of the names in the
prefatory indexes. Unlike Little Domesday, where in
Norfolk and Suffolk the earls precede the archbishops,
bishops, and abbots, the churchmen in Great Domesday
invariably follow the king. To this rule the county of
Nottingham is the single exception; in both the list and
the text Earls Alan, Hugh, and the count of Mortain are
respectively nos. II, III, and IV. Nor is the explanation
far to seek. The compiler first copied from the circuit
return the list of tenants-in-chief, and then proceeded to
abbreviate its text, automatically rearranging the order so
as to make the archbishops, bishops, &c., follow straight
on after the king. The result was that nos. II, III, and IV,
the fees of the three earls, were entirely omitted in the
text, and had to be added on a specially inserted leaf
(f. 282). Another case wherein the exception proves the
rule is connected with the third circuit, only one of whose
five counties bears the otherwise invariable heading to
the prefatory list, viz. 'Hic annotantur tenentes terras
in Middlesexe' (f. 126 b). An examination of the small
gathering of six leaves which suffices for Middlesex (viz.
ff. 126–31) reveals that the outside bifolium (i.e. ff. 126
and 131) is blank except for the index which occurs on the
verso of f. 126, the main text of the county beginning on
f. 127. At first sight it looks as though the index was forgotten, and a double-leaf added to repair the oversight.
But in every other county, bar one,[1] we find that the text

---

[1] Hampshire. The recto of the first leaf for Wiltshire (f. 64) is also blank, and
the text begins on the verso; but it is clear that the original intention was to
begin on the recto extracts from the surveys of the chief boroughs. The index was
first written on the verso of the leaf, and then the compiler fearing he would not
have enough material on his boroughs to fill the whole recto of the first leaf,
began his account of Malmesbury and Wilton on the verso, above the index. He

begins on the recto of the first leaf of the quire and that in addition to the index this leaf carries the description of the chief town or towns, or at least that a space is left for such an entry. Add to this the fact that the other county which begins with a whole blank leaf, recto and verso (apart from the index), is Hampshire and the conclusion is forced on us that these blanks were left for a description of London and Winchester respectively, which for some reason were omitted at the last moment. This is a conclusion of great interest, for it suggests that both London and Winchester were 'surveyed', and that the decision to omit them was probably due to their length and complexity. In these as in other cases (e.g. Sussex where they perhaps decided to leave Lewes in the text as a 'mediatized' borough) the index was first written like those of the remaining counties of this circuit without the *Hic annotantur* heading, which was probably added later. Indeed, it may very well be that the compiler 'thought up' this heading, when he had completed his summary of the circuit, to call attention to and explain the forlorn little list on the otherwise blank folio preceding the county summary.[1] The curious absence of the *Hic annotantur* heading to the preliminary indexes in this circuit suggests, in fact, that the compiler began his task with the third circuit, and so with the county of Middlesex, and that the decision to omit London suggested to him the idea of *heading* his indexes to show the county to which they belonged. The idea was approved and consistently followed in his abbreviation of the county summaries of the remaining circuits.

The discovery that the preliminary index of tenants at the head of each county was copied from the circuit return is of special interest for the south-western circuit

then found he had too little space and the result is the most crowded and untidy page in the whole of Great Domesday (f. 64^v)!

[1] In this connexion it is worth noting that the prefatory indexes to Essex, Norfolk and Suffolk in Little Domesday have no such *Hic annotantur* heading.

for which we have much of the full text in Exon Domesday though not the finished return sent to Winchester. By comparing for these counties the index with the text that follows it is possible to trace in detail, first, the final grouping made in the local return of tenants whose lands though already recorded under the holders names in Exon, were still not separated into counties, and, secondly, the editorial alterations made by the abbreviator in Vol. I of Domesday Book. As an example, we may examine the county of Somerset. The chief difference between Exon and the fair copy sent to Winchester lies in the classification of the humbler tenants. In Exon these are tentatively divided into French thegns, English thegns, and king's serjeants (*servientes*). For these the fair copy substitutes, as elsewhere, just two headings, viz. king's serjeants (XLVI) and thegns (XLVII); but in so doing promotes several of the more important men, like Ralph Paganel and Ralph de Limesi, to baronial rank by separately recording their 'honours' (nos. XXXI and XXXII). In addition Samson the chaplain's manor of Combe (f. 467) was found to be held in mesne tenure from the bishop of Bayeux, and so removed from the category of French thegns to form a separate fee (no. IV) of the bishop. In this discovery, which could only have been made by the men on the spot, lies the best proof[1] that Exon was recopied locally to form the return of this circuit; and the fact that the handwriting of the compiler of Great Domesday is found in the revised entry regarding Combe strongly suggests that the changes were only made after consultation with headquarters at Winchester.[2] It may be that similar help was given to other circuits. However that may be, we are not surprised to find that the editorial changes made by the abbreviator in Great Domesday are quite trifling. They have been exhaustively examined by Eyton,[3]

[1] Cf. above, p. 110.   [2] Above, p. 112.
[3] *Somerset Domesday*, vol. i, p. 54. Changes similar to those made in Somerset

and most of them seem due to either carelessness, or, more probably, to haste. In Somerset the compiler certainly made a sad mess of the fee of Humphrey the Chamberlain; and it is clear that with the full return before him little or no reference was made to the prefatory list or index till the abbreviation of the text was completed, and the time had come to number and rubricate both index and text. It was then obvious that the text had departed somewhat from the index, and a good deal of ingenuity was required to reproduce the forty-seven titles of the index in the text that followed it.

In these examples we can trace the workings of a single mind actually evolving a set pattern of presenting his material in Great Domesday. Of his techniques in the actual task of abbreviation something has already been said in examining Exon Domesday. It was impossible to standardize completely the formulas used in the varying local returns, but at least these could be compressed and made more terse, as, for instance, the verbose description of manors in Exon Domesday, which was drastically cut down in the shorter text. We may reasonably suppose that the same process was employed in dealing with the returns of the other circuits. But all we can now do with these is to draw some tentative conclusions from the prefatory indexes, copied into Great Domesday from the circuit returns, which show so many differences from the revised text which follows them. Of these the most certain is the consistent refusal of the Domesday compiler to recognize mesne tenants as holders of land entitled to separate titles.[1] For this reason the abbot of St. Mary's, York, whose lands were separately listed in the circuit returns, was denied a separate heading in Great Domesday, his lands being entered under the fees of the tenants-in-chief from whom

were also made in Devonshire. There in addition to the three Somerset headings we find a further one for the lands of 'French knights'. Above, p. 107.

[1] Cf. above, p. 110, 191.

he held them, viz. Hugh the Earl (f. 305) and Berengar of Todeni (f. 314). The abbot was probably included as a tenant-in-chief in the local return by reason of his possession of or claim upon St. Olave's Church, Marygate; but this claim was not made good, and we have a writ[1] of William I confirming the claims upon it of the count of Brittany. So, too, as mentioned above, the fee attributed to Rainald fitz Erchenbald in the preliminary index for Surrey (no. XXXIII) was transferred in the text to Alfred of Marlborough, whose mesne lord Rainald was.[2] Another trace of editorial correction in the shortened text occurs in Devonshire where the successive headings XXIV, Walter de Clavile, and XXV, Walter, refer to the same man. In this case we can trace the error right back to Exon where the fees of Goscelm and Walter de Clavile are combined under a single heading owing to the fact that one manor was held conjointly by the two. This was put right in the *text* of Domesday, though the error is still found in the prefatory list. But of all discrepancies between the circuit returns and the final shortened version in the text of Great Domesday, the most frequent relate to the holding of the smaller tenants-in-chief in the last two or three headings of the prefatory lists, and the reader who consults, say, the counties of Sussex, Berkshire, Dorset, Lincolnshire, and Buckinghamshire can watch the compiler at work regrouping the humbler people.

One other source of information regarding the actual making of Great Domesday is found in the actual make-up of the quires, which contrasts sharply with that used in the smaller volume. With very few exceptions the latter uses quires of eight leaves: there are only five inserted leaves in 450 folios; there are few gaps or blanks left and each county is complete in itself. Taken in conjunction

---

[1] *Regesta*, vol. i, no. 226.
[2] The same principle explains why in Cheshire the feudatories of Earl Hugh are neither listed nor numbered in the text.

with its varying script and the paucity of its marginal
entries, these features prove that Little Domesday was,
substantially, just a fair copy of an already largely completed return. Vol. I, Great Domesday, is very different,
and for the simple reason that it was not a copy but a
wholesale abbreviation of the first return. Here, too, the
rule is to allot a separate quire or quires to each county,
but in four important instances the rule is broken. Cornwall begins in the middle of the last quire for Devonshire;
Shropshire and Cheshire are similarly combined; also
Gloucester and Worcester. Finally Yorkshire and Lincolnshire, which together fill more than ten quires, are so
intimately interconnected as almost to suggest that they
formed a single circuit on their own.[1] In the first of these
instances the presentation of two counties as a single and
separate section of the whole has, I am sure, significance.
Perhaps this conjunction was just one of convenience
suggested by the close connexion between these particular shires. Devonshire and Cornwall, for instance, are
grouped together in the earliest surviving Pipe Roll
(31 Henry I). With these notable exceptions the shires in
Great Domesday are self-contained, so to speak, each with
one or more quires; and it is clear from a close examination of inserted leaves that it was not always possible to
work straight through from the beginning of a county to
the end. The greatest difficulty was evidently found with
the shires in circuit no. VI which have many gaps, suggesting unusual difficulties encountered in abbreviating
the first return. On the other hand, in the counties in the
fifth circuit with the exception of Staffordshire[2] there is
a more complete harmony between the prefatory indexes
and the numbers in the text.

---

[1] These quires too are carefully lettered A to K, a feature found nowhere else
in Vol. I.
[2] One of several reasons for doubting whether, after all, Staffordshire is
rightly included in circuit no. V. The fourth circuit seems the right place for it.

We have to remember that the quires or gatherings for each county in Great Domesday were not at first thought of as pages in a single volume, but as booklets, each of which, whether made for a single county or for two, was complete in itself and could be referred to separately. So they remained long enough for the outside leaves to become dirty with much handling, and when they were converted by binding into Great Domesday no attempt was made to retain the 'circuit order'. Instead the book begins with Kent, and that it was meant to do so is shown by the extra-large illuminated D of Dover, with the account of which Kent starts. Next followed the counties in order westwards to Cornwall. Then begins a second 'band' of counties north of these, starting with Middlesex and working westwards to Hereford. Another east-to-west band follows, beginning with Cambridge and extending to Cheshire, which, as it were, turns back to Derby and Nottingham. The volume ends with Lincolnshire and Yorkshire which formed a single 'booklet'. Had the smaller volume ever been added to Great Domesday we can say with some confidence that Essex would have immediately preceded Middlesex, while Norfolk and Suffolk would have preceded Cambridge.

The more closely, then, we examine Great Domesday, the stronger is the impression of a single mind imposing on diverse materials a single, if rough, pattern; and this view is supported by the official pamphlet, *Domesday Re-Bound*, based on a minute examination of the make-up of the volume. It is there suggested that the whole book was written by a single scribe; that the work was planned to begin (as it does) with Kent, but that the actual writing started with Middlesex; and finally that it bears an impression of haste, 'a haste not due to carelessness but to urgency', because, perhaps, it has to be presented to the king. The work is somehow finished 'barring always Essex, Norfolk and Suffolk which exist already in a reasonably final form and which there is no time to incorporate'.

Between the smaller volume and Great Domesday the official pamphlet repeatedly affirms 'a clear contrast'. The gatherings are more regular than those in the larger volume; the horizontal rulings are more simple, and the scribes, for there are a number of them, with very few exceptions keep to the number of lines per page which they indicate. The materials of the two volumes are different; that of the larger volume is sheepskin, while the smaller is calfskin; and the orderly procedure in drafting suggests that Little Domesday is simply a fair copy of its original. The rubrication and pigment are wholly different in the two volumes; and in the composition of Little Domesday there is a clear indication of an organization working 'locally or at least independently of that which produced the major volume'.

These suggestions, based on the facts revealed by rebinding and tabulated in Appendixes I and II of *Domesday Re-Bound*, fully endorse and underline the conclusions here advanced regarding the making of Domesday Book. With the views of Maitland and Round they are wholly at variance, for they clearly imply that the actual Inquest and both volumes of Domesday Book were completed, or rather brought to a halt, at the death of William the Conqueror.

The most revolutionary suggestion made in the official pamphlet is that which would attribute to a single scribe the writing of the whole of Vol. I. The weight of palaeographical opinion, so far as one can discover, leans to the view that several scribes were engaged on Great Domesday; but the more one broods on the script the more difficult it becomes to find any passage which can be confidently ascribed to any writer other than that of the rest, or indeed any other part of it. One is driven, almost reluctantly, to the view that a single scribe wrote the whole volume, and—even more important—that this scribe was also the compiler, whose task was to abbreviate the local returns, already drawn up, like Little Domesday, and indexed according to the names of the holders of land. If so, it must have been a very senior official, and a trusted one who bore the responsibility of discarding the greater part of the information so meticulously set out in the 'original returns'. This script, which is highly distinctive, indeed unique, has an old-fashioned air, more characteristic of a native than a foreign scribe. It is quite possible that his name occurs in the book he wrote, though unlikely that we shall ever identify him.

The proof that the compiler was also the scribe lies, firstly, in the two substantially identical but verbally very different entries of the fee of Robert Hostiarius in Leicestershire (f. 235 and f. 237); secondly, in the fees of the bishop of Bayeux (f. 87 b) and Robert Fitz Gerold (f. 97) in Somerset, of which varying versions, in the same script, are found in Exon Domesday; and thirdly, in the curious evidence brought together in *Domesday Re-Bound* regarding the horizontal ruling of the gatherings, that is to say the number of lines per page. The compiler seems to have begun in a large careful hand, allowing only 44 lines to the page. This he employed in dealing with the circuit which included Middlesex, Hertford, Buckingham, Cambridge, and Bedford; and so continued with circuit no. VI, through Huntingdon, Nottingham, Derby, and Lincolnshire. In Yorkshire we find the number of lines to the page increased to nearly 50, and since we presume that the commissioners worked outwards (and in this case northwards), the change took place while he was abbreviating the last county in his local return. Next, perhaps, he turned to abbreviate the return of the first circuit—Kent, Surrey, Sussex, Hampshire, and Berkshire, where we find consistently 50 lines to the page. All this suggests that the compiler was feeling the necessity for compression by getting more on the page, and in his abbreviation of circuit no. IV, Oxford, Leicester, Northampton, the number of lines to the page runs in places to nearly 60. Finally, and most strangely, in circuit no. II, that of the south-western counties, and V, the Welsh border, the compiler eventually ceased to rule any lines at all. This change we might attribute to laziness or carelessness, but this in fact is not the impression left by the writing for these counties, which is still most competently done. Rather, the change seems due to haste, haste to get the job finished and therefore at all costs to compress within the space allotted the shortened version of his material. This is especially noticeable in the south-western circuit, and a glance at the facsimile of the first folio for Wiltshire, for example, shows that the compiler, forced to get in to his page more than it would hold, actually ignored the lines he had ruled across it. There are no less than thirteen gatherings which are not ruled at all. They comprise much of the south-western counties and all of those on the Welsh border, and we can hardly doubt both that they were the last written and that they are left unruled to expedite the completion of the book. By ignoring the ruled page an entry could be written in as large or as small a script as there was room for, and to these striking variations in the size and carefulness of the script is chiefly due the tendency of palaeographers to presume a number of different scribes. The key to the problem lies in the fact that the scribe was abbreviating a much larger original, also arranged by counties, and had to estimate before he began the size of quire he needed, so that each county section of his abbreviation should form a separate, self-contained booklet.

XIV

AFTER DOMESDAY

WHEN William I died in September 1087 the Treasury at Winchester was in possession of the full local return by circuits, and of an abbreviation of these returns for all circuits but that of East Anglia. The full returns of this circuit, now called Little Domesday (Vol. II), were therefore unequally yoked to the short version in Vol. I to form 'Domesday Book', the official and permanent record of the inquiry. It is an extraordinary thing that the final outcome of this vast inquiry should have been so fortuitous; and no explanation, it seems to me, is adequate but that death put an end to the proper completion of Vol. I. Those who have seen in Little Domesday a first attempt, and an unsatisfactory one, discarded in favour of Vol. I, forget that it would have been the easiest thing in the world to abbreviate Little Domesday, involving the addition to Vol. I of not more than 30 or 40 folios to the 400-odd of which it already consisted. Nor, of course, is it really credible that a first attempt at codifying the returns would have been allowed to run to 450 folios before it was seen to be either cumbersome or inadequate.[1] The mongrel form of Domesday Book, in two volumes which obviously belong to different stages of the Inquest, is, in short, the best proof that the enterprise was abruptly halted by William's death.

To a certain extent we can test this conclusion by the royal writs of William I and William II, which throw light on the way in which the administrators who carried out the Inquest thought about it and referred to it.

[1] It is, however, possible, if unlikely, that the multitude of small free and socage tenants in East Anglia was considered to defy abbreviation.

Among the archives of Westminster Abbey is preserved a most rare and precious original charter or writ by which William I informs Ralph the sheriff and all his ministers in Surrey that for the good of his soul he has conceded to the abbey and to Abbot Gilbert 8 hides of the manor of Pyrford (Surrey) quit and free henceforth from scot and all his custom and money rent called in English *geld*. The document, which still carries the great seal, is witnessed by William bishop of Durham and Ivo Tailebois. It also, and this is most unusual in Norman writs, bears a date and one couched in terms of the Survey, viz. 'Post descriptionem totius Anglie'. This grant must have been made before 9 September 1087, and we turn anxiously to the Pyrford entry in Great Domesday (f. 32), which is both elaborate and unusual. The manor is there a part of the Westminster Abbey fee, and we are told that it was assessed in Harold's time, first at 27 hides, and later at 16. Then, and this to me is the most unusual feature of the entry, a scribe, not necessarily the one who made the original entry, has written in the margin: 'Modo geldat pro viii hidis.' Mr. Bishop and Mr. Chaplais, who have reproduced the writ in facsimile,[1] remark on this entry:

> The grant recorded in our writ amounts to a total exemption from geld of the manor of Pyrford. This explains why the writ bears a dating clause—and why the date should be given with reference to the Domesday Survey. It is obvious that otherwise royal officials would have interpreted the writ as a mere confirmation of the reduction from 16 to 8 hides which is recorded in Domesday Book.

They may be right: they probably are right: but one wonders whether the extraordinary little note in the margin was not *added* by a clerk to explain the effect, as he understood it,[2] of the king's writ, viz. a reduction of

---

[1] *Facs. of English Royal Writs to A.D. 1100* (1957), plate XXIV.
[2] If the marginal note had been derived from the full local return, we should

obligation from 16 to 8 hides. Whatever view we take, there seems to be little doubt that Great Domesday was already in existence by the close of the reign.

For William II's reign we have several royal writs which refer to the Survey. One of these, datable as 1091–96, notifies the bishop of Bath, the sheriff, and all of Somerset, that the king has found from William bishop of Durham and the records (*breves meos*) that William I granted Lydeard (St. Lawrence) and Angersleigh to Winchester and Bishop Walchelin, and confirms the grant.[1] Here again all the information referred to in the writ is found in Great Domesday in a famous entry which says in Latin:[2] 'And King William granted these lands to be held by St. Peter and bishop Walchelin as the king himself admitted (*recognovit*) at Salisbury in the hearing of the bishop of Durham whom he ordered to write down this grant in the records (*in brevibus*).'

William I's grant was apparently made in the course of the Survey and we can only suppose that the bishop of Durham was one of the *legati* for the south-west circuit. Here again, then, there is no reason to doubt that Great Domesday was already in existence. These examples of William I and William II's writs both refer to Great Domesday, and both it will be noticed are connected with William, bishop of Durham, who died in 1096. Another writ of William II refers to land in East Anglia, and this, too, is witnessed by a bishop of Durham who I think is William. If so, it belongs to the years 1093–5, though we cannot exclude the possibility that the reference is to Ranulf Flambard who became bishop of Durham in 1099. This writ requires that the abbot of St. Benet Hulme be put in seisin of certain lands, which are duly mentioned in

---

expect not the word 'geldat' but 'modo defendit se pro viii hidis', the formula for geld liability current on this circuit (no. I).

[1] *Regesta Regum Anglo-Normannorum*, vol. ii, p. 404.

[2] f. 87 b 1; also in Exon Domesday (p. 163).

Little Domesday, and adds: 'And know that this land was recorded (*inbreviata*) in my records (*meis brevibus*) to the use of St. Benet, and that these records (*breves*) are in my Treasury at Winchester.' For the early years of William II's reign, then, royal writs referred to what *we* call Domesday Book as the king's *breves* in the Treasury; and this usage, as we have seen above,[1] is exactly that of the very clerks who were responsible for the local returns, as well as the compilers of Great Domesday. They referred to the *breve* of an individual tenant-in-chief or a religious house meaning the full description of his manors; or to the king's *breve* meaning the *Terra Regis*; or to the *breve* for Hereford meaning the complete record of the shire. A tenant could even refer to the day on which he was *inbreviatus*; and the king could tell one of his *legati* to inscribe a grant *in brevibus*. The evidence of both volumes of Domesday on this point is also, as we have already seen, confirmed by both the I.C.C. and the I.E. What just did they mean by *breve* or *breves*? We must not try to make *breve* a technical term: it means no more than written records or surveys, and is in fact the Latin equivalent of the writings which the Anglo-Saxon Chronicle tells us were later brought to the king when the Inquest was completed. The same word was used, in other contexts, for the royal writs; the hundred we read again and again has seen neither the *breve* nor *sigillum* which would prove a claim. And if we must not think of it as a technical term, still less may we suppose that it was used in opposition to Domesday *Book*. The only original documents of the Survey still surviving are uniformly written on quaternions or quires; and we have no authority for supposing that the returns were made in any other form, least of all in rolls (*rotulis*). For all we know these quaternions may have remained unbound for some years. Bound or unbound, it is clear that the enormous collection of written documents

[1] P. 129.

which were associated with the Inquest in the public
mind, and of which samples and fragments survive still
in Exon Domesday, in the *clamores* of Lincoln and Yorkshire, and in the *invasiones* of East Anglia—all these
slowly faded from the public and the official memory as it
was realized that in every query the answer from which
there was no appeal was succinctly and conveniently contained in the two, not so big volumes—Little Domesday
and Great Domesday. Thus gradually men began to think
of the Domesday Survey not in terms of a *descriptio* or of
breves, but as a book. Long ago[1] Round called attention
to the settlement of a plea before Henry I's queen, where
we read: 'Sciatis quod Faritius abbas de Abendona in curia
domini mei et mea, apud Wintoniam in thesauro . . . per
Librum de Thesauro diratiocinavit quod . . .' This incident he dated between 1108 and 1113: but since then an
earlier reference has come to light in a writ of William II,
which seems to belong to the very end of the reign:
'Willelmus rex Anglorum Durando vicecomiti et baroni-
bus de Hantescyre salutem. Facite ut monachi sancti
Petri de episcopatu Wintoniense habeant in pace terram
de Helinge quam Imma regina eis dedit, sicut *liber regius*
hoc testatur. T. episcopo Dunelmensi.'[2] For William,
bishop of Durham, who, as we have seen, took part in the
actual survey, the records of it were simply *breves*, documents: but for Ranulf Flambard (if this bishop of Durham
is Ranulf) the reference is to the 'royal book'. But it was
not yet called Domesday Book, a description first met with
in the *Dialogue concerning the Exchequer*, written by Richard
fitz Nigel, the Treasurer, *c.* 1176. 'This book', he says,

is metaphorically called by the native English, Domesday, i.e. the
Day of Judgment. For as the sentence of that strict and terrible last
account cannot be evaded by any skilful subterfuge, so when this
book is appealed to on those matters which it contains, its sentence

---

[1] 'The First Mention of Domesday Book' (*Feudal England*, p. 143).
[2] *E.H.R.* xxxv (1920), p.388.

cannot be quashed or set aside with impunity. That is why we have called the book 'the Book of Judgment' [Domesday], not because it contains decisions on various difficult points, but because its decisions, like those of the Last Judgment, are unalterable.[1]

Thus, early references to the record of the Survey as a book are exceptional and we seem to owe them to some of the officials who actually participated in its execution. In the reign of Henry I we hear no more of a book or of *breves*: and royal writs as well as the chronicles uniformly describe it as the king's *carta*[2] which is in the Treasury or at Winchester. Thus, men who knew that it was a book and remembered how it had been made had died off, while the popular name of Domesday Book had not yet won its way into general use. Yet whenever quoted, either in royal writs or by individuals, the facts given are always to be found in one or other of the two volumes of 'Domesday Book'. There is, I think, no instance in any royal writ of an allusion to, or a quotation from, the full local 'original returns'. They were forgotten, and by the end of the twelfth century, when the public records were beginning to be more systematically preserved than hitherto, they had disappeared. Traces of them, however, remain in those local monastic compilations, falsely called 'satellite surveys', and notably in the Domesday Monachorum of Christchurch, Canterbury, the records of St. Augustine's, Canterbury (circuit no. I), and the Ely documents analysed above (circuit no. VI). A more intensive scrutiny of them and some others might yet reveal when and how portions of the full returns came into the possession of some of the larger monasteries.

It is an odd coincidence (if it *is* a coincidence) that the bishop of Durham is so often connected with the 'Domesday' writs quoted above; and it is unfortunate that we cannot be sure whether the latest, which refers to the

---

[1] *Dialogus de Scaccario*, ed. C. Johnson (Nelson, 1950), p. 64.

[2] *Hereford Domesday* (Pipe Roll Soc., N.S. xxv, 1950), pp. xxvi–xxvii.

liber regius, is really witnessed by the famous, or infamous, Ranulf Flambard. For the chronicler Orderic Vitalis tells a strange tale of Ranulf Flambard, employing measurement 'by the rod', revising the Domesday Survey. A writ of William II (1093–9),[1] addressed to his justices of England (of whom Ranulf was one), cogently supports Orderic's story. In it they are directed by the king, who was abroad, to assess (*admensuretis*) the abbey of Thorney 'for gelds, scots, knight service, and all customs . . . as leniently as any honour is assessed which has the same amount of land'. Round, who first called attention to this writ, pointed out that 'it points to a *pro rata* as against an arbitrary assessment', and is the more noteworthy because Thorney Abbey was not one of those which in the twelfth century owed knight service.[2] All this suggests that William II, though clearly interested in the results of the Domesday Survey, was turning his energies to some sort of *revision* or reassessment of feudal services, now that his father had, so to speak, got the facts down on paper; and that this revision was based on new and more scientific principles. If so, he is unlikely to have carried any farther his father's work on Domesday Book—a consideration which almost rules out any likelihood of either volume of Domesday Book having been put together in his reign. Moreover, since Round wrote about it, fresh evidence has turned up of the same activity in the reign of Henry I. This is a writ of the year 1103[3] in favour of Ramsey Abbey addressed to the bishop of Lincoln, Earl Simon, the sheriff of Huntingdon, and all other sheriffs in whose shires Abbot Bernard has lands. The abbot is to measure the services (*admensuret servicia*) of his military tenants as may be advantageous to his church, as those of the tenants

---

[1] *Regesta,* vol. i, p. 136 (LXXII). Cf. R. W. Southern in *Trans. R. Hist. Soc.,* 4th series, xvi (1933), pp. 101 f.

[2] *E.H.R.* xxix (1914), p. 349, reviewing *Regesta,* vol. i.

[3] *Regesta,* vol. ii, no. 650. The original of this charter survives (B.M. Add. Ch. 33642).

of other abbeys are measured ('sicut vavassores aliorum abbatum regni mei admensurati sunt'). It is, then, certain that a new turn was given to the principles of feudal taxation in the reign of Rufus, and that it persisted into that of his brother. The interest of the Crown was perhaps beginning to focus on the *servitia militum* and subinfeudation; but we clearly still have much to learn on these matters. It is none the less relevant to insist that the first evidence of an intention to reassess the geld belongs not to the reign of William I, but to the later years of Rufus, and then only as one of many customs (*consuetudinibus*). Moreover, the reassessment was thought of, not in terms of fiscal hides, villages, and hundreds, but of feudal honours measured by the hide. In short, so far from being the motive for the Survey the idea of reassessment was perhaps suggested by it and then only as a part of a financial reorganization based on wholly different principles.

We have reached the end of the making of Domesday Book; but there is an epilogue to the story. In finance, as in other things, the medieval mind was prone to attempt more than it could perform, or at any rate than it could use. Medieval treatises are very often unwieldy in length, and the cult of completeness and comprehension which inspired the original conception of the Domesday Survey reminds us of their huge histories, their exhaustive treatment of theology, and their immense abbeys and cathedrals, few of which were carried to completion. But they were also very practical people—they had to be—and though they rejected compromise in theory, they specialized in epitome and précis: in vade-mecums and 'inquire-withins'. The universal history of Matthew Paris, which began with the Creation and only ended at the year of his death, was twice abbreviated, to make it in the end a handy little volume. Much the same happened to the theological works of Kilwardby; and so it was with Domesday Book, which itself began as an abbreviation,

the necessity for which was no doubt brought home to
the king's administrators before ever the 'original returns'
reached Winchester. This first declension from the ideal
was some time later repeated, and Domesday Book was
itself officially abbreviated. We know this from the 'Breviate of Domesday',[1] written in the Exchequer in the
second quarter of the thirteenth century and still preserved in the Public Record Office. This splendid volume,
finely written and illuminated, shows no evidence of
having been much used and has attracted almost no
attention, since it was assumed to have been compiled as
well as written in the thirteenth century. But we can now
safely carry back its compilation to the twelfth century,
and more likely early than late. It may even be nearly
contemporary with Domesday Book itself.

The chief evidence for its early date comes from the
precious cartulary of Heming, sub-prior of Worcester
under Bishop Wulfstan (d. 1095). It contains some valuable facts regarding the Domesday Survey, and it is a
reproach to modern scholarship that we have still to rely
on the edition of Thomas Hearne published in 1723. For
a century before the Norman Conquest the church of
Worcester had enjoyed exceptional rights in the 300 hides
which formed the hundred of Oswaldslaw, and these are
set out on f. 172 b 1 of Great Domesday in a long note,
which says 'hoc attestatur totus comitatus'. This is quoted
by Heming, writing about the turn of the century, as
follows:

This testimony was confirmed under oath by the whole county,
at the exhortation and by the labour of the most pious and prudent
father bishop Wulfstan in the time of William I in the presence of
the magnates of that king viz. Remigius bishop of Lincoln, earl
Walter Giffard and Henry de Ferrers and Adam the brother of
Eudo, the king's *dapifer*, who had been sent by the king to make an

---

[1] See *Herefordshire Domesday* (Pipe Roll Society, 1950) for a fuller description
of the Breviate.

inquest and to describe the possessions and customs, both of the king and of his magnates (*principum*) in this province and in many others, at the time when the king had a description made of the whole of England.[1]

Here, then, we have the names of the *legati* of the fifth circuit, and Heming continues: 'Ad huius rei confirmationem exemplar eius in autentica regis cartula scriptum est que in thesauro regali cum totius Anglie descriptionibus conservatur.' A little later Heming gives us the text of the relevant portions of Domesday Book from the various counties in which the church of Worcester held lands under the heading: 'Descriptio terre episcopatus Wigornensis secundum cartam Regis que est in thesauro regis.' But a close examination shows that in Heming we have only an abbreviated text of Domesday Book, and one which, despite many small differences, is often virtually identical with the Breviate of Domesday. Both consistently omit all manorial particulars—the ploughs in demesne and those of the villeins, the number of villeins, bordars, &c., the woodland, meadow, the 'valets', and so on, but carefully retain the names of the tenants and the number of hides each held. Was Heming drawing upon the official abbreviation of Domesday already made at Winchester, or himself abbreviating the full text? We cannot be sure, but his text at least proves that there was already a demand for such a skeleton survey, and further research may show that the text of the Breviate was in more common use locally in the twelfth century than that of Domesday Book.

However remote and obscure the motives and methods of the Domesday Inquest, the subject at least is topical. Royal Commissions are still with us, and both we and our rulers can safely take for granted the administrative process by which they reach their results. Indeed, so easy has

---

[1] *Chartularium*, i, p. 288.

it all become, that today they are chiefly employed by
governments to avoid or at least to defer doing something
about the problems that embarrass them. But the farther
we go back the more important it becomes to discover not
merely what was done, but how it was done; and the most
remarkable fact about the Domesday Inquest is perhaps
that it was done at all. It is our best evidence of the iron
will of the Conqueror, and the measure of the difference
between the authority wielded by him and even the
greatest of his predecessors.

The final result of the Inquest, preserved in Domesday
Book, is a vast mass of statistics which has no parallel in
the Middle Ages. Yet, however objective the result, the
motives which prompted the Inquest remain obscure, for
they were unrecorded by contemporaries, and today can
only be recovered if at all by reconstructing the administrative process of the Inquest and the difficulties that had
to be overcome. But more than the motives for the Survey
is in question. Professor H. C. Darby's *Domesday Geography*, of which only the first two volumes have appeared,
suggests the further possibility that a clear grasp of just
how the facts were assembled may throw some light on
what for his purposes are the crucial considerations regarding Domesday statistics, viz. their accuracy and their
validity.

In this book Professor Darby and his collaborators,
proceeding county by county, attempt by a series of most
ingenious maps to plot the distribution and density of
population, woodland, pasture, fisheries, mills, and salt-
pans as recorded in the Survey. It is still too early to
assess the value of the information that this minute survey
will afford, but for one of these map-series, viz. woodland,
he has published a preliminary account of the whole
country, which throws some light on the way the Inquest
was conducted. Taking 'Domesday Woodland'[1] and the

[1] *Economic Hist. Review*, 2nd Series, iii (1950), pp. 21–43.

published volumes of the *Domesday Geography* as our source let us attempt a broad survey of the inferences to be drawn from the study of woodland over the whole face of England.

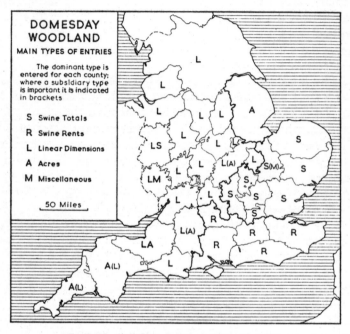

England: distribution of types of wood entries.

There are, it appears, four different methods of recording the amount of woodland. The wood may be measured:

1. By its length and breadth.
2. In acres.
3. By the numbers of swine that could be fattened on its mast.
4. By the swine rents which it yielded.

Normally each county is characterized by one type of entry; but as a rule the dominant type of entry is accompanied by some subsidiary entries of a different character. The dispersion of these four methods is shown by a most instructive map, which suggests two comments:

Firstly, that the method of recording woodland is in close harmony with the hypothesis (for it is no more) that England was divided into distinct circuits of commissioners for the purpose of the Inquest. Thus, swine totals are the dominant type of entry for the eastern circuit, which comprised Essex, Norfolk, and Suffolk; while the first circuit consisting of Kent, Sussex, Surrey, Hampshire, and Berkshire employs and alone employs, as its dominant type of entry, method no. 4 (swine rents). The third circuit (Middlesex, Hertford, Buckingham, Cambridge, and Bedford) like no. VII also measured by swine totals, and in all other circuits the dominant type of entry is by length and breadth. To this rule, it will be noted, there is but one exception, viz. Lincolnshire. Since nothing is more certain than that Yorkshire and Lincolnshire belonged to the same circuit, the exception reminds us that there were limits to the degree of uniformity which could be secured by the commissioners of each circuit in the face of local practice.

Secondly, this map seems to bear out the distinction drawn above[1] between the more advanced and intensive social and agricultural development of eastern and southeastern England and that of the midlands and the west, for the measurement of length and breadth, characteristic of the latter, is both more rough and ready and less exact than that used in the other half of England. Indeed, measurement by length and breadth raises some insuperable questions of interpretation, and seems to be characteristic of scantily populated regions which lacked the intense local life of eastern England. Property there was

[1] Above, p. 75.

broken up into many small, independent tenures, each of which had to be accurately recorded.

No praise can be too high for the skill and caution with which Mr. Darby has drawn these little maps of the woodland, population, meadow, and so on in each county. Their purpose is merely to show the relative density of each class of phenomena; and he is careful to point out, for example, that the swine totals are no more than a way of estimating the value of woodland. They do not imply that the numbers of pigs, often very large, for which there was woodland, really existed, and they have to be carefully distinguished from the actual pig totals in each manor. Every type of map, too, is carefully considered in the light of the known geographical and geological conditions; and the whole enterprise when completed will give life and meaning as never before to the massive but dead statistics in Domesday Book.

The outstanding problem for Mr. Darby and his team is thus the accuracy of their statistics. On this question the two published volumes, it must be confessed, have little to tell us. Yet it seems to me that Mr. Darby's preliminary study of woodland has already thrown some light upon it, by providing us with valuable clues as to the way in which the information was obtained. It is clear from the map that the most common and widely dispersed method of measuring woodland was by its length and breadth, and that the other three types are exceptional. Entries by length and breadth are characteristic of the north of England, the south-west, the Welsh border, and the midlands as far as Huntingdon where a characteristic entry reads: 'Wood for pannage 1 league in length and four furlongs in breadth.'[1] Such an entry presents many difficulties.

[1] *Domesday Geography of Eastern England*, p. 335: the entry for Bluntisham, 'Silva pastilis i leuga longo et iiii quarentenae lato'. In Exon Domesday woodland is uniformly recorded not as *silva* but as *nemus*, for which the shortened version in vol. I of D.B. systematically substitutes *silva*, and *silva minuta* for *nemusculi*.

There was not at this date a standard league or furlong. These varied according to local usage; but, granting this, what was in the minds of the clerks who recorded woodland in this way?

Is it giving extreme diameters of irregularly shaped woods, or is it making rough estimates of mean diameters, or is it attempting to convey some other notion? We cannot tell, but we certainly cannot assume that a definite geographical figure was in the minds of the Commissioners. We cannot hope to convert these linear measurements into acres by any process of simple arithmetic; and it would be rash to make any assumptions about the superficial extent of woodland measured in this way.[1]

And what is to be said of the entries which record only a single dimension? Thus at Lingen in Herefordshire we are told that there is half a league of woodland (f. 260) and at Elton (f. 183 b) two furlongs. The measurement of woodland by length and breadth hardly makes sense, and has defeated the ingenuity of Round, Eyton, and more recent scholars. As a result the woodland maps in *Domesday Geography* do not pretend to do more than show relative density, or, in other words, that there was more woodland in one place than in another. In view of the importance of woodland in the manorial economy this uncertainty is astonishing, and suggests that these statistics are no more than the traditional estimates, or the guesses of the manorial owners' representatives whom we know to have attended the Inquest. Out of them the commissioners made what sense they could. At Barrow-on-Soar in Leicestershire (f. 237), for instance, the wood is measured by length and breadth, but is also valued:[2] 'Wood, one league in length and four furlongs in width which renders five shillings.' This is borne out by an illuminating entry for Bernoldune[3] in Herefordshire:

[1] Ibid., p. 335.
[2] *Domesday Geography of Midland England*, pp. 337–8.
[3] D.B., vol. I, f. 187 a 2.

'There is a large wood there, but its size (*quantitas*) was not mentioned (*dicta*).' Such an entry is a confession of failure by the commissioners who, as Mr. Darby says 'were trying to be accurate'; but in fact it tells us no more and no less than the normal entry by length and breadth. We must renounce any idea that a new, measured survey of woodland accompanied the Domesday Inquest, for in scores of examples where the woodland was small enough to have been accurately measured in acres we encounter such brief entries as *silva modica, silva parva, silva parvula, silva minuta,* and—more exactly—*silva nil reddens*.[1] The mere fact that four different ways of measuring wood-land are found in Domesday Book goes far to prove that the Inquest did no more than record the information of local representatives, and if so, that its figures must not be taken too seriously, especially when the amount was considerable. What we know of medieval figures suggests that they are more trustworthy or less untrustworthy as they grow smaller; and this applies to woodland measure-ment. We can perhaps accept as accurate the 'wood for six pigs and a half' recorded at Barnes (f. 9a2) in Kent, but the entries of wood for 1,000 swine or more in East Anglia are as suspect as the records of armies of 50,000 men which we meet in the chronicles.

As the *Domesday Geography* approaches completion, the entire series of density maps for population, woodland, meadow, pasture, fisheries, mills, &c., may be expected to throw further light upon the statistics they are intended to illustrate; and from them too it may be possible to define more clearly how the Inquest was actually carried out. Meanwhile it is worth observing that in one county only, viz. Lincolnshire, is woodland normally recorded by acreage; that the less pretentious measurement by swine totals is at least more reliable than that by length and breadth; and that the recording of swine rents used in

[1] See the subject index to Domesday Book (1811), *sub* 'silua'.

circuit I was from the commissioners' point of view the most satisfactory of all, as it gave an exact estimate of money value, which was their immediate aim. Lastly, it is curious that in Kent[1] we seem to reach the point of transition from swine totals to swine rents, for a close examination reveals both systems in operation. Neither form of entry is adequately described as dominant. Whatever the reason for this, it suggests that in the last resort the authorities were solely dependent upon the actual cultivators of the estates for the form as well as the accuracy of their statistics.

The conclusion that manorial statistics came and could only come from the actual owners or farmers of manors, corrects a widespread tendency in all writings on Domesday Book to exaggerate the part played by the hundred juries. Their chief function, beyond question, was to testify to ownership and to unlawful seizure of property.[2] Nor is there any reason to think that the woodland and similar statistics involved any surveying by the commissioners of individual manors. The details of woodland, no doubt, presented greater difficulties than, say, the simple totals of stock on demesne or the number of villeins, bordars, cottars, and slaves; but they do not stand alone. Other types of statistics, and notably the estimates of ploughs for which there was land,[3] seem to have been arrived at by similar rule-of-thumb methods. These too present insuperable difficulties which were exhaustively

---

[1] See 'Domesday Woodland', *Econ. Hist. Rev.*, 2nd series, iii (1950), p. 27. I say 'transition' since, most curiously, the reference to swine rents only occurs towards the end of the county (ff. 11–14).

[2] Above, p. 78.

[3] See *Domesday Geography of Eastern England*, p. 44, for a discussion of the difficulties these present in Lincolnshire. These entries, according to Maitland, furnish 'apparently unasked information' (*Domesday Book and Beyond*, p. 420); but surely they spring from the last clause of the terms of reference (above, p. 60): 'et si potest plus haberi quam habeatur'. Maitland expresses the 'horrible suspicion' (p. 427) that 'the number of team lands is but remotely connected with the agrarian arrangements of 1086'.

discussed by Maitland in *Domesday Book and Beyond*. The ordinary formula for recording plough teams was *terra est pro x carrucis*, and the very fact that the entry is so often left unfinished[1] indicates that the information was sought from individuals and not from juries, who had to give some answer to the questions put. Maitland cites a hundred in Rutland[2] in which there were 12 carucates *ad geldum* and land for 48 ploughs, but which were in fact being cultivated by 530 tenants using 127 ploughs! The 'valets' or values of manors are sometimes equally suspect, and Maitland notes that it was 'common' for a first-class manor in Yorkshire to be worth exactly £56![3] 'Everywhere', he adds, 'we are baffled by the make-believe of ancient finance.' His comment suggests that sooner or later the Domesday geographers will have to face the question of the validity of their statistics; and if so, this will involve some clear working hypothesis of the detailed process by which the commissioners compiled them.[4]

[1] Above, p. 80.

[2] *Domesday Book and Beyond*, p. 471 (D.B., vol. I, f. 293 b 2). It is worth noting that for the hundred of Oswaldslaw in Worcester the problem was solved by a comprehensive note that in none of the manors listed was there land for more ploughs than were actually in use (D.B., vol. I, f. 174 a 1). For this statement, as Maitland points out (op. cit., p. 424), the bishop of Worcester was ultimately responsible; but what he had in his mind was not a reassessment of geld but a possible increase in the *valet* of each manor.

[3] Ibid., p. 473.

[4] In chapter I of the *Domesday Geography of Eastern England* Mr. Darby impartially sets out the conflicting views on this subject, but without deciding between them or offering a fresh hypothesis.

APPENDIX

[Reprinted with corrections, from 'The Date of the Geld Rolls in Exon Domesday' (*E.H.R.* lxv (1950), pp. 7–15).]

THE next step is therefore to set out the positive evidence of indebtedness to Domesday which can be traced in the geld accounts. In this matter historians are under a great debt to Eyton's immense research; and we must regret that his inquiries were limited to two only of the five south-western counties. It was, indeed, a note in Eyton's *Key to Domesday* that first seriously aroused my suspicions regarding the date of the geld rolls. Peter, bishop of Chester, was dead before Domesday; his lands appear *in manu regis*, and his successor Robert was appointed at the midwinter court of 1085. Now the geld roll for Cuferdestroue hundred in Dorset, among its exemptions from geld of land in demesne mentions 'unam hidam quam tenuit Petrus episcopus',[1] and Eyton notes, 'Peter, Bishop of Chester, consecrated in 1070, is usually said to have died in 1085. This entry in the Inquest of April 1084 makes it probable that he was then dead.'[2] It certainly does imply that Peter was dead some time before the geld roll was made; but one hesitates to discard Stubbs's date of 1085 on this slender evidence. If the geld roll belonged to 1086 the difficulty disappears.

More complex is the rather tangled evidence regarding a certain Escelinus or Schelin, with whom Eyton dealt very fully. The Dorset account[3] states that Escelinus holds 1 hide in demesne in the hundred of Albretesberga, and Eyton reasonably located this hide in Medessan [Edmondsham], of which a detailed account is given in Exon Domesday. From this it appears[4] that Queen Matilda held the manor at her death, after which it passed to the king, who now (*modo*) holds it. It pays geld on 2 hides and the king has 1 hide in demesne. It is worth 60s., 'et quando Eschelinus recepit totidem valebat, qui hanc mansionem tenebat de regina'. Exactly parallel with this case is that of Wichampton in the hundred of Bedeberia. The geld roll says[5] that Escelinus holds 1 hide and 3 virgates in

---

[1] Exon Domesday, f. 24. [2] *Key to Domesday*, p. 122, n. 6.
[3] Exon Domesday, f. 18. [4] Ibid., f. 29 b. [5] Ibid., f. 18.

demesne, and that 'de duabus partibus unius hide quam tenet Eschelinus nunquam habuit rex geldum'. Exon Domesday tells us[1] that the king holds Wichampton for 4 hides and two parts of a hide, of which 2 hides and 1⅔ virgates (i.e. the sum of Escelinus's two holdings in the geld account) are in demesne. The manor renders 100s. a year, 'et tantumdem prius valebat quando Eticelinus recepit qui eam tenebat de regina qui nunquam reddidit geldum regi de duabus partibus unius hide quam in hac mansione supra nominavimus'. Exchequer Domesday abbreviates these two entries in Exon according to its ordinary practice. Both manors are shown[2] as held · by the king and Escelinus is not mentioned.

Now these passages raise certain difficulties whether we assign the geld rolls to 1084 or 1086. Eyton is conscious of this when he writes of Wichampton

> The Queen had enfeoffed Eschelinus therein before the year 1083. Eschelinus still held the estate in 1084 but under the king. Eschelinus then claimed exemption on two parcels thereof;—on one (*viz.* 1 hide 3 virgates) as demesne;—on the other (*viz.* 2⅔ virgates) by prescription. . . . Before Domesday the king had ousted Eschelinus from Wichampton. The Domesday Commissioners found the king in seisin of the whole manor, *viz.* 4 hides 2⅔ virgates. They put the King's demesne there at 2 hides 1⅔ virgates, which is exactly the measure of the two parcels exempted from geld in 1084.[3]

The queen died in 1083. It is therefore odd to find Escelinus claiming demesne in these manors, either in 1084 or 1086, and Eyton, to explain it, supposes a forfeiture. Nor can we doubt that Escelinus ceased to be the 'owner' of these estates after the queen's death, for Domesday Book records another Dorset manor, Hame, with 3 virgates and the third of a virgate, then held by Torchil, and it adds 'Hanc terram dedit regina Schelm (*sic*). Modo habet rex in dominio.'[4] On the other hand, Domesday Book shows Escelinus (or Schelin) as the holder of the great manor of Alford (Acford)[5] in Dorset, which gelded for 16 hides. It also shows him in Somerset as the holder of Fodington.[6] It gelded for 1 hide and 1½ virgates, and was held entirely in demesne, for in the Somerset geld account Escelinus claims 1 hide and 1½ virgates as demesne in Bruton[7] hundred. We have, however, a fuller record of this tenancy in Exon

---

[1] Exon Domesday, f. 32.   [2] D.B., f. 75 b 1.
[3] *Key to Domesday*, p. 105.   [4] D.B., vol. I, f. 84 a 2.
[5] Ibid., f. 83 a 2.   [6] Ibid., f. 99 a 2.   [7] Exon Domesday, f. 82.

Domesday which notes, 'reddit per annum XX solidos et quando Escelinus accepit *ad firmam de rege* valebat tantumdem.'[1] This entry occurs under the heading 'Lands of French thegns in Somersetshire', and though all the other entries give a *valet*, in this one alone is the tenant said to have held the manor at farm. The suggestion may therefore be made that at Wichampton and Edmondsham, Escelinus was holding *ad firmam* from the king in regard to two estates which he had held in fee under Queen Matilda. However that may be, it is important to note that all the facts contained in the geld roll were available in the circuit return to the Domesday Inquest, whence they passed to Exon Domesday. We can hardly doubt, for example, that it was from this source the clerk making out the geld roll, gathered the fact that at Wichampton from two parts of a hide the king had never (*nunquam*) had his geld. What other source, in fact, could there be for such information except the Domesday Inquest? And if Escelinus's connexion with these manors had altogether ceased before Domesday Book, why should the compilers have bothered to make their full and careful notes about so small a matter that was past and done with?

Turn next to Devonshire, where Domesday Book, summarizing a fuller entry in Exon Domesday, records of the manor of Lei, held by Anscitil from William Chievre or Capra 'Huic manerio addita est dimidia virga terrae et celata est ita quod rex non habet inde geldum.'[2] This default is duly recorded under the hundred of Framintone in the geld accounts 'et pro dimidia virga quam tenet Anscitillus de W. Capra non habuit rex geldum.'[3] Why, we may ask, should this half virgate be described as concealed if it had been carefully recorded during the very last collection of geld in 1084?

It is noteworthy how precisely the geld roll follows the original geographical survey in the above entry by writing *non habuit geldum*. In two Dorset examples of hidden land geld roll and original survey agree in writing *nunquam gildavit*. The first of these relates to the hundred of Bera, where the geld roll states 'et de dimidia hida quam tenet Walterus Tonitruus de uxore Hugonis *nunquam habuit rex geldum*',[4] which appears to derive directly from the following entry in Exon Domesday:

---

[1] Ibid. f. 466 b (cf. R. Lennard, *Rural England* (1959), p. 111).
[2] D.B., vol. I, f. 110 b; Exon Domesday, f. 399 b, reading *non habuit*.
[3] Exon Domesday, f. 65 b.   [4] Ibid., f. 20.

Uxor Hugonis habet i mansionem quae vocatur Pidela . . . ibi est dimidia
hida et quatuor agri et i ortus quae *nunquam* gildavit sed celatum est. . . . Ibi
habet Walterus Tonitruus qui ipsam mansionem tenet ij carucas. . . .[1]

The second Dorset entry in the geld account occurs under Beieministre hundred 'de i virga quam tenet Willelmus Malbeénc de
comite Hugone nunquam habuit rex geldum.'[2] The striking word
here is once more the *nunquam*, and in Domesday Book we find the
reason, for in the margin a note has been added 'ibi (i.e. Catesclive)
est una virga terrae de qua celatum est geldum tempore regis
Willelmi.'[3] Eyton has most scrupulously quoted the note in Domesday as well as the geld roll entry, but without any suggestion that
the two might be connected. The natural inference is that the
entry in the geld roll is based on the discovery of this hidden virgate
by the Domesday inquest. If not we must suppose that it was discovered in 1084 and rediscovered in 1086.

The probability that the geld rolls belonged to 1086, suggested
by these instances, was raised to the level of virtual certainty by a
more complicated case of relationship, found in the first account for
Wiltshire. Under the hundred of Warminster is recorded 'et hic est
inventa 1 hida que non reddidit geldum postquam Willelmus rex
habuit regnum. Eam tenent Anfridus et Rainboldus.'[4] The hide is
explained by the two following entries in Domesday Book:

Rainboldus tenet de Ernulfo Opetone. . . . In hac terra est dimidia hida
comprehensa quae geldabat T.R.E. Sed postquam rex W. in Angliam venit
geldum non reddidit.[5]

and

Ansfridus tenet de Willelmo Opetone . . . pro dimidia hida non reddidit
geldum postquam W. rex venit in Angliam.[6]

The use of an identical formula in these passages requires a clear
choice between two alternatives. Either Domesday Book, through
the circuit return behind it, borrowed from the geld account, or the
geld account borrowed from Domesday; and since Domesday gives

[1] Exon Domesday, f. 56 b. It is worth noting that no mention of the hidden
half hide occurs in the Exchequer Domesday entry (f. 83 b 1).
[2] Ibid. 19 b. Still another example is found in the virgate which Robert holds
of the wife of Hugo from which the king has never had his geld (Exon Domesday, ff. 22 and 58 b).
[3] D.B., vol. I, f. 80 a 2.   [4] Exon Domesday, f. 1 b.
[5] D.B., vol. I, f. 70 a 2.   [6] Ibid., f. 71 b 2.

us details regarding the tenure and the amount of land held respectively by Ansfridus and Rainboldus, it is obvious that the geld account is indebted to the inquest and not vice versa. In this connexion it should be mentioned that the second and third accounts for Wilts. record the same information in rather different ways. No. 2 says: 'Et hic tenent Honfridus et Rainboldus i hidam quae non reddidit geldum tempore regis Willelmi.'[1] No. 3 says simply 'Ansfridus et Rainbaldus retinuerunt geldum 1 hidae.'[2] The use of three different phrases[3] to record the same facts supports the conclusion reached above, since it goes to show that the three Wilts. accounts were made up independently of one another from the originals of the Domesday inquest. J. H. Round, in his careful collation of the Inquisitio Comitatus Cantabrigiensis, the Inquisitio Eliensis, and the Domesday text for Cambridgeshire, drew attention to the constant variation of phrase to describe the same facts used by the various scribes employed on transcribing the geographical materials. Exactly the same process is seen at work in the Wilts. accounts. Take, for example, the very next entry in the account for Warminster hundred. The first two versions each include among the exempt demesne 'S. Stephanus de Fonteneio ij hidas quas tenet adhuc Alricus predecessor eius'.[4] The third version of the account reads as follows: 'Alricus prepositus S. Stephani de Funteneio retinuit geldum de ij hidis'.[5] At first sight it would appear that one or other version is a misreading of the original statistics. But it may

[1] Exon Domesday, f. 8.   [2] Ibid., f. 14.

[3] e.g. Roll 1, f. 1 b: 'In hundredo Extredeberie . . . Ecclesia Beccensis retinuit geldum per monachum qui villam custodit de x hidis quae date fuerunt ecclesiae pro anima regine.' Roll 2, f. 8: 'Monachus de Bec retinuit geldum de x hidis', etc. Roll 3, f. 14: 'Monachus de Bech', etc., as roll 2. Cf. D.B., vol. I, f. 68 b 1: the Church of Bec holds Devrel which gelded T.R.E. for 10 hides but which Queen Matilda later gave to the Church of Bec. Cf. similarly the three accounts for the hundred of Thornhill: also the 2 hides of the bishop of Winchester in Dunton hundred (f. 2 b) 'de quibus homines ibi manentes fugati sunt propter forestam regis'; and ff. 9 and 15 b: 'ij h. de terra Walchelini sunt ibi wastae propter forestam regis.'   [4] Exon Domesday, ff. 1 b, 8.

[5] Ibid., f. 14. Cf. D.B., vol. I, f. 72 b 2: 'the church of St. Stephen holds 2 h. and 1 v. in Mideltone which gelded *pro tanto* T.R.E.' If this estate is the one referred to in the geld roll, we may have here the third clerk's authority for treating it as geldable. With this, again, compare the virgate held by Godric *venator* in the hundred of Mere which all three accounts treat as exempt demesne. In Domesday Book the corrector has later interlined the words *et geldat* above the entry 'Godric venator tenet unam virgatam terrae in Mera' (D.B., vol. I, f. 74 a 1).

well be that both give a part only of a much fuller copy, and that each version is right so far as it goes. We cannot be sure about it, any more than we can explain why the third accountant removed the 2 hides from the category of exempt demesne to that of geldable land which has failed to pay. Instances could be multiplied indefinitely.

In the face of this evidence, it is, I believe, perverse to reject the overwhelming probability that the geld rolls are dependent upon information contained in the raw material of the Domesday inquest. There remains a great deal in these accounts which has not been, and perhaps cannot be, explained, since both the Exon and Exchequer Domesdays omit all reference to the hundreds. There are, too, differences, and no doubt mistakes. The geld roll for Bedeberia hundred (Dorset), for example, mentions the third part of one hide held by Piccotus of the count of Mortain,[1] from which the king has never had his geld. The Domesday correlative, as Eyton would say, is almost certainly 'Ibi [i.e. Wichampton] habet *Hubertus* unam virgatam terrae et terciam partem unius virgatae de qua nunquam dedit geldum.'[2] Such discrepancies are to be expected, and Round has called attention to two 'duplicate' yet irreconcilable entries in Somerset Domesday, relevant here since they relate both to Somerset and the count of Mortain. They describe one hide at Prestetone held of the count of Mortain,[3] which in one place is said to be held by Robert FitzIvo and in the other by Hugh of Valle Torta. Moreover, they differ as to the value of the estate and in various other particulars, and clearly represent two separate and varying accounts given to the king's commissioners. We are not here concerned with Round's explanation of the flat contradiction these entries present; but at least we need not be surprised when we meet a similar difficulty in the geld account regarding another tenant of the count of Mortain. Was it Hubert or was it Piccot who in 1086 held the third part of a hide from the count at Wichampton? We cannot say.

Another objection, which at one time seemed almost fatal to the view here set out, should be mentioned, though it was eventually removed in a very simple manner. The geld roll for Albretesberga hundred in Dorset states that the king has not had his geld 'de i hida et iij hidis [virgis] quas tenent (*sic*) Uluuardus Albus de aecclesia

---

[1] Exon Domesday, f. 18 b.   [2] D.B., vol. I, f. 79 b 1.
[3] *V.C.H. Somerset*, i, p. 427. The relevant passages will be found in D.B., vol. I, f. 92 a 2 and f. 86 b 2, and Exon Domesday, f. 103.

Glastiniensi'.[1] Ulward Wite, a Saxon thegn who held lands before
the Conquest in many counties and retained some of them under
William I, was certainly dead in 1086, for Exon Domesday groups
his Somerset lands under the heading *Terra quae fuit Uluuardi Wite*,[2]
and the lands still held by his widow are carefully distinguished. It
therefore looked as if the geld roll which apparently shows him as
actually holding land, must precede Domesday; and so Eyton inter-
preted this entry. I was, however, impressed by the fact that even
Eyton, after a careful survey of Ulward's far-flung lands, found
difficulty in reconciling this entry with the complicated details of
Ulward's various tenancies.[3] The possibility occurred to me that the
scribe, having first written *hidis* and then substituted *virgis*, and
then *tenent* for *tenet*, was nodding over his task. I concluded that
he meant to write *tenuit*; but the truth when I found it was more
prosaic. The manuscript *does* read *tenuit*, and *tenent* is just a mistake
of the editor or the printer. There is then a perfect correspondence
between geld roll and Domesday in respect of Ulward Wite; and
the incident is still another warning not to be hypnotized by the
deceptive air of infallibility which clings to the special type[4] and
grand, wasteful printing of the Record Commission edition of the
Domesday manuscripts.

In spite, then, of ignorance and error, there is a formidable array
of positive evidence which suggests the direct dependence of the
geld accounts upon the original material of the Domesday Inquest.
We can, however, go farther and clinch the argument by a comparison of the information conveyed to us respectively by the geld
rolls and Domesday regarding Manasses Coquus, Manasses the
cook. The Dorset geld roll shows him as the holder of 3 virgates in

---

[1] Exon Domesday, f. 18.   [2] Ibid., f. 116.
[3] *Domesday Studies, Somerset*, pp. 120, 176-7. Cf. pp. 85-87 and *Key to
Domesday*, p. 112. His name also occurs in a list of holders of exempt demesne in
Milbourn hundred (Somerset). See Exon Domesday, f. 180 b. Eyton comments
thus: 'But this survivor of the Saxon Thanes of the West was deceased before
Domesday, *if not at the date of the Inquest*, and his lands, saving his widow's
dower, were in *manu regis*' (*Domesday Studies, Somerset*, vol. i, p. 177).
[4] The special type used for Record Commission publications will explain,
though it cannot excuse, a blunder in 'The Making of Domesday Book' (*E.H.R.*
lvii. 175). On p. 400 of Exon Domesday we read (in record type) 'praeter hanc
prae scriptam mansionem est addita alia mansio'. Misled by the separation of
two syllables of a single word, I read this as *per scriptam mansionis* from which
followed an untenable inference.

Brunesella hundred, and we duly find him in Domesday Book holding 3 virgates in Staplebridge. The Somerset account, on the other hand, which tells of the land (p. 70) *quam tenuit Manasses* clearly supposes him to be dead; and dead he is in Somerset Domesday, where his wife is shown in possession of his estates. In short, Manasses is alive in the Dorset geld roll and in Dorset Domesday, but dead in the Somerset geld roll and also in Somerset Domesday. Eyton, who prints all the passages in full, remarks

It seems clear that Manasses the cook was deceased at the time of the Gheld-Inquest [25 March 1084], though the Dorset Inquest speaks of him as living, and only non-solvent in respect of some land of the monks of Sherborne which he had held.

It is curious that the Dorset Domesday treats the same land as if Manasses were living in 1086, while the Somerset Domesday clearly implies his death.[1]

It is curious indeed if we assign the geld rolls to 1084; but the difficulty disappears if we draw the obvious inference from the facts, viz. that Manasses died in the course of the Inquest (1086), and that the geld rolls are contemporary, or, more precisely, slightly later than the Inquest.

It remains only to summarize briefly the arguments advanced above. Firstly, the geld rolls (with a single exception) are, physically, as it were, a part of Exon Domesday, written for it by the same scribes as wrote the rest of the volume. Next, they record the collection of a six-shilling geld which had already been raised in two instalments; but despite the efforts of Walter and his colleagues to collect money discovered as due by Bishop William and his colleagues, there is still a certain amount of money outstanding. The geld is, in fact, still in process of collection. Thirdly, the geld rolls suggest a special effort to check the collection of a traditional and customary render in the light of a great body of information derived from an inquest; and this inquest looks very like that of 1086. I do not understand how else we can explain the fact that the three Wiltshire accounts, though all differ in detail regarding the number of hides in each hundred and in their order and phraseology, are unanimous regarding the total money paid into the treasury. Finally, we have discovered unmistakable examples of the indebtedness of the geld roll compilers to the primary, geographical material—Round's 'original returns'—of the Domesday Inquest.

[1] *Domesday Studies, Somerset*, vol. i, p. 68. Cf. *Key to Domesday*, p. 117, n. 2.

BIBLIOGRAPHY

TEXTS

Domesday Book, 2 vols., 1783.
—— *Indices*, 1811.
—— *Additamenta*, 1816, including 'Exon Domesday' and the 'Inquisitio Eliensis'.
—— *General Introduction*, by Henry Ellis, 2 vols., 1833.
Inquisitio Comitatus Cantabrigiensis and *Inquisitio Eliensis*, ed. N. E. S. A. Hamilton, 1876.
Northamptonshire Geld Roll. See A. J. Robertson, *Anglo-Saxon Charters*, pp. 230–7.
Domesday Monachorum, ed. D. C. Douglas, for R. Hist. Soc., 1944.
An Eleventh-Century Inquisition of St. Augustine's, Canterbury, ed. A. Ballard, 1920.
Textus Roffensis, ed. Th. Hearne, 1720.
Hemingi, Chartularium Ecclesiae Wigorniensis, ed. Th. Hearne, 2 vols., 1723.
Victoria County History contains translations of the Domesday text, with historical introductions for most of the counties covered by Domesday Book. Especially useful have been those for Buckingham, Essex, and Somerset (J. H. Round); Norfolk (Charles Johnson); Cambridgeshire (L. F. Salzman) and Wiltshire (R. R. Darlington, who includes a translation of the Geld Account).
Regesta Regum Anglo-Normannorum, vol. i [1066–1100], ed. H. W. C. Davis; vol. ii [1100–1135], ed. C. Johnson and H. A. Cronne, 1956.
Anglo-Saxon Chronicle, ed. B. Thorpe (Rolls Series), 2 vols., 1861; ed. J. Earle and C. Plummer, 2 vols., 1891–9; and in translation ed. G. N. Garmonsway, 1953.
Facsimiles of the text of Domesday Book, county by county, issued by the Ordnance Survey, 1861–4.
Domesday Re-Bound, H.M. Stationery Office, 1954.
The Domesday Geography of England: vol. i, *Eastern England*, by H. C. Darby, 1952; vol. ii, *Midland England*, ed. H. C. Darby and I. B. Terrett, 1954.

OTHER WORKS

A. BALLARD, *The Domesday Inquest*, 1906.

F. H. BARING, 'The Exeter Domesday', *E.H.R.* xxvii (1912), pp. 309–18.

JAMES BENTHAM, *History of the . . . Church of Ely*, 1771.

W. DE GRAY BIRCH, *Domesday Book*, 1887.

HELEN M. CAM, *The Hundred and the Hundred Rolls*, 1930.

H. C. DARBY, 'Domesday Woodland', *Econ. Hist. Rev.*, 2nd series, iii (1950), pp. 21–43.

D. C. DOUGLAS and G. W. GREENAWAY, *English Historical Documents*, vol. ii. P. E. Dove, *Domesday studies*, vol. i, 1888.

R. W. EYTON, *A Key to Domesday: Analysis of the Dorset Survey*, 1878.

—— *Domesday Studies: Analysis of the Somerset Survey*, 2 vols., 1880.

—— *Domesday Studies: Analysis of the Staffordshire Survey*, 1881.

H. P. R. FINBERG, 'The Early History of Werrington', *E.H.R.* lix (1944), pp. 237–51.

—— *Tavistock Abbey*, 1951.

R. WELLDON FINN, 'The Evolution of Successive Versions of Domesday Book', *E.H.R.* lxvi (1951), pp. 561–64.

—— 'The Immediate Sources of the Exchequer Domesday', *Bulletin of J.R.L.* xl (1957), pp. 47–78.

—— 'The Exeter Domesday and its Construction', ibid. xli (1959), pp. 360–87.

V. H. GALBRAITH, 'The Making of Domesday Book', *E.H.R.* lvii (1942), pp. 161–77.

—— 'The Date of the Geld Rolls in Exon Domesday', ibid. lxv (1950), pp. 1–17.

R. S. HOYT, 'The Terrae Occupatae of Cornwall and the Exon Domesday', *Traditio* ix, 1953, pp. 155–99.

CHARLES JOHNSON, *Dialogus de Scaccario*, Nelson, London, 1950.

R. LENNARD, 'A Neglected Domesday Satellite', *E.H.R.*, lviii (1943), pp. 32–41.

—— 'The Hidation of "Demesne" in some Domesday entries', *Econ. Hist. Rev.*, 2nd series, vii (1954), pp. 67–70.

—— *Rural England 1086–1135*, 1959.

F. W. MAITLAND, *Domesday and Beyond*, 1897.

F. W. MAITLAND, *History of English Law* (with Frederick Pollock), 2 vols., 1898.

J. F. A. MASON, 'The Date of the Geld Rolls', *E.H.R.* lxix (1954), pp. 283–9.

I. S. MAXWELL, 'The Geographical Identification of Domesday Vills', *Institute of British Geographers, Transactions and Papers, 1950* (1952), No. 16, pp. 95–121.

EDWARD MILLER, 'The Ely Land Pleas in the reign of William I', *E.H.R.* lxii (1947), pp. 438–56.

A. L. POOLE, *From Domesday Book to Magna Carta*, 1955.

J. H. ROUND, *Feudal England*, 1895.

—— 'Danegeld and the Finance of Domesday', in *Domesday Studies*, ed. P. E. Dove, vol. i, 1888.

PETER SAWYER, 'The "Original Returns" and Domesday Book', *E.H.R.* lxx (1955), pp. 177–97.

—— 'The Place-Names of the Domesday Manuscripts', *Bulletin of J.R.L.* xxxviii (1956), pp. 483–506.

—— 'Evesham A, a Domesday Text' (*Worcester Hist. Soc.* 1960, *Miscellany* 1).

F. M. STENTON, *Anglo-Saxon England*, 1943.

CARL STEPHENSON, *Medieval Institutions*, ed. Bryce D. Lyon, 1954.

W. H. STEVENSON, 'A Contemporary Description of the Domesday Survey', *E.H.R.*, xxii (1907), pp. 72–84.

CHARLES S. TAYLOR, 'An Analysis of the Domesday Survey of Gloucestershire', *Bristol and Gloucester Arch. Soc.*, 1888.

P. VINOGRADOFF, *English Society in the Eleventh Century*, 1908.

—— *The Growth of the Manor*, 1911.

INDEX

Abingdon, Fabricius, abbot of, 209.
Abington, Great, *see* Abintone.
Abington (Northants), 95.
Abintone, Abington, Great (Cambs.), 172.
Acford, *see* Alford.
Adam, brother of Eudo Dapifer, 36 n., 213.
Aiulf, the sheriff, 89.
Alan, Earl, 125, 127, 133, 157, 195.
Alan, of Burwell, 9 n., 127.
Albretesberga, hundred, 223, 228.
Alexius I, Emperor, 57.
Alford (Dorset), 224.
Alresford (Hants), 170.
Alricus, 227.
Alvediston (Wilts.), 89.
Amari, M., 55, 56, 57.
Anfridus, 153, 154.
Angersleigh (Soms.), 207.
Anglo-Saxon Chronicle, 1, 3, 25, 30, 44, 50–53, 89, 91, 97, 208.
Anscitil, 225.
Ansfridus, 226, 227.
Apulia, 58.
Armingford, hundred, 132, 133, 172.
Asheldham (Essex), 163.
Aylesford (Kent), 152.

Badlesmere (Kent), 153–5.
Badlingham (Cambs.), 125.
Baldwin, Abbot, *see* Bury St. Edmunds.
Ballard, Adolphus, 8 n., 39, 146 n., 151.
Baring, F. H., 28 n., 29.
Barlow, Frank, 47.
Barnes (Kent), 220.
Barrow-on-Soar (Leics.), 219.
Barstable hundred, 158.
Barton (Cambs.), 134.
Bath, abbey of, 34; bishop of, 207; priory of, 19 n.

Bayeux, Odo, bishop of, 110, 111, 153–5, 157, 197, 203.
Bec, church of, 227 n.
Bedeberia hundred, 223, 228.
Bedfordshire, 8, 71, 131 n., 172, 191, 203, 217.
Beieministre hundred, 226.
Bera hundred, 225.
Berkshire, 8, 71, 75 n., 162, 191, 194, 203, 217.
Bernard, abbot, *see* Ramsey.
Berningham (Norfolk), 79.
Bernitone hundred, 72 n.
Bernoldune (Hereford), 219.
Bewsborough hundred, 153.
Bigot, Roger, 129.
Bishop, T. A. M., 206.
Bluntisham (Hunts.), 218.
Book of Fees, 151.
Borough Green (Cambs.), 134 n.
Borowarlest last, 152.
Braintree (Essex), 164.
Bramford (Suffolk), 70.
Breve, breves, meaning of, 81, 121, 129–30, 135, 140, 143, 186, 207–8.
Bruce fee, 181 n.
Brunesella hundred, 230.
Bruton hundred, 224.
Buci, Robert of, 191.
Buckinghamshire, 8, 71, 131 n., 161, 172, 199, 203, 217.
Burch, *see* Borough Green.
Burci, Serlo de, 93.
Burgh Apton (Norfolk), 140.
Burwell (Cambs.), 127.
Bury St. Edmunds, abbey of, 46, 65; Baldwin, abbot of, 183; Samson, abbot of, 184.
Byzantine administration, 56, 57.

Caen, 142.
Cahainges, William de, 134.
Calabria, 57, 58.

REPRINTED LITHOGRAPHICALLY IN GREAT BRITAIN
AT THE UNIVERSITY PRESS, OXFORD
BY VIVIAN RIDLER
PRINTER TO THE UNIVERSITY